P9-AOU-079

GODS WITH
BRONZE SWORDS

GODS WITH BRONZE SWORDS

Costa de Loverdo

Translated by Nancy Amphoux

Doubleday & Company, Inc. Garden City, New York 1970

Published under the title LES DIEUX
AUX EPEES DE BRONZE ©
René Julliard, 1966

Library of Congress Catalog Card Number 70–114752

Printed in the United States of America

CONTENTS

PREFACE 1

FOREWORD: THE REPORTER'S EQUIPMENT 6

The mythological process · Deciphering · Heinrich Schliemann's act of faith · The testimony of Agathon · The key to history · The key to legend: linguistic symbolism · The connection with the gods · The technique of historical investigation

Chapter I
GENEALOGY OF THE HEROES 15

The migration of the "men from the west" · The giant Atlas · The Egyptians · The disappearance of Atlantis · The war between Atlantides and Greeks · Arrival of the Indo-Europeans · Rise of the Phoenicians · The Inachos · The people of Deucalion · The Hellenes · The Cretans take to the sea · Birth of the Minotaur · The reign of Minos I · The struggle for the trading centers · The Achaeans learn to sail · Phorcys' empire in the west · The baptism of Europe · The ancestors of the heroes

Chapter II
PERSEUS 31

"To Argos where the horses graze" · The cask of the Danaans · In the Kingdom of Danaos, sixteenth century B.C. · The struggle for succession · The fateful oracle · The prisoner and the shower of gold · Birth of Perseus · Diktys, the man with nets · "Bring me Medusa's head!" · The pirates of Seriphos · The white-haired Hesperides · The nymphs · Erytheia, sentinel of the ocean · The Gorgons · Medusa · The chase · In the land of Cassiopeia and Andromeda · The Cyclops · Back to Seriphos · Perseus' revenge · The Oracle of Hera is fulfilled · Great-walled Tiryns · Mycenae the Golden · The reign of Perseus · Epidaurus · Dionysos · Death of Perseus

Chapter III
BELLEROPHON OF CORINTH 57

Corinth, queen of the isthmus · The isthmus · Born of the blood of Medusa: Chrysaor and Typhon · . . . and winged Pegasus · Bellerophon · The Chimaera · The labors of Bellerophon · The ride of the winged Pegasus · The Echinades · Meganese · Pegasus' hideout · Death of Echidne · Bellerophon strikes back, but so do the gods

Chapter IV
AMPHITRYON 70

Tantalos and his torment · Pelops the emigrant · Doped horses and a rigged race · The race · The "father" of the Peloponnesus · The wars between the brothers · Amphitryon in exile · The "fox" · Athens, thirteenth century B.C. · Minos II, the oppressor · Down with the Teleboans

Chapter V
THE BIRTH OF HERAKLES 80

The Perseid law of succession · Hera, goddess of fertility · The Argive Heraeum · Birth of the master of the labors · "On the fetus in the seventh month" (Hippocrates) · Herakles, vassal of Eurystheus · Herakles and the serpents

Chapter VI
HERAKLES AS A YOUTH 89

The education of Herakles · First sign of his fatal flaw · Physical appearance · Herakles' first "lion" · Early prowess in love · Troezen · A chance encounter: the boy Theseus · Jason is born

Chapter VII
EARLY ACHIEVEMENTS 95

Orchomenos · Herakles, Theban strategist · A fit of madness · Delphi · The secret of Delphi · The oracle's decree

Chapter VIII
FROM THE NEMEAN "LION" TO THE AUGEAN STABLES 105

Herakles and Eurystheus · The palace at Tiryns · The Nemean "lion" · Mount Tretos · Herakles' weapons · The great fight · Death of the lion · The pelt · The terror of Eurystheus · Lerna · The "hydra" · The battle · Death of the hydra · Medieval Antiquity · The centaurs · The Erymanthian "boar" · Demeter · Eleusis · Orpheus, the lyre-playing hierophant · The Mysteries · The Cerynean "hind" · The hunting of the hind · The Stymphalian Marsh · The "birds" · Athena again · The Peloponnesus pacified · The wealth of Augeias · Herakles, toreador · The "stables" · Herakles and Dexamenos

Chapter IX
FROM THE CRETAN "BULL" TO THE "GIRDLE" OF HIPPOLYTE 137

The Cretan "bull" · Capture of the bull · Herakles at Olympia · The stadium · The first games · Twentieth century A.D.: the ruins · The museum · The "mares" of Diomedes · The Amazons of the Thermodon · Hippolyte's "girdle" · Herakles at the gates of Troy

Chapter X

THE YOUTH OF THESEUS 151

Theseus sets forth · The Scironian rocks · Athens, twentieth century A.D. · The Acropolis · The Parthenon · Athens, twelfth century B.C. · The "bull" of Marathon · The Calydonian "boar"

Chapter XI

JASON AND THE ARGONAUTS 160

The challenge · The Golden Fleece · The Hellespont · Phineus, the blind navigator · The good ship *Argo* · Dodona · The voice of Zeus · The muster roll of the Argonauts · The expedition sets sail · Herakles marooned · Navigating the Aegean · The Harpies · Through the strait · In the Black Sea · The land of the Golden Fleece · Medea, authority on poisons · Jason's ordeal · Success · Pursuit · Byzantium · The mouth of the Danube · The river with two estuaries · Down the Rhine · The Argonauts reach the ocean · Return to the Mediterranean · In sight of Crete · Theseus and the Amazons

Chapter XII

FROM THE CAUCASUS TO THE PILLARS OF HERCULES 183

Death of the "eagle" · The tenth labor · "Delenda Erytheia" · The "sons" of Chrysaor · The sacred cattle of Erytheia · Preparations for the voyage · Herakles, general · Herakles, politician · The army sets sail · Herakles in Egypt · The "golden goblet" of Tartessus · The battle at the Pillars of Hercules · The enigma of the fleet · The tectonic theory · Herakles in Celtica · The founding of Alesia · In Cisalpine Gaul: Monaco · Livorno, and on to Rome · The Phlegraean Plain · The eruption of Vesuvius · The battle with the Giants · Herculaneum · Lake Avernus · From Scylla to Charybdis · Eryx the Phorcid · Death and rebirth of the nymph Scylla · End of the Corsican

Phorcids · News from Greece: the abduction of Persephone · Of "nymphs" and "sirens" · The "nymph" Cyane · The fate of Syracuse · The tomb of Archimedes · Herakles conquers Sicily · Akragas · The Mysteries of Agrigentum · The temple of Zeus · Herakles, demigod of Sicily · Up the Italian boot · The "gadfly" of Epirus · Crossing the Strymon · The cities of Herakles · The sword of bronze · Prelude to Magna Graecia

Chapter XIII
FROM THE GOLDEN APPLES OF THE HESPERIDES TO THE GATES OF HELL 212

Who were the Hesperides? · The "golden apples" · The conquest of the gardens · The "weight of the world" · Athena returns the apples · And now to Hell · Cerberus · Two illustrious inmates: Theseus and Persephone · The key to Hell · The road to Cape Taenarum · The caverns of Hades · Cerberus' sentry box · The Laconian Styx · Theseus' release · Herakles and Cerberus · End of the Delphic mandate

Chapter XIV
FROM THE CAPTURE OF TROY TO THE DEATH OF HERAKLES 225

The contest in Oechalia · The incident at Delphi · Herakles goes to Omphale · The rediscovery of Troy · Beneath the wall of Laomedon: Priam's treasure · The first Trojan War · The first "Odyssey" · Another homecoming, another war · Eurytus, another "monster" · The Pylos of Neleus · The rage of Herakles

Chapter XV
THE DEATH OF HERAKLES 237

The Horn of Plenty · The philter of Nessos · Herakles in Thessaly · The poisoned tunic · The martyrdom · The pyre on Mount Oeta · Herakles among the gods

Chapter XVI
THE TWILIGHT OF THE HEROES 243

Death of Jason · The incident at the Panathenaia · Theseus and the Minotaur · The "labyrinth" at Knossos · Daedalus and Icarus · Ariadne's thread · The baptism of the Aegean · The tragedy of Phaedra

Chapter XVII
THE SWORD OF IRON 251

CHRONOLOGICAL TABLES 253

PRINCIPAL SITES OF THE HEROIC AGE 256

BIBLIOGRAPHY 258

INDEX 261

"Both the heroes of these tales and the geographical setting in which they take place actually existed."

CAMBRIDGE ANCIENT HISTORY

GODS WITH
BRONZE SWORDS

PREFACE

About the gods of the swords of bronze:

Dear Costa de Loverdo:

I am only too pleased to take a moment away from the routine of my university classes to accompany you into your beloved realm of historical vision. This is no longer the exclusive domain of the poets, moreover: today men of science are also required to plumb the sources of creative imagination.

Although some scholars may still be reluctant to do so, the public, untouched by the quibbles of professional archaeology, have no such scruples. In their attempts to understand the way in which we reach our discoveries, some people even suppose us to be in possession of secret processes and documents. Sometimes, the natives of the sites you know so well in my country may be heard alluding to the "occult tomes" which the "foreign gentlemen" consult before proclaiming, "This is the place. Dig here." In their fanciful accounts, the treasure is always uncovered just below the surface, the foreign gentlemen scoop it all up and are whisked away as though by magic, never to return.

Now, you and I have never seen such sorcerers; yet there is a grain of truth in these naïve tales, as in all legend: in many instances, what they call "secret documents" and "magic formulas" are nothing more or less than the writings of the ancients. You, as a historian, have said it often enough: each text is potentially able to furnish some clue to the classical world. The poems of Homer, plays of Aeschylus, dialogues of Plato, an ancient inscription, even a Byzantine anthology can be useful to those who know how to read them. Most precious of all is the account of his travels which Pausanias, in his way a serious archaeologist, wrote in A.D. 160; he is remarkable both for his faithful reporting of the traditions that had come down to his generation, and for the scrupulous attention to detail with which he described the vestiges whose origins most other men of his time were busily forgetting. Schliemann, the great "patron" of your *Swords of Bronze,* believed in the *Iliad* as an orthodox Hebrew believes in his Pentateuch, but he never failed to consult Pausanias for confirmation.

He went to Mycenae in 1876 because Homer said Agamemnon and his army were slaughtered there, and because Pausanias noted down the exact location of their tombs. This "fanatic," who put as much faith in their affirmations as in a coroner's death certificate, then ordered his men to dig.

You tell how he actually found the illustrious dead of his dreams, together with their fabulous treasure, in the designated place. In that dramatic moment he kneeled to kiss the remains he thought were Agamemnon's and the ground he believed to be hallowed. True enough, as you observe, he had made a chronological error of some three hundred years or more, and the remains were not those of the Atreidae but of their forefathers, contemporaries of your Bronze Age heroes. But thanks to him, they were resurrected; and with such a find, who cares about a trivial anachronism? Who cares about the violent abuse heaped upon his genius by a few scholars who could not forgive him his lack of Ph.D.s? Avatars of this type so often occur among the true innovators in the world of science. His critics have now sunk into oblivion, and what remains is the fact that the "visionary fanatic" discovered the civilization Homer sang of, opening up the whole field of research based on the writings of the ancients and touching off the sequence of great discoveries of modern archaeology.

Perhaps an example—this one only a few years old—would be in order here, to show how faith in the veracity of the texts, a principle you so rightly embrace, continues to reward all who possess it a hundredfold.

In 1939 the archaeological exploration of Messenia—the region corresponding to Homer's Pylos—was undertaken jointly by Greece and America. Professor Blegen discovered the famous palace attributed by many to Nestor, together with a large number of tablets written in "Mycenaean" script. The war stopped all progress, and work was not resumed until 1952, when I was put in charge of the Greek team. While Professor Blegen, a great scholar, was completing the excavation of the palace, I decided to try out a new method, which consisted mainly in seeking to increase my understanding of the kingdom of Nestor—at least in so far as its essence could be extracted from its shell of mythology—by studying the ancient texts.

First, I had to find out who Nestor really was. The Homeric texts show him as an old, old man, famous for his great wisdom, his interminable discourses, and the prodigious capacity of the goblet from which he drank (Schiller frankly spoke of him as an old tippler, "*der Alte Zecher*"). Because of his great age, he did not actually fight in the battles, nor did his army play a prominent part in the Trojan War, although his son Antilochus was a fine charioteer and close friend of Achilles. And yet, wherever we look in both the *Iliad* and the *Odyssey,* the features of Nestor stare back at us.

Perhaps, therefore, we must not be satisfied with this bare caricature. How had the old king achieved such prominence in Homer, when he had done so little? Where were we to look for a key to the enigma?

In addition to the *Iliad,* there was another poem: the *Kypria Epic,* the general tenor of which is known to us through the *Chrestomathia* of Proclus. In it, Menelaus returns from Crete to find Helen, Paris, and the royal treasure gone with the wind. The Trojan War is declared. Menelaus and Agamemnon agree to seek alliance with Nestor, and Menelaus goes to Pylos in person to persuade Nestor to help them.

What kind of help do they want? Ninety vessels! Only ten fewer than were supplied by Agamemnon's own empire, which in those days was the most powerful in the Mediterranean. Thus it becomes clear that the kingdom of Nestor was second in sea power, and therefore in wealth, in all Greece. And this was the working hypothesis we adopted during the remainder of the Greek excavations at Pylos.

Our expectations now being greater than before, our research was scaled accordingly, and results soon confirmed the allegations of tradition—the "veracity of the Homeric tales," as Schliemann would have put it. Under the blows of our picks, Messenia emerged as the seat of a "Mycenaean" civilization more comprehensive and highly developed than Mycenae itself. Scores of mounds and tombs were uncovered, and in 1956 one of them was found to contain, among other objects, those priceless swords with the golden hilt guards, damascened in gold and incrusted with silver or nielloed by smiths who were masters of their art—swords such as were brandished by your heroes of the *Swords of Bronze.*

In 1960 I was already convinced that the Messenian site of Peristeri would give us a new Mycenae, and in 1962 I dared to prophesy the excavation of treasures as great as any found by Schliemann. Some thought my prediction very rash, but was it really, when tradition affirmed that Pylos was the home port of a fleet that could amass wealth on a scale comparable to that of the kings of "Golden Mycenae?"

Once the expropriation formalities were finally completed and digging could proceed systematically, the earth yielded a marvelous golden diadem and, among many other examples of the goldsmith's craft, three goblets; one is seventeen centimeters high and has a diameter of twenty centimeters, irresistibly evoking Nestor's famous goblet of legendary size.

These finds are only a few months old and may fairly be seen as the initial confirmation of our hypothesis. Our work is continuing, but, more precious than the treasures they may lead us to is the function of the texts as a source of inspiration and enthusiasm—to us, the archaeologists, as well as to you, the historian. For both of us, the ancient texts and traditions contain the ferment of discovery.

This is the profitable path you have chosen to follow in your search for the heroes, recreating the stormy epic of the founders of Hellas, the battles and exploits of those you call the gods of the swords of bronze.

Professor S. Marinatos
Athens, March 1966

Publisher's note: Professor Marinatos, of the Academy of Athens, has been responsible for many noteworthy discoveries; among other things, he has provided a solution to the puzzle of the sudden collapse of the Minoan civilization of Crete. He was the first to attribute it to an eruption of the nearby crater of Thera—a hypothesis that has since been confirmed by geology, vulcanology, and seismology, as the author states in the opening chapters of this book.

FOREWORD

The Reporter's Equipment

In memoriam
Heinrich Schliemann

Ten years of study, in libraries and laboratories, in Athens and Paris; several more spent exploring sites in the Peloponnesus, Attica, Boeotia, Phocis, Egypt, ancient Phoenicia, Crete, Sardinia, Corsica, Sicily, Provence and Italy; scratching at the surface of the earth and the floors of caves, with geologist's hammer and archaeologist's pick; on foot, on mule back, by jeep, boat, and airplane, and sometimes in a bathysphere: this was the toll that the gods of the sword of bronze exacted from their historian.

Schliemann and Sir Arthur Evans and their successors, the great "inventors" of Troy, Mycenae, and Knossos, were ideal guides along the way, but there were other inventive spirits, too—Madeleine de Loverdo or P. H. Hirmenech—who never became famous or have now been forgotten.

At the end, another link was forged in the long chain that reaches back into the dark unknown and will one day emerge in the broad light of day.

The Mythological Process

By definition a "mythographer" is a person who writes about myths, but that will not help us to agree on a definition of "myth." Dictionaries offer various alternatives: "characteristic or narrative of an age of heroes or fable" or "tradition presenting, in allegorical form, some great natural, historical or philosophical event."

It is the historian's task to extract the original fact from its envelope of fable.

Everyone agrees that stories transmitted orally become transformed into legends of the miraculous. At Roncesvalles, for example, we are invited to admire the ten-meter-high rock cleft by Roland in his attack upon Durandel. You could drive your donkey through the gap, supposedly made by one blow of his sword. Does that mean the knights of Charlemagne must be relegated to the ranks of pure fable?

For a long time, however, this was the treatment given to protohistory by qualifying it as mythological.

Deciphering

It used to be: "Pegasus? A flying horse that crossed the Mediterranean with one flap of its wings? Poetic delirium!"

That was the whole problem: the ancient writings are the work of preliterary troubadours, not of historians in the twentieth-century manner. But if this is poetry, then in terms of poetic metaphor the wings of sea-borne Pegasus would be sails, skimming the crests of waves, the sails of swift vessels that give wings to navigators. This suggests a fleet, whose heraldic device would be a winged horse. If so, there is no longer anything astonishing in the idea that Pegasus should go across the sea.

In this instance the process can be demonstrated, moreover, simply by tracing a drawing of a ship from the side of an amphora dating from the eighth century B.C., the period in which the texts were being written. There the wings are, beyond any doubt.

The same metaphor applies in respect of Daedalus and his son Icarus, who used "wings" to escape from the labyrinth. One need only recall that Daedalus was "the first man to use sails on ships in place of oars."

Similarly, seventy-five years ago Max Müller, head of the school of the same name, never wrote the name of Herakles without adding, "whose solar origins are universally admitted." The proof? Herakles' Labors move from East to West, like the sun.

But in that case, what of his return to the Peloponnesus, necessitating a trip in the opposite direction? Here Müller showed his ignorance of the process by which myths are created: the pagans deified any mortal whose deeds were memorable. The mechanism is always the same: we Christians create our saints according to very similar criteria.[1]

For the subject of the myth, too, the end result is always the same: a seat in heaven.

Heinrich Schliemann's Act of Faith

For archaeologists of the last century, Greece began with the first Olympic games (776 B.C.), as though the spectators who watched them were a product of spontaneous combustion rather than of a protracted evolution.[2]

Then came the German Heinrich Schliemann. His was a strange destiny: a merchant grown rich in the indigo trade, who was obsessed by an unaccountable passion for ancient Greece. He never wearied of saying that one universe was still to be discovered—that of the mythical world of Homer, who nobody believed had actually existed.

Then came the revelation, with a flabbergasted world looking on as Priam's Troy returned to life under the picks swung by teams of men whom the graduate of nowhere had hired to dig on the mound of Hissarlik (Aegean coast of Asia Minor). He had trusted Homer, and he was right.

Then Schliemann went to dig at Mycenae, "a few feet from the Lion Gate." One starry night he clambered out of the pit covered with dust and, by the dim light of torches, wrote a telegram to the King of the Greeks that still sends shivers down archaeologists' spines: "I have just looked into the eyes of Agamemnon . . ."

In that, he was mistaken: the golden mask he thought portrayed the Greek commander of the army at Troy was a likeness, not of Agamemnon, but of one of the Perseids, and it was they and their whole saga that had just been resurrected on Helladic soil.

A successor to carry on Schliemann's great work was found in

[1] Herakles was deified for his Labors; St. George was beatified for "slaying the dragon."

[2] Microbiology was the first field in which, thanks to Pasteur, this view was shown to be false.

Sir Arthur Evans, who excavated the palace of the Minoan kings at Knossos—and now it was the Minotaur's turn to see the light of day again.

The limits of history were driven back, this time to the very beginning of the Bronze Age, almost five thousand years ago.

The Testimony of Agathon

It required a mountain of evidence to convince the judges of the old school. One of the most persuasive items was found at Dodona, the ancient sanctuary of northern Greece. This was the testimony of Agathon of Zante, who invoked the oracle more than a thousand years after Jason had come that way, and declared himself to be a descendant, in the thirtieth generation, of the prophetess Cassandra.

The inscription is engraved in bronze. Archaeologists date it from about 300 B.C. Now, thirty generations before that puts us not far from the year 1230, when, according to accounts of the Trojan War (these days, no one seriously doubts that it took place, and took place precisely in the thirteenth century B.C.), Cassandra was alive.

As far as the basic issue is concerned, judgment has now been passed. "Both the heroes of these tales and the geographical setting in which they take place actually existed."

But we must go still further back through time.

The Key to History

The laws that preside over human movements are immutable, and as a result, in both their causes and effects, destinies repeat themselves unendingly.

For example, there is the law of gravity, which places castles on hilltops so that an attacking army will reach the castle wall in a state of exhaustion after its climb. If some acropolis is missing, therefore, we will look for it on high ground.

Similarly, migrations go through the passes and not over the peaks of the mountain range they are traversing, because the terrain compels them to do so. Their starting point may be unknown, but not the route they took in transit, for that was foreordained.

It is also true, with some exceptions, that movement flows away from chill and mist in the direction of more gentle climes: like plants, humans obey the law of heliotropism, and botany and archaeology have in common the phenomenon that draws the corolla after the life-giving sun. In the same way, the peoples of desert regions grope their way to the rivers, like roots in search of the source of life. They go to the sea, too, to find wider horizons.

Wherever the nomad feels at home, solid constructions begin to replace his ephemeral tents; and towns grow up where there is a justification for them: at the intersections of roads and valleys.

Now wherever there is a town, there must also be town politics, an assembly of dignitaries, a forum, and a parliament, just as there must be strategy and tactics wherever there is war, and cemeteries, liturgy, and temples wherever there is death.

Another example: man is drawn into battle by hunger, love or hatred, ambition or greed—and sometimes, by following the line of least resistance, for it is easier to steal a purse than to work to fill it. Therefore, we want to put what we possess in a safe place, and so walls are built and flanked with towers.

In both their causes and effects, these simple truths survive unchanged in every age and season. Murder and plunder, larceny and war are the eternal solutions to the same problems, and with a minimum of perceptiveness it becomes possible, through analysis of the end product, to identify its causes, which vary with the specific historical context. The motives of human beings, like their needs and passions, never cease to be the same.

And this is why, as they say, history repeats itself.

Therefore, by studying the traces left by its heroes, we can arrive at an understanding of the Mycenaean expansion.

The Key to Legend: Linguistic Symbolism

Some ten years ago, the juxtaposition of a legend and a text by St. Paul gave me a clue to the location of a city which had vanished in circumstances so mysterious as to make one wonder whether it could ever have existed.[3]

[3] "Préface à la redécouverte de la ville de Dion" (*Bulletin de l'Association G. Budé,* October 1955). "Les villes ensevelies d'Athos" (*Géographica,* June 1956). "Mont Athos" (*La Colombe,* 1955, Appendix).

This study led me to tackle the problem of the Homeric texts. I soon saw that one of the keys to Greek protohistory lay in the interpretation of that picture language, wrapped in periphrasis and packed with symbols, which had caused pre-Schliemannians to mistake fictionalized journalism for pure fiction.

I also saw that a knowledge of modern demotic Greek was absolutely essential to an understanding of the texts that were its remote ancestors.

The misfortunes of the Asian Pelops were a typical example: the archaeologists had written him off as a mythical being because he was "boiled and eaten" by his father, Tantalos (the one of the famous torment), and yet survived to tell the tale. But modern Greeks still say that someone who is supplanted by a superior or persecuted by someone else has been "eaten" and "boiled." Here there is no myth: only an image, the same applied to Pelops, who was dominated and oppressed by his tyrannical father.

Similarly, the custom of adopting as a heraldic emblem some animal that possesses the traits one hopes to be known for among one's contemporaries is as old as mankind. In the days of the cave men, chiefs chose as their totem whatever animal might best characterize them or enhance their prestige in the eyes of their subjects. Courage is a lion; cunning, a fox. The fleece is the natural emblem of a pastoral tribe. In the days of Herakles, there were the Nemean lion, the Erymanthian boar, the Golden Fleece. Not so very long ago we had Richard the Lion-hearted; William de la March, Boar of the Ardennes; and Bossuet, the "eagle" of Meaux.

Extortion is also expressed symbolically: the ruling classes are said to "bleed" the people—like the "hydra" of Lerna, no doubt, demanding tribute from passing merchants. Today, when taxes go up, we say we are being "skinned alive," "milked dry," "strangled," etc.

The Connection with the Gods

Similarly eighteenth-century archaeologists thought the relationship between a king whose daughter was a country must be "mythological" (e.g., Pharoah, "Father" of Lydia), but now the same text is interpreted as expressing a relationship of sovereign to fief. It is commonly said, for instance, that France is the "elder daughter" of the Church.

This idea of figurative kinship is most important, for the monarchs of old used it to establish their claims to divine origin. The offspring sired by "Zeus" are legion: Minos, Perseus, Herakles; and Alexander a thousand years later. Where necessary, the oracles, often members of the royal family, were called in to confirm the claim: illegitimacy, when it could be attributed to a god, was anything but a blot on the family escutcheon. It was a title to glory, and a means of consolidating one's hold on the throne. We shall probably never know who Alexander's terrestrial father was; he was sired "by Zeus" out of Olympias, in Philip's absence. But as for Perseus: "Zeus," disguised as a "shower of gold"—the shower her covetous uncle Proetos caused to rain upon her guards—stole into the prison where Danaë was languishing, sequestered by her father. The image is still in common use today.

Of course, the further back one goes in time, the more uncertain become one's conjectures, but Perseus is only five reigns older than the Atreidae, who are now accepted historical figures.

Denying his existence, or that of Jason or Herakles, when excavations have confirmed those of Agamemnon and Priam, would be tantamount to conceding that a given set of grandsons had lived, but not their grandsires.

"In archaeology, whatever makes sense and is rational in the traditions is accepted as true until disproven."[4]

And, if one knows how to read them, it is plain that Homer, Pherecydes, Apollodorus of Athens, Hesiod and Diodorus Siculus never supposed for one moment that the heroes whose exploits they were recounting were "mythical."

The Technique of Historical Investigation

The working hypothesis of both Schliemann and Evans may be summed up in one sentence: where the ancients are concerned, there is no legend without some basis in fact.

[4] Hirmenech (*Hercule, étude préhistorique*).

With that as my point of departure, and my training as a professional engineer, I had at my disposal the whole arsenal of technology that modern science has given to archaeologists and mythographers. And what an arsenal it is! It has now become possible to feed the coded specifications of an amphora fished out of the Corsican sea into a computer that will then feed back the specifications of a similar amphora lost in the ocean two thousand years earlier.[5]

Not only can the possible location of an object be given in advance, but also its state of preservation.

Using radioactivity, an object's age can be determined with the precision specific to the Geiger counter and the infallible electron.

Spectrography and chemical analysis are ready to oblige with categorical replies when asked to scrutinize a stony mass congealed three thousand years ago or a crust of smoky deposits baked onto a cavern vault by a Middle Bronze Age potter's fire.

The results we obtain by such methods are nothing short of miraculous. For instance, the ancients say that a darkness obscured the sky over Egypt. Science, called in to investigate, provides an explanation: geologists have now ascertained that the crater of the island of Thera (Santorini, in the Cyclades) erupted in the sixteenth century B.C., breaching an entrance for the sea. Proceeding from there, vulcanologists explain how the prevailing winds might have carried the ash thrown into the stratosphere in the direction of the Nile delta. Meteorologists, next to be consulted, can even specify the time of year: Boreas, the north wind, blows toward Africa during three months only. Thus a combination of mythology, geological analysis, and weather balloons can enable the twentieth-century historian to puzzle out the origin of the "darkness over Egypt."

These results shed light on a related enigma—Cretan, in this instance. The tales of earthquakes and clouds of fire that reduced the palace of King Minos at Knossos to a heap of rubble must now

[5] Making due allowance for parameters such as the difference in mean temperature of the water in the Mediterranean and the ocean, the depth at which the object was lying, degree of deterioration caused by different species of marine fauna, etc.

be believed: Marinatos has proved that this holocaust occurred at the same time as the other events I have mentioned.

Similar instruments of research, used to amplify texts alluding to other localities, are now bringing Perseus, Bellerophon, Herakles, Theseus, and Jason back to life as well.

Chapter 1
GENEALOGY OF THE HEROES

"The son of Danaë of the lovely locks
Was Perseus, son also of Zeus, the sire of heroes."

HESIOD

History is a family affair. What manner of man was it who gave the Greek heroes their particular drives, ambitions, and attitudes?

In so far as we can tell, the Aegean civilization developed from two streams of very dissimilar origins, which converged and overflowed onto its shores between four and eight thousand years before Christ.

The Migration of the "men from the west"

Plato, writing in the fourth century B.C., refers to a traditional anecdote whereby a priest of Saïs in Egypt is said to have told Solon, around three hundred years earlier, "Our sacred writings affirm that eight thousand years have passed since this country was first civilized."[1]

The original settlers, however, came from far away to the west: "In those days there was an island outside the passage you [Greeks] call the Pillars of Hercules. This island was larger than Libya and Asia combined."

He is referring to the parts of Asia and Africa known at that time (an area larger than France).

"From the depths of the Atlantic . . . this insolent power" invaded the Mediterranean coast. Herodotus (fifth century B.C.) de-

[1] All quotations from Plato are taken from *Timaeus* and *Critias*.

scribes the "rampart of sand" leading from the Ocean Gateway to Egyptian Thebes. It was ". . . marked off at intervals equal to a ten-day voyage by mountains composed of large crystals of salt, from which fresh water flows." The first of these projections, starting point on the coast of the Atlantic, "is near Mount Atlas, a narrow, rounded mountain whose peak is always hidden in the clouds; the natives call it the pillar of heaven."

The Giant Atlas

And so it is. Not far from Gibraltar stands an isolated foothill of the Atlas range, a solitary mountain near the Atlantic coast, its summit virtually always lost in the clouds, the very image of a "pillar of heaven." The *Nautical Instructions* of the United States Navy give an impressive rendering of it.

This is also the giant Atlas, "bearing the sky on his shoulders."

To the east of Morocco lie the Chott Depressions, with oases providing a water supply for caravans. In view of the surrounding terrain, they offer the only possible route.

Then comes the Sahara, but the Tassili frescoes, dating from the eighteenth dynasty, prove that even in the second millennium (and a fortiori six thousand years earlier) the desert was lavishly fertile and there was fresh water in abundance: large herds of cattle are pictured on the cavern walls, and even a hippopotamus hunt.

The Egyptians

It was probably these newcomers who taught the Egyptians how to work metal (especially copper). By analysis of the level on which objects are found in the many-layered alluvial deposits of the Nile, the successive stages of civilization may be defined as accurately as the age of a tree from the rings of its trunk. The information obtained by this means does not conflict with the date given by the priest of Saïs, and it is tempting to attribute the sudden flowering of civilization in the Nile delta to the arrival of the emigrants from the Atlantic.

The Sphinx of Giza may be their work. An inscription from the fourth dynasty (nearly five thousand years ago) speaks of it as a monument "found by accident, buried in the sand and forgotten for many generations.[2]

If so, these first settlers may well be said to be "almost as old as the bones of the continents themselves."[3]

The Disappearance of Atlantis

Fact or fiction?

Recent investigation places a higher coefficient of truthfulness upon Plato's much-scorned account. None of the opponents' arguments will stand up any longer, either as far as his actual statements are concerned (embroidered and distorted, but not imaginary) or in terms of geology.

During the eighth millennium, he says, the Atlantic island disappeared. But how?

In those days the planet was undergoing a major crisis: only recently freed from its load of quaternary ice, earth's fragile crust was still adjusting to the new conditions.

The Nile confirms this. The fact that there is a first layer of sediment means that there was a first flood, and that means a first rainy season in Ethiopia (which is what causes the floods). The rainy season, in turn, is caused by winds blowing from the Indian Ocean at regular intervals. And the sudden advent of such winds is inconceivable without some prodigious upheaval in the direction of India and the Pacific.

Also at that time, the line of least resistance in the earth's crust that snakes across Iran, Asia Minor, and the floor of the Mediterranean, and continues out into the mid-Atlantic, was rent by convulsions.[4]

"In the days that followed, dreadful earthquakes and cataclysms occurred. In the space of one terrible day and night . . . all of a sudden . . . the Atlantid island sank into the sea and disappeared."

[2] F. Lenormand, *Histoire d'Orient.*

[3] E. Shuré: *Les Grands initiés.*

[4] We have witnessed the fragility of this scar in our own century: in the tremors in Iran, Turkey, the Peloponnesus, the Ionian islands; at Orléansville, Agadir, in the Azores (?), in the activity of Santorini (Cyclades), the Lipari Islands, Vesuvius, Etna; in the birth of a volcano at Cape Capelinhos (Azores)—all in the last twenty years.

In its place there remained only the volcanic archipelagoes we know today as the Azores, Madeira, and the Canaries.

The big island had sunk into the waves, but the Atlantides themselves were not extinct; they still held their mainland possessions, which comprised, according to Plato, ". . . on our side . . . Libya and Tyrrhenia."

These survivors also retained some of the characteristics of their original island culture—in particular, a set of symbols, and an aggressive temperament.

In the Bronze Age, they pushed eastward and collided with the heroes of Athens and the Peloponnesus.

The War between Atlantides and Greeks

"It was then, O Solon, that the heroism and enterprise of your powerful city [Athens] began to dazzle every beholder. It conquered the invader, raised the trophy, preserved the freedom of men who had never known slavery and, bearing no grudge, freed the other peoples, including my own, who were living in the shadow of the Pillars of Hercules."

The priest of Saïs said this war had been fought eight thousand years before his time. But it is maintained that in those days Athens had not even been founded. This is an optical illusion, however, rather than a mistake. The war was indeed fought in the second millennium, not in the eighth, and by that time Athens was already an old city. Also, the adversaries were not the original Atlantides and Athenians, but the descendants of the survivors of the Atlantic catastrophe—and Perseus, the hero who "slew the Gorgon"; Bellerophon, who "bridled Pegasus"; and Herakles, who "overpowered Geryon"—all acting for the account of Athens the Bellicose, as explicitly stated by Homer, Apollodorus, Diodorus and Pindar.

Solon went to Egypt in the sixth or seventh century B.C., eight thousand years after the first events related here (migration of the Atlantides and destruction of their island). This means that the conversation at Saïs took place seven hundred years after the second set of events (fourteenth century B.C.—the westward thrust of the Atlantides' descendants, encounter with the Greeks, and further geological upheavals, now substantiated).

At that remove the two periods, which had many features in common, had already merged into one in the mind of the Egyptian priest, moving closer together on the broad horizon of oral tradition, like parallel lines or superimposed photographs. It would have been truly amazing only if they had not done so.

Arrival of the Indo-Europeans

During these same remote millennia another wave of migration flowed down from Central Asia to the shores of the Mediterranean, drawn by its eternal springtime.

These people came between the Urals and the Caspian, across the steppes north of the Black Sea and down the valleys of the rivers that rise in the heart of the continent: the Dnieper, the Dniester, and the Danube.

The Pelasgians were among them. After reaching the Balkans, they turned south and, somewhere around the fourth millennium, began to populate what was later to become Greece.

Other bands, assembling in Iran, came by way of Mesopotamia. At the time of the first two Egyptian dynasties, they reached the shores of the Aegean. They were the Lydians, Lycians, Cilicians, Mysians, and Carians, the pioneers of history in these regions and thus, in a sense, its raw material. Later they were to found the city of Troy. Their names were Tantalos, Pelops, and Priam, and they also contributed to the formation of the Greek people.

Using techniques they had learned on their way through Mesopotamia, where the Sumerian civilization was developing, they planted and cultivated Syria, the slopes of the Taurus Mountains, and the islands off the coast of Asia Minor. But all these peoples, originating far inland, were wary of the sea.

However, at the beginning of the third millennium, a race of master seamen began to filter into their territory. These were the "red men"[5] in their "long ships," who invented navigation in the Mediterranean.

[5] Phoenician means "red man."

Rise of the Phoenicians

Paraphrasing a classical author already lost in his day, Justin wrote that "the Phoenicians stopped at the edge of the Syrian swamps" (the Jordan Trench, Dead Sea).

But where did they begin? Herodotus gives us the answer: "The Tyrians knew their ancestors had come from the Erytheian sea, on the shores of the sea where we now are [i.e., the Mediterranean]. Even in those days their long ships were carrying Egyptian cargo. . . . [The Tyrians] say their temple of Melkarth was founded around 2300 years ago [that is, in 2800 B.C.]."

After settling on the coast of Lebanon, they sent their fleet into the distant Aegean archipelagoes, and especially to Crete, whose inhabitants had previously made all their weapons and tools out of stone; to them they brought the arts of working copper and bronze.

Whenever, as periodically happened, Egypt enlarged her empire and took over their land, the Phoenicians sailed under her colors: cartouches of the Pharaohs Sneferu and Sahu-Ra (3200–2900 B.C.) have been found at Knossos.

Communications between Egypt and Crete were obliged to go by way of Phoenicia and the Cyclades, as ships in those days could only sail downwind, and, there being no regular winds from Africa, the direct south-north route was only occasionally practicable.

From Crete, which became their home port, the Phoenicians set sail for the mainland to the north, and, at the beginning of the second millennium, one of their captains happened into a sheltered bay in what came much later to be called the Peloponnesus, and disembarked there, at the mouth of a capricious river, in the land of the Pelasgians.

The Inachos

Today its ravaged bed, flushed by sudden fits of temper when its gravel mingles with the alluvial silt, can be crossed on an iron bridge on the Corinth road just north of Argos. It has retained the Greek form of its Phoenician name, Inachos.

Inachos founded a dynasty. Phoroneos succeeded him, and Ephyra, the latter's "daughter," who "bestrode" the Peloponnesian isthmus, later became famous under the name of Corinth. Apis, whose name is sufficient proof of his Egyptian ancestry, was the next king.[6]

Then came Argos, who bequeathed his name to the city and region around it (Argos means "plain").

The Inachids reigned for 420 years—or 378, depending on who is doing the computing. But the river remained the real master of the place. Today the plain it crosses is covered with olive groves and fine orchards, and the roads are lined with eucalyptus. But in the second millennium it was often flooded and, according to Thucydides' description of primitive Greece, the Pelasgian tribes inhabiting it were nomads: "There was no commerce . . . The inhabitants did not amass wealth, nor did they till the soil, for, having no fortified cities, they could never be sure an invader would not come and seize all they possessed . . ."

And, true enough, the newcomers were beginning to tread on one another's toes.

The People of Deucalion

In the sixteenth century B.C. a fresh wave of inland tribes from the far-off Caucasus rolled over the peninsula. These were the people of Prometheus, hitherto "bound" and subjugated by an "eagle" (some sovereign who had taken the bird of prey as his device?).

"Wearying of crude Scythia where his father kept him confined," and fed up with "eating out his liver" (or "champing at the bit," as we might say), Deucalion, the son of Prometheus, fled down the path taken by the Pelasgians before him, and settled in Thessaly, between Olympus and Thermopylae. If the Paros marble[7] can be trusted, he reigned there in 1574.

[6] Apis was the sacred bull of the ancient Egyptians, a product of both Osiris and Ptah. The priests drowned it in a fountain dedicated to the sun, and its mummy was worshiped.

[7] This inscription, a copy of some Athenian documents, appears to have been engraved around 264–263 B.C. On it, events are dated according to the terms of office and reigns of the City's magistrates and kings.

The region was then devastated by a natural disaster, the flood that bears Deucalion's name (occurring, according to the Paros chronology, in 1529). Geologists agree that at some time in the middle of the second millennium, the Peneus River was suddenly dammed by an earthquake at the point where, swollen by its four tributaries, it was about to flow into the sea. A tidal wave swept the coast, and heavy rains flooded the valley that year.

The surviving Thessalians retreated up one side of Mount Parnassus (8067 ft.), the lofty peak whose other slope looks down on the sanctuary of Delphi.

Deucalion and his wife Pyrrha then consulted the goddess Themis, who instructed them to "go outside the temple . . . and throw your grandmother's bones over your shoulder."

Deucalion understood that bones—those of the earth—meant stones. "So they picked up stones and, after throwing them over their shoulders, saw that the stones thrown by Deucalion were changed into men and those thrown by Pyrrha were changed into women."

In fact, when the waters finally receded and they were able to do so, the survivors simply went back down among the stones uncovered by the flood, which then "came to life" by virtue of their presence.

Pyrrha gave Deucalion a son: Hellen.

The Hellenes

Thucydides writes: "Until the time of Hellen, son of Deucalion, the appellation 'Hellenes' does not seem to have existed. Every tribe, and especially the Pelasgians, called Greece by some name related to its own. But when Hellen and his sons had gained control of Phthiotis, and other cities were coming to them for help, they all began to call themselves and each other Hellenes, as a result of their closer relations."

Homer never gives the name of Hellenes to all the Greeks, only to those from Phthiotis.

The "sons" of Hellen were Aeolos (Aeolians), Doros (Dorians), and Xuthos. His grandsons were Achaeos (Achaeans) and Ion

(Ionians). Hellen also had a brother, Aethlios, whose great-grandchildren were named Aetolos (Aetolians) and Epeios (in Elis).

What we are seeing here is the "family tree" of the Hellenes, and also the order in which the northern tribes penetrated into Greece, following the original Pelasgians; we also have the geographical distribution of their territories.

These tribes were to sire some illustrious offspring: first Jason, then Achilles, then Alexander.

But before this could happen, the land dwellers' blood had to mingle with that of the Cretan Phoenicians, the "red men" who were now emerging from the sea on all sides.

The Cretans Take to the Sea

While these migrations were taking place, the Phoenician colony (*minoa*) of Crete had grown so strong that it was becoming a serious threat to the parent settlement on the mainland. With its own fleet, it launched boldly out into piracy, along the coast of Tyre.

In the opinion of the ancients, the Phoenician and Cretan legend of Europe dates from the end of the sixteenth century. At that time Syria was ruled by "Agenor, son of Poseidon and Oceanid Libya . . ." That is, a sovereign born of the "sea god" (hence, a sailor) and hailing from Atlantid Libya (a perfect description of the Phoenician "red man"). "He had three sons, Cilix, Cadmos and Phoenix [whose name is that of Phoenicia itself], and one daughter, Europe . . . who was a peerless beauty, so fair that she was suspected of stealing Hera's cosmetics [Hera, wife of Zeus]."

Homer adds, "She, whose father was the illustrious Phoenix." Was she his "daughter" or his "sister?" In any but a literal sense, it makes no difference, since the object here is simply to specify the nationality of a princess from Phoenicia, the land of Phoenix.

The "myths" say that Zeus, the god of gods (who was born on Mount Ida in Crete), abducted her from the Phoenicians. Others say the rape was perpetrated by the "Cretan bull," and in many classical renditions she is seen coming ashore on the back of that sacred animal.

But Victor Bérard, a great authority on the subject, wrote that "the bull of the rape of Europe is the islanders' pirate ship, terror of the mainland Phoenicians, its prow adorned with the head of the beast of Crete. In the Odyssey, the ship is called 'straight-horned' because of this feature."[8]

From that day forward "the Tyrians added a 'feast of the evil evening' to their religious liturgy."

The root of Europe is *ereb,* a Semitic vocable referring to the west, the setting sun, or the evening. Europe—the twilight of Phoenician supremacy, which was gradually passing into the hands of the Cretans.

Birth of the Minotaur

The southeastern coast of the big island is bordered by sheer mountain faces cleft by deep ravines, some three thousand feet high and only a few yards wide. The mountain slopes are covered with maple, oak, pine, and cypress.

There is one gulf, however, protected from the sudden, violent winds of Africa by a range of coastal hills on the south side of a narrow valley that runs parallel to the sea—a land of the vine and olive.

Into this gulf flows the Elektras, the "yellow river" carrying the ocher-colored earth down from the heights. This is also the plain of Phaestos, today a wilderness of ruins. Among the toppled stones one gray monolith still stands, in the form of the stylized horns of the bull, emblem of the marauding ships.

The princess came ashore. She went up the little river, then its tributary—a swift stream by whose banks gaunt flocks nibble at the rusty grass that grows from the stony ground among the flowering oleander. The snowy peak of Psiloriti (Mount Ida) towers more than eight thousand feet above; when there is a thaw, the torrent swells in an instant.

This is Lethe, the "river of forgetfulness."

Nearby lie the ruins of Gortyna, ravaged by earthquake and the internal quarrels of the Cretans. But in the Hellenic fifth century,

[8] Victor Bérard, *Les Phéniciens et l'Odyssée.*

the laws laid down by the Wise Men of Greece were inscribed on its walls, and Pausanias was taken to see the plane tree that shaded the transports of Europe and the "Cretan bull."

Their union produced the first great king of the island *minoa,* and Minos I, naturally enough, was his name. As both king and high priest of the cult of the bull, he wore the sacred animal's mask during all religious ceremonies, and so became the first Minotaur of an august line.[9]

The Reign of Minos I

Minos I was a wise lawmaker who, like Moses two centuries later, went up the sacred mountain (Mount Ida) to receive counsel and the laws from his "father" Zeus. He was a just man, and at his death he was appointed "judge of the underworld," alongside his brother, the famous Rhadamanthus: "Then I saw Minos, noble son of Zeus; with the golden scepter in his hand, this king sat in judgment upon the dead . . ." (*Odyssey,* XI.)

At Knossos, near Herakleion, Minos built himself a palace; beneath the foundations of later structures its pillared crypts are still standing, along with fragments of floor pavements, and storerooms showing traces of hundreds of amphoras.

Thucydides wrote: "Minos gained control over most of what we now call the Greek sea. He subdued the Cyclades and was the first to establish colonies on most of the islands, chasing out the Carians who had been living there. He set up his own children as governors. Moreover, as was only natural, he did his utmost to root out piracy, in order to ensure the safe collection of the taxes he levied."

It was now the Cretans' turn to accuse the Phoenicians of piracy.

The Struggle for the Trading Centers

The stake in this match was the profitable commerce that was growing steadily more important throughout the Mediterranean.

In the second millennium, the "long ships" carried grain in earthenware jars, oil and wine in sealed amphoras, wood, spices,

[9] Minos, king of the *minoa,* is a generic noun, like "pharaoh" in Egypt.

incense, and chemicals (natron, of which the Egyptians required large quantities to embalm their dead); but the choicest merchandise, the cargo of any craft able to navigate the open sea, was ore.

The sixteenth century was the culmination of the Mediterranean Bronze Age—and bronze is made from copper and tin. The former was within easy reach, on Cyprus (*kypros,* a word meaning "copper"), but tin was mined in Iberia, on the coast of the Río Tinto in the country of the Tartessians, and in the Cassiterides Islands (*cassiteros*—tin), which have since disappeared, probably during some seismic upheaval around 1500 B.C.[10]

The Achaeans Learn to Sail

Phoenicians and Cretans, thus, were plying between opposite ends of the Mediterranean. Soon they were joined by a third, and rival, thief. The Achaeans, "sons" of Hellen, had now reached the sea and, passing through Central Europe on their way, had learned how to make bronze.

But it was the Phoenicians, according to Strabo, who taught them "to sail by the Bear." Their fifty-oar long ship now became the model for the fleets that were to give the land dwellers their turn to rule the sea.

Like their predecessors, they began as pirates, but by the middle of the fifteenth century they were sufficiently well organized to raid Crete and loot the palace of Minos, who had been so sure of his fleet that he had not even bothered to build a wall around his residence.

Then the crater of Thera (Cyclades) erupted and let in the sea; the island, a cone-shaped mountain around eight miles in diameter and three thousand feet high, literally blew up, hurling cubic miles of rock into the atmosphere. Ash flew 100,000 feet up in the air, and water gushed through the breach and into the cavity, which has a surface of fifty square miles, and reached a depth of over twelve hundred feet; whole fleets maneuver there today.

In Crete, sixty miles away, "even sacred grottoes like Arkhala

[10] They must have been located somewhere to the west of the British Isles, in a line with the English veins where they disappear into the sea.

Khori were destroyed." The ground was covered by volcanic ash, and towering tidal waves swept over the coast from the north.[11]

In the course of this unprecedented catastrophe, Minos' magnificent palace burned and was destroyed.

Phorcys' Empire in the West[12]

The seafaring peoples at the western end of the Mediterranean also profited by these events. A prince named Phorcys ruled over these remote descendants of the Atlantides "of Libya and Tyrrhenia." "Poseidon [god of the sea] married Ghea [Mother Earth] and gave birth to Pontos [the ocean]; he in turn begat Phorcys . . ."

According to Varron, this was the great protohistorical[13] King of Corsica who, as the son of Ghea and Poseidon, was both a "land dweller" and "sailor."

His stronghold lay in the valley of the Taravo; since 1954 teams from the French Centre National de la Recherche Scientifique have gradually been disinterring the imposing vestiges of a Bronze Age civilization "anterior, in any case, to the second millennium."[14]

On the way up the valley, driving along the narrow road that winds upward to the peaks, a row of menhirs suddenly appears at the edge of a wood. Some of them are carved with swords of unmistakable provenance: they are those used in the Middle Bronze Age.

Elsewhere among the foliage of beech and oak, strange anthropomorphic silhouettes loom up, several meters high: mute sentinels modeled by some great people who lived there in the night of time.

In the fourteenth century B.C., Corsica was the center of a vast colonial empire.

"Phorcys married Ceto, daughter of Poseidon [daughter of a sealord], and their children were the Nymphs, the Graeae, and the Gorgons."

To the ancients, "nymphs" were personifications of springs and,

[11] I. Velikovsky, *Worlds in Collision.*
[12] See map of the Phorcid Empire of the "monsters."
[13] Protohistory: period preceding classical history.
[14] R. Grosjean, C.N.R.S.

by extension, the towns built near them. These two, named Thoosa and Scylla, were "young," that is, new, and "born" of Phorcys—hence, founded by him. Located on the shores of Sicily, they drained the big island's hinterland and dominated the sea arm that separated it from the mainland.[15]

The Graeae, on the other hand, or "old women"—Enyo, Pemphredo and Deino—were "old" colonies, probably dating from the first Atlantid migrations, which had founded them in passing. The Greeks also called them "Hesperides" (*hesperos,* evening) because they lay in the direction of the setting sun. Phorcys perished in his attempt to conquer or defend them, and was nicknamed "the African" on that account.[16]

A fourth "Hesperide"—Erytheia, also of Atlantid origin—lived on a little island of the same name, outside the Pillars of Hercules.[17]

As for the "Gorgons" (Stheno, Euryale, Medusa), "they lived beyond Ocean, at the end of the world, near the home of night[18] . . . They bore a striking resemblance to their elder sisters, the Graeae."

How is it that the Graeae are called "elder" sisters? Weren't they colonies of Atlantis and therefore, of necessity, "younger"? The contradiction is only apparent: the cataclysms of the eighth millennium had occurred in the interim, and by the time of Phorcys some inhabitants of the merchant towns of Libya and Tyrrhenia, survivers of the disaster, had found their way back to their vanished fatherland and repopulated its remains. This made the Atlantic Gorgons legitimately "younger" than the Graeae.

Lastly, an outpost in Hellenic waters, lurked Echidne (the spider), a "monster" who spun her web from a stronghold in the Echinades Islands. She held the most important strategic position of all, for the archipelago, protected from the open sea by Leucas and Ithaca,

15, 16, 17, 18 Genealogy of the Phorcid "monsters"

Phorcys m. Ceto
(Corsica)

Nymphs	*Graeae*	*Erytheia*	*Gorgons*	*Echidne*
(Thoosa, Scylla)	(Deino, Pemphredo, Enyo)		(Stheno, Euryale, Medusa)	
(Sicily)	(Africa)	(Cádiz)	(Ocean)	(Echinades)

spans the mouth of the river Achelous and dominates the entrance to the Gulf of Corinth, the marine lifeline of the ancients.[19]

From this Echinadian hideout, the Phorcids, who could be dislodged only by a really formidable fleet, boldly set out to conquer the eastern territories.

Checking these invaders and then repulsing them was to be the great task of the Greek heroes. They had to "slay the monsters," in the colorful speech of the classical poets of mythology.

The Baptism of Europe

Like the Phorcids, the mainland Phoenicians took advantage of the temporary eclipse of the Cretans to gain a foothold in the markets of Greece, the home of their Achaean pupils in the art of navigation.

The land beyond the sea to the north still reminded them of the rape of Europe; first Crete, then Greece, then the northern shore of the Mediterranean and finally the whole continent behind it inherited the princess's name.

Europe, the land of Europe; Ereb, the land of the setting sun—the two ideas merged into one in the minds of the Tyrians.

Thus the continent acquired its name.

The Ancestors of the Heroes

According to the "Paros marble," a Phoenician (or Egyptian) named Cecrops landed in Attica around 1580 B.C. and settled at the back of a sheltered bay not far from a rocky plateau that could serve as a fortress.

The port was Piraeus; the flat-topped boulder, the Acropolis. A thousand years later, Pericles was to cover it with dazzling temples, but the city's initial impetus came from a hero, one of Cecrops' descendants—Theseus, the son of Aegeus, who was to conquer the second Minos.

It was now the turn of Europe's brother Cadmos to seek *his* fortune; in 1519 he landed in Boeotia, killed a local "dragon" and named his town Thebes, after the capital of Egypt—another indica-

[19] See note on previous page.

tion of his origin. Today archaeologists digging on the site of the Boeotian city are turning up large numbers of Phoenician tablets, which may have much to tell us.

Then, in 1510, Danaos, another Phoenician, "attempted to steal the crown from his brother Aegyptos, and was forced to flee Egypt." He settled in Argolis, evicting the last remaining Inachids there, and founded a new dynasty, which was to produce Perseus and then, fifteen generations later, Herakles.

Chapter II
PERSEUS

"After him rushed the elusive monsters,
The Gorgons, slavering to seize him;
Perseus hacked off Medusa's head
And fled them, shuddering with fear."

HESIOD

"To Argos where the horses graze . . ." (*Iliad,* XV.)

Argos lies at the back of a blue gulf on the eastern side of the Peloponnesus. It is a small town, whose low houses, clean-lined and cool-hued, cluster around a big shady square, and most of the time it is ablaze in the sun.

Two russet hills overlook it. On the road from Corinth, they are visible a long way off: Mounts Larissa and Apsis. The name of the latter means "shield," an exact description of the mountain's swelling shape. (But it was baptized after the time of Danaos, in whose day the shield was still unknown.)

In the hollow between them stand the foundation walls of temples of Apollo and Athena Oxyderkes (clairvoyant). The theater was carved out of solid rock at the foot of Larissa. It held twenty thousand spectators: ninety tiers of seats climb up the steep slope, a stairway for giants.

Higher up the same arid hill gleams an immaculate little pure white monastery; its patron saint is the Virgin, who inherited the throne of an older fertility goddess—Hera, wife of Zeus.[1]

[1] In the second millennium, the tutelary goddess of Argos was called Hera Akraia, Hera of the Cliff. In our day, presiding over the same precincts and lodged in the same grotto, she is called Panaghia Vrashou, Madonna of the Rock.

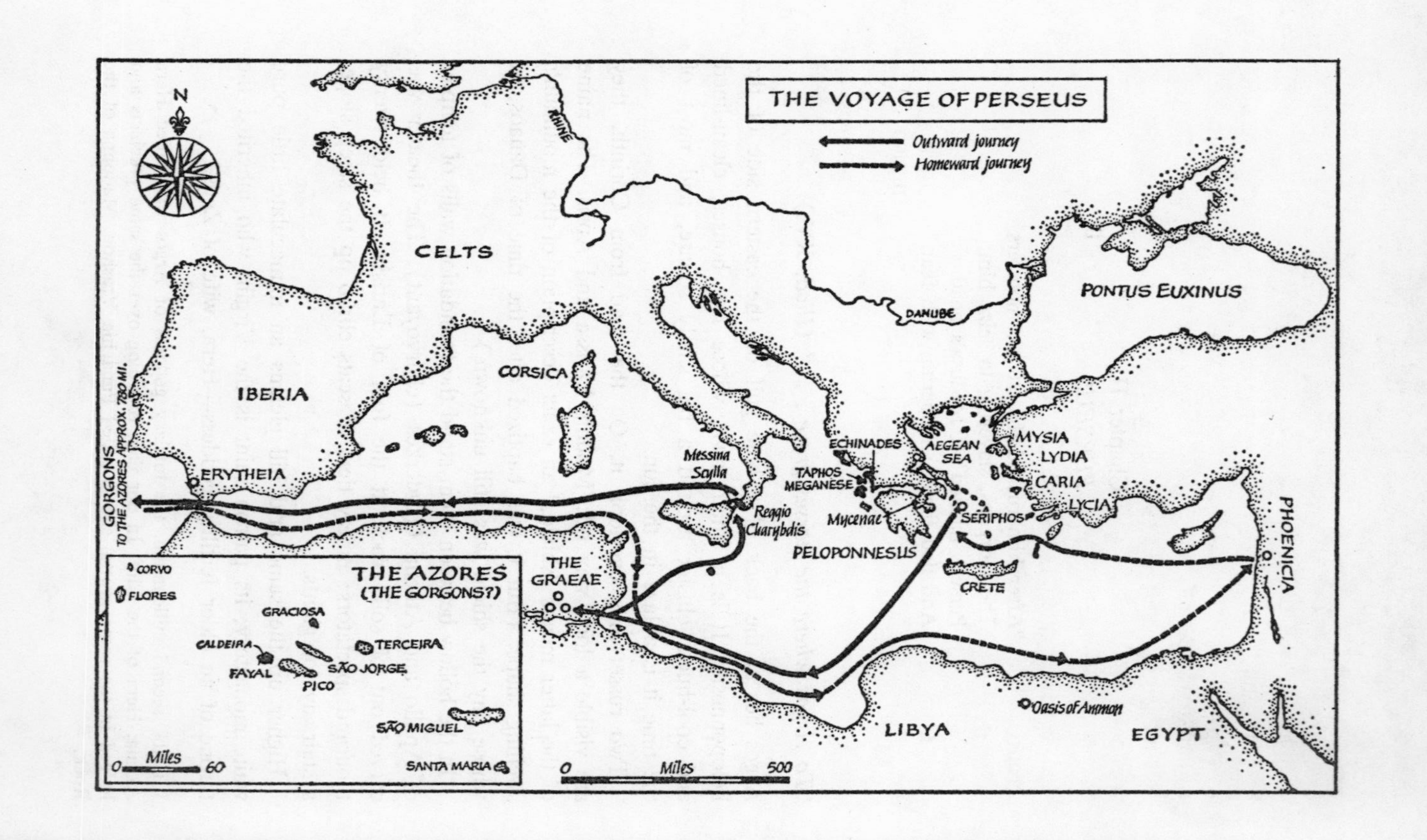
THE VOYAGE OF PERSEUS
Outward journey
Homeward journey
N
CELTS
RHINE
DANUBE
PONTUS EUXINUS
IBERIA
CORSICA
ERYTHEIA
GORGONS
TO THE AZORES APPROX. 780 MI.
Messina
Scylla
Reggio
Charybdis
ECHINADES
TAPHOS
MEGANESE
Mycenae
PELOPONNESUS
AEGEAN
SEA
MYSIA
LYDIA
CARIA
LYCIA
SERIPHOS
CRETE
PHOENICIA
THE
GRAEAE
LIBYA
Oasis of Ammon
EGYPT
0
Miles
500
THE AZORES
(THE GORGONS?)
CORVO
FLORES
GRACIOSA
CALDEIRA
FAYAL
TERCEIRA
SÃO JORGE
PICO
SÃO MIGUEL
SANTA MARIA
0
Miles
60

Hera is a name to remember, for in the second millennium her temples dictated the policies of kings, supported by the superstition then prevalent.

When Danaos came, there was nothing but a prehistoric town: foundations of walls and houses have been unearthed on the summit of Apsis, and the merest embryo of a fort stood on the acropolis of Larissa.

The natives encountered by the Phoenicians were Pelasgians who had been conquered by Inachids. They worshiped Hera in her grotto, while their necropolis at the foot of Apsis slowly filled with their dead.

The Cask of the Danaans

At the level of the hamlet, the river Inachos continued its war upon the plain, which retaliated by drying up the stream during the torrid summer months.

The thirst of this land is unquenchable. It is like a bottomless cask: no matter how much water pours into it, it will never be full. Danaos and his followers brought irrigation canals, reservoirs, and drainage traps from the Nile Valley, but their efforts were in vain, the plain of Argos has remained the "cask of the Danaans."

In the Kingdom of Danaos, Sixteenth Century B.C.

"Then came men from Tiryns who built strong walls . . ."

Tiryns stands on a rocky promontory near the coast, eight and one-half miles from Argos. In the sixteenth century its houses were only partly protected by an outer wall; it was the descendants of Danaos who completed the fortifications and transformed the settlement into the "city of towers."

Two miles south of this bastion, a precipitous cape looms over the gulf: Nauplia, the "sailing ship." In the Bronze Age it provided a sheltered harbor for pirates and fishermen, the original and eternal "sons of Poseidon," god of the sea.

Completing the scene, two archaic towns perched on rugged hilltops eight or nine miles inland, also awaiting the ramparts Perseus was to build around them with the help of the Cyclops. The first was called Midea; the second was soon to become the more powerful of the two, seat of an empire and greatest shrine of the goddess Hera, "who suddenly caused the thunder to growl, in honor of rich Mycenae's king" (*Iliad,* XI).

But now, the two principalities faced each other as rivals, on opposite sides of the Inachos.

The Struggle for Succession

Danaos was succeeded on the throne of Argolis by Lynkeos, and then, perhaps a little before the year 1400, by Abas, whose twin sons Acrisios and Proetos "began to fight before they ever left their mother's womb . . . When they grew up, they quarrelled over possession of the crown, and it was during this war that the shield was invented" (Apollodorus).

Acrisios won, and drove Proetos out of Argos to seek refuge at the court of Iobates, King of Lycia, on the coast of Asia Minor. He married Iobates' daughter, whom Homer calls Anteia, but the tragic poets say her name was Stheneboea. His father-in-law then sent the couple back to Argolis, at the head of a fleet of ships and an army.

The scholiast on Euripides explains that "as Proetos was receiving help from Lycia, his brother Acrisios, intimidated by his army, consented to share the kingdom, and it was agreed that he should keep Argos, while Proetos would have Tiryns."

The Fateful Oracle

Acrisios was worried, for no throne is ever truly secure until an heir has come to sit on its steps, and he had no male issue. Pherecydes writes: "Acrisios married Eurydice, daughter of Lacedaemon, and had a daughter named Danaë, after Danaos, founder of the dynasty. He consulted the oracle, to learn whether he would ever have a son. The god replied that he would not, but that his daughter would, and that this boy would be the cause of his grandfather's death."

Prophecy of a clairvoyant? Nobody knows. The oracles of old were often relatives or close friends of the kings,[2] and their dictates

[2] Just as, for obvious reasons, many kings of the Middle Ages and Renaissance made cardinals of their cousins and friends.

coincided with the interests of the reigning power too often to be accepted entirely on faith. The curse to be carried out by Acrisios' grandson may well have been devised by his hated brother and transmitted for a consideration—the stake, which was the fertile plain of Argos, was well worth the money.

If this was a stratagem, it was a master stroke: indirectly, the oracle was discouraging Acrisios on pain of death, from aspiring to any form of descendance. If anything should happen to him, Proetos would automatically inherit his brother's crown and thus become master of all Argolis.

The Prisoner and the Shower of Gold

Acrisios did not know what to do. The men of that time were ruled by superstition: how could he be certain that the warning had not really come from the god? In his doubt, he abstained.

Apollodorus goes on: "Acrisios ordered a cellar of bronze [or lined in bronze] to be built in the courtyard of his palace, and in it he locked Danaë and her nurse, so that she might not bear any children." But no prison is too stout for Zeus.

"Zeus, being enamored of Danaë, came through the roof disguised as a shower of gold . . ."

Now, rain cannot penetrate a bronze-lined roof, as Apollodorus is the first to admit: "Some authors say she was seduced [not by Zeus, but] by Proetos . . ."

Passion or politics? Proetos was Stheneboea's husband, but Danaë's charms were such that their memory lingers on in Homer six hundred years later: "Danaë, the beauty with the magnificent ankles . . ." (*Iliad,* XIV).

"Proetos had no difficulty in seducing the recluse, for she was perishing of boredom and never saw a living soul."[3]

Pregnancy has offered a door to freedom from an oppressive family for many another girl since; and all that the consummation of Proetos' passion cost him was the shower of gold which fell, in all probability, into the money pouch of the guards and not upon the prison roof.

[3] L. R. Lefèvre, *Hèraklès.*

Birth of Perseus

"Danaë gave birth to a son, who was called Perseus."

Through the efforts of her devoted nurse the birth was kept secret for a time, or perhaps the slave who brought the women's food was given a share of the shower of gold to hold his tongue. Also, Acrisios, who was probably ashamed of his dastardly treatment of his daughter, never went to see her. Nevertheless, the secret could not be kept indefinitely. Walking past the bronze room one day, the king heard sounds of laughter and an infant's wailing.

What he felt at that moment gives us another clue to his character: it was stark terror, for the prophecy was beginning to be fulfilled.

Pherecydes describes the king's reaction: "Acrisios summoned Danaë and her nurse, ordered the latter to be killed on the spot, and, leading Danaë up to the altar of Zeus Hercios, asked her privately who was the father of her child. She replied that it was Zeus." Here the "shower of gold" served its purpose once again. The chronicler adds: "Acrisios would not believe her and shut both her and her child inside a trunk, which he cast into the sea."

Instead of killing his daughter and grandson himself, Acrisios left them to drown, following the custom of the Nile—the Egyptian blood of his forefather Danaos had apparently not lost all its power.

A trunk: the seafaring vessels of that time (the "long ships") had neither deck nor cabin, so the king must have had one built especially for the purpose, so that his prisoners could be locked inside it. "And the waves bore the trunk away toward the island of Seriphos . . ."

Diktys, the Man with Nets

Seriphos rises out of the blue sea some sixty miles east of Argos —a mountainous, roughly circular island studded with boulders and gouged by ragged inlets.

The ships that call there—the "milk train" of the Cyclades, so to speak—put in at Leivadi, the principal harbor, on their way from Piraeus to the larger island of Milos.

Seriphos: fifty square miles, with summits of 1400 to 1500 meters. There is so little topsoil that the inhabitants actually import it and spread it on the ground in the hollows, where it is further protected by walls (rain, when there is any, is torrential), but nevertheless fig and olive trees and some very fine grapes are grown on the island.

The musk-scented oleander blossoms along the banks of the streams, and hot springs bubble up here and there. A vein of iron ore lies beneath the depression in the center of the island, and it was mined long before the classical period in Greece.

Three thousand souls cling to this rock for life, half of them in a little town whose whitewashed houses seem like so many dazzling cubes scaling the hillside, and the other half in five tiny villages and a monastery.

With its deep bays and towering headlands, and the caves hollowed out of its coast, however, the island made an ideal shelter for the pirates of antiquity.

The "trunk" containing Perseus and Danaë drifted along in the current of the Gulf of Sarona to a beach where Diktys, brother of the ruler of the island, "was fishing. He brought them to shore in his nets . . ."

Diktys—the name means "man with nets." "Danaë's voice reached his ears, and he opened the trunk. Upon learning the identity of its occupants, he took them home with him and treated them like members of his own family." (Apollodorus.)

The remainder of Perseus' childhood was spent at the court of Seriphos, but not uneventfully. In her riper years, Danaë was still an attractive woman. "Polydectes, the brother of Diktys and king of Seriphos, fell in love with her . . ." and courted her assiduously; perhaps he also saw marriage with Acrisios' daughter as a means of gaining a foothold on the Argive throne.

"But Perseus [in the meantime] had grown up and Polydectes could not satisfy his lust," for the young man, inspired by proper filial concern for her honor, kept a very close watch over his mother.

How was Polydectes to get him out of the way?

"Bring me Medusa's head!"

While paying court to Danaë, Polydectes was also considering (or pretending to consider) another alliance—with Hippodameia, daughter of Oenomaos, a ruler in Olympia.

Was he hesitating because he could not decide which marriage would be more advantageous to him? Or was he simply being spiteful? "He asked his friends, Perseus among them, to give him some present that would help him to win the hand of Hippodameia. Perseus said he would help, even if it meant going to cut off the Gorgon's head. So Polydectes asked all the others to bring horses, but Perseus he asked to fetch the head."

Pherecydes, writing six hundred years before Apollodorus, gives an even more detailed account of the challenge: "Polydectes invited several people to a feast. Each guest came bringing a horse. Perseus brought one too, but Polydectes would not take it; instead, holding him to his promise, he asked him to bring the Gorgon's head, and threatened to rape his mother Danaë if he did not produce it."

With this provocation, the young man set off on an expedition "to the western extremity of the earth, where the Gorgons live—those monsters abhorred of men, whose hair is made of live snakes and upon whom no man could ever look without dying." (Aeschylus.)

By taking the young man at his word, Polydectes hoped he had found a means of sending him to his death.

The Pirates of Seriphos

"Perseus withdrew to one end of the island to meditate . . ."

Perhaps it was the Cape of the Sword, or Cape Cyclops, two naked outcroppings of rock divided by an inlet, south of the main town. In any event, it is virtually certain that one of the pirate expeditions so common at that time was then engineered on Seriphos, for no sooner had he begun his meditations than "Hermes came to him and inquired into the cause of his melancholy."

Was this the god (of tradesmen and thieves) descending to Seriphos from Mount Olympus? Or was it the tradesmen and thieves themselves, making overtures to the young hero in the name of their patron saint? Whichever it was, Perseus responded, and "Hermes, after hearing the cause of Perseus' troubles, encouraged him and offered to act as his guide."

This solved half his problems, and the remainder were soon dispelled as well—for behold no less a personage than Pallas Athena herself now set foot on the rocky promontory: Athena, whose city had undertaken to conquer the seas. She was anxious to put an end to the Echinadian pirates who were intercepting supply ships bound for Athens at the entrance to the Gulf of Corinth, for she could have no hope of ruling the western seas as long as the "Graeae," "Nymphs," and "Gorgons" were afloat and in control of the intermediate points of anchorage.

Medusa's island lay at a great distance, out in the ocean of the setting sun, but the Greeks were familiar with the settlements along the way—those same "Graeae" and "Nymphs," peopled by the very race Athens had determined to destroy.

A masterful scheme was now hatched. Was it the product of the solitary musings of one young man? One is tempted rather to believe that it was his counselor who masterminded the plot: the warlike Athena, "daughter of Zeus and goddess of wisdom," whose battle stratagems litter the pages of ancient history.

So it was that, "guided by Hermes and armed [en route] by Athena," leaving Danaë as a hostage with the King of Seriphos (to ensure his return and the sharing of the loot), Perseus now set out to sea.

The White-Haired Hesperides[4]

Apollodorus writes: "Perseus went first to the land of the Graeae." Enyo, Pemphredo and Deino, the "Hesperides of Atlas," and "daughters of Phorcys," lived, according to Ovid, "on the shores of Lake Tritonis."

Lake Tritonis was a body of water in the Sahara—still existing in those days—which has been in the process of desiccation ever since, leaving only the Algerian and Tunisian Chotts as its last remaining traces in our day.

[4] See map of Perseus' travels.

In addition (still according to Ovid), Enyo, Pemphredo, and Deino were "closed cities," which suggests that they may have been oases. They had "white hair," like the peaks of the Atlas Mountains in winter. Like, for instance, the peaks of Tebessa and, especially, Aures (2372 meters). In short, the Graeae lived near both the coast and the median line of the Chotts (as they were then, in the second millennium), within view of the hidden peaks of the Atlas Mountains; this description fits the region of the El Djerid Chott (Gulf of Gabès).

According to Apollodorus of Athens, the Graeae "had only one tooth among them, and used it in turn." This refers to their common army, "a fang longer and stronger than the tusk of the strongest boar." Also, they had "only one eye for the three of them." We might say "view" or "policy."

In other words, these were three federated colonies, which Perseus and his followers had to subdue. Why? Eratosthenes explains: "They were the guardians of their sisters, the Gorgons."

Perseus' plan of attack now becomes clear. "He seized their tooth [i.e., rendered them powerless] and their eye [imposed his views on them], promising to return both if they would tell him the way to the home of their sisters the nymphs." (Apollodorus.)

Cowed by his threats, having become his hostages, the Graeae led Perseus straight to the island of the Trident.

The Nymphs

Thoosa and Scylla, the "younger" daughters of Phorcys, occupied a position of prime importance in Sicily. Scylla was the more strategically placed, for, as her name indicates, she is literally the (watch)dog of the strait. Opposite her, on the mainland, stands Charybdis.

The "man-eating maëlstroms" celebrated in the *Odyssey* seem to have been traversing a period of calm just then.[5] Their appearance was deceptive, however. The two miles separating the "two reefs" of Reggio and Messina are always fraught with danger. Modern fishermen, their light sails dancing over the troubled cross-

[5] They became active a little later, in the thirteenth century, just long enough to bequeath us a legend.

currents in search of the local swordfish, know it only too well: Scylla is an evil-tempered nymph, and the fire-belching Liparis and Etna's glowering crater are only too close at hand. If the "Earth-shaker"[6] should awaken, disaster strikes like a thunderbolt.

When it does, as in 1908, white Messina becomes a heap of rubble and the specter of cholera glides up from the ruins. It wasn't so very long ago—the old men are still talking about it on the sunny quays of Reggio di Calabria, among the ferry docks at Villa San Giovanni, and across the strait, in the gray-domed church that stands as a figurehead on the island of the Trident.

Perseus negotiated the strait between the two promontories without mishap: "One thrusts a sharp peak up into the fields of heaven [Messina]. The other, you will see, is much lower [Reggio]."[7]

This brought him "to that admirable island of the sun, Son of the On-High, where they saw crowds of his wide-browed oxen and fat ewes."[7]

Without further ado, the hero proceeded to the next phase of his plan. What had he come there in search of? Apollodorus tells us: "These nymphs possessed winged sandals and a pouch—thought to be a sort of traveling satchel, for food and clothes were kept in it."

Magic sandals? Here again, wings are the poets' favorite metaphor for wind-driven sails. "Winged sandals" are sails for swift action, a fleet. And the "pouch" in which food and clothing were stored is nothing other than a ship's hold.

Yet more essential to him is the "helmet of Hades" of the Sicilian nymphs, of which Homer has the following to say: "Athena [ever quick to devise fresh stratagems] placed on her brow the helmet of Hades, to avoid being seen by stalwart Ares [god of war]." (*Iliad.*)

This is "putting on the mask"—the nymphs are "sisters" of the Gorgons, and in their fleet Perseus would in a sense be invisible to the latter.

[6] *Odyssey,* XI.
[7] *Odyssey,* XII.

This form of camouflage was a favorite ruse of the Athenian divinity's strategist-priests. A century later they used it again, with the wooden horse which rendered the Greek soldiers "invisible" to the Trojans. "It was built by Athena with the help of Epeios: a snare which the godlike Ulysses brought inside the town filled with pillagers." (*Odyssey,* VII.)

Erytheia, Sentinel of the Ocean

Thus camouflaged, the raiding party sailed past Erytheia (the fourth Hesperide, "sister" of the three Graeae and, like them, a "daughter of the setting sun").

"Erytheia was an island on the edge of Ocean, now called Gadire . . ." Apollodorus corroborates Pherecydes here, and Strabo agrees: this is the island on which Cádiz was subsequently built. Its position offered the Phorcids the same advantages that led them to occupy the Echinades and Scylla: for defense, its insularity; for offense, control of the strait, through which the richly laden cargo ships were all obliged to pass.

Among the ancients, Erytheia was a naval keyhole, like its modern neighbor, the fortress of Gibraltar.

Thanks to the "mask of Hades," Perseus sailed unmolested past this ally of the Gorgons; Phorcys' sentinels could see nothing more than Scylla's fleet rounding the cape.

The Gorgons

"Perseus then took wing and, accompanied by Athena, reached the Gorgons." (Apollodorus.)

Stheno, Euryale, and Medusa, recolonized a few generations before by their "sisters" (Hesperides and Nymphs), "lived" in the middle of the ocean.

Had the Phorcid sailors rediscovered the route to all three of the archipelagoes—the remains of the "mother" island—or only to one or two of them? Like their Phoenician contemporaries, their sole guide was the constellation of the Bear. With no other aid, could they successfully plot a course into the Atlantic?

About Madeira, we know nothing, but fourteenth-century Portuguese conquistadors returning from the Gran Canaria brought back a mysterious bronze statuette resembling the "giant Atlas" (a man bearing the globe on his shoulders).[8] However, this is a very feeble glimmer to light up the whole face of history.

The only unsubmerged land to present a relatively simple navigational problem (the ships had merely to set a course due west from Erytheia in the direction indicated by the priest of Saïs) was the tripartite volcano-studded archipelago known today as the Azores.

What an amazing archipelago it is: its roots are sunk in over six thousand feet of water, and yet those roots have felt the sun's rays, for the sea bottom is carpeted with a type of lava that crystallizes only in the open air and contains diatom fossils of a type found in fresh water alone.[9]

Occasionally we too have witnessed an Atlantic submersion: in 1812 a new island, Sabrina, broke surface only to disappear in the course of a submarine eruption. In 1958 another sunken crater awoke, belching thousands of millions of cubic yards of fiery debris, and then, during a seismic convulsion lasting eighteen hours (460 tremors were recorded), the subterranean dome built up by the spewing lava proceeded to collapse. Atlantis is no longer a mystery, at least as far as the "how" of its disappearance is concerned.[10]

The Azores are a paradise. Passengers on the transatlantic flight from Lisbon see them, beyond the mighty swell of the ocean, set into its gray infinity like a scattering of precious jewels.

Santa Maria is covered by scrub, alive with small game: a vast plateau of lava where oxcarts creak down black roads lined by amaryllis and agave, indifferent to the buzzing of international aircraft. São Miguel is a green island, hidden beneath its forest cover. Terceira is a reef girded by cliffs, blistered by chaotic craters and covered with tropical vegetation. São Jorge is a black boulder plowing through the sea, with sheer cliffs and plunging overhangs, where a new crater was formed as recently as 1808, but it is

[8] A. Gaudio, *Canaries* (Julliard, 1958).

[9] Discovered during the laying of a submarine cable in 1923, and during the 1947 and 1949 expeditions of the oceanographic ship *Atlantis*.

[10] Old lava covers the ocean floor over a surface of thousands of square miles and is several thousand feet thick in places; this gives some idea of the magnitude of the cataclysm that caused the Atlantic island to vanish in the way Plato described.

also a vast green pasture, where cattle graze between hedges of flowering hydrangea.

Graciosa, "the graceful," clasps to her green bosom the chasm of Furnas, its floor hidden under a dark lake. Windmills wheel in the smiling countryside and flocks of turkeys strut about. Faial is her twin, called the "blue" island because of its hydrangeas.

This is the home of La Caldeira, "The Caldron" (1012 meters), a huge lunar crater, its flanks glistening with streams. It still mutters from time to time, and then its "sons," the fishermen, cross themselves in terror lest the Gorgon-volcano should awaken, just as their "brothers" of the Sicilian swordfish fleet dread the ire of the nymph Scylla, when Etna or the Liparis begin to growl.

Pico, "the peak," wears its handsome hood of snow until April. Its summit is as far above the ocean floor as that of Mont Blanc and is often lost in cloud, but it can be reached on mule back. Once there, its *misterios* (mysteries) can be identified as rivers of calcinated stone.

Then there is Flores, still farther west, with deep valleys, green meadows, and swift streams—an island draped in flowers, corseted by cliffs, its coating of dark earth furrowed by deep gorges (they, too, covered with hydrangeas). Scattered among the plateaus and crater lakes, the inhabitants' crude lava dwellings disappear among the banana and pineapple plantations.

Lastly, there is Corvo, smallest and least-frequented of the nine, a reef isolated by storms from November to May, the last Atlantid shoal looking out to the new continent.[11]

The three groups of the Azores—mountain peaks with alternating torrents of water and lava coursing down their sides, an Eden perpetually threatened by volcanic hell: were they Stheno, Euryale, and Medusa?

Medusa

The Gorgons of ancient bas-reliefs do not always present the contorted and awesome aspect of a volcano in eruption. Some

[11] The lava figure that used to point the way to the Infanta's navigators stood on Mount Gordo, overlooking the lake.

show the features of a woman whose expression is as gentle as a subtropical island in repose.

When they are calm, nothing is more comely than their scattered locks, symbol of the swift mountain streams. But when the lava begins to flow instead of water, "their heads bristle with serpents" (Apollodorus). The flow of lava is also like a tongue protruding between the peaks (teeth) of some hideous maw. The heedless man who lets himself be lapped up by it unawares is petrified, like the cowering forms found in Pompeii, fossilized by the ashes of Vesuvius.

The ancients even described the sounds that accompanied the eruptions. When she wants to imitate "the shrieking of the Gorgon, Athena blows on a bone pierced with holes." The sound is exactly like the strident moaning of gases forcing their way through fissures when the volcanic crust begins to crack.

Such were the Gorgons, but the portrait is also that of La Caldeira on Faial, with water and lava pouring down the Caldron's slopes by turns. In addition to these grim attributes, which made the Gorgons into "monsters abhorred of men," they also possessed more conventional forms of defense used in their day: "They had boars' tusks [like their "sisters," the Graeae], hands of bronze [weapons made of bronze] and wings of gold." (Apollodorus.) Once again: wings—sails gilded by the setting sun; in other words, a fleet.

Of the three sisters, Medusa alone was reputed to be mortal (in danger of submersion?), and so it was she whom Perseus attacked. At his approach, the charm of the "helmet of Hades" worked again, and he found Medusa "asleep"; the ships came from Scylla, so the island's defenders suspected nothing.

Nevertheless, Perseus kept his eyes open, for the fleets of the other Gorgons might appear at any moment, and he would then find himself in an ambush. "Turning away and looking into a shield of bronze in which the Gorgon's face was reflected [the image makes one think of our rear-view mirrors], he cut off her head with the aid of [again] Athena, who held his hand."

Three generations later, bronzesmiths immortalized the scene on

Herakles' shield. Hesiod writes: "Above the Gorgons was depicted a fearful scene of fighting men, some trying to save their town and family, others raging to destroy them. Many had fallen, more continued to struggle." One can almost hear the clang of their swords of bronze.

The plunder was piled into the "pouch." Apollodorus tells how Perseus bore off the greatest trophy of all, the "Gorgon's head"—emblem of the Phorcids, and as such, represented on all their weapons. In that age it was the custom, after a battle, to take the shields of the fallen, bearing their insignia. (In our day, the victor appropriates the enemy's flags.)

The museum at Olympia has preserved a precious copy of the Medusa-head shield, dating from the eighth century B.C. and originating probably in the Echinades. Glaring out from the tarnished bronze, the face is surrounded by plaits of hair and serpents, the tongue protruding between the fangs bristling in the open mouth. Three wings, symbolizing the "winged" fleets of Stheno, Euryale, and Medusa, curve out from the rim of the shield.

The Chase

With Medusa murdered, Perseus hastened back to his ships: the surprise attack, followed by plunder and flight, is the unvarying tactic of the pirate (and modern commando).

He had not been able to prevent a few ships of the Gorgon fleet from escaping during the raid, so Euryale and Stheno now "awoke."

Perseus fled. "The son of Danaë of the lovely locks, the heavenly horseman Perseus was seen . . . He wore the winged sandals on his feet, and the sword of bronze hung from a black belt slung across his shoulders; he flew, swift as thought . . ." (Hesiod.)

Until quite recently we used to say, "I fly" when we were in a hurry, and Perseus had particular reason not to linger, because "after him rushed the dread, the fearful Gorgons, eager to seize him."

Too late; by the time they had reached Medusa's side, the Greeks had eluded them and were on their way home.

In the Land of Cassiopeia and Andromeda

Still wearing "the helmet of Hades," Perseus re-entered the Mediterranean; Erytheia had not been given the alarm, and let him pass. On his way along the coast of Africa, now familiar ground to him, he stopped among the worshipers of Amon (the Egyptian sun god; hence, in Egypt). In those days the ruler of the land was named Cepheus, and Cassiopeia was his queen. Their daughter Andromeda was betrothed to her uncle Phineus.

"Cassiopeia boasted that she was more beautiful than the Nereids, daughters of Poseidon." (Apollodorus.) These "daughters" of the sea god were probably the invaders described in Egyptian inscriptions as "peoples from the sea."

"Vexed by the challenge" of Pharaoh's wife, Poseidon "submerged the land," suggesting an exceptionally high rise of the Nile; he also sent a sea "monster" of the species Perseus knew so well.

Cepheus went to an oasis in nearby Cyrenaica to consult the Oracle of Amon, whose political role in Egypt was as important as that of its Greek counterparts—with whom, moreover, it had certain associations.[12]

"The Oracle announced that their troubles would cease if Andromeda were exposed to the elements, so the Africans compelled Cepheus to do as it commanded." The "peoples from the sea" must have demanded Cepheus' daughter as a hostage, with the priests of the sun god acting as go-between in the negotiations.

"Bound to a rock," therefore, Andromeda stood waiting for the Nereids' ship, when Perseus, "seeing her, fell in love with her and promised to kill the monster if the king would give him Andromeda as his bride. Cepheus agreed to the bargain, so the hero lay in wait for the monster, fulfilled his promise, and freed Andromeda." (Apollodorus.)

But as soon as the threat of the "monster" was removed, Phineus claimed his ex-fiancée back again, and Perseus, who was not at all pleased by this, promptly killed him too.

[12] The prestige of the Oracle of Amon was equal to that of Delphi, Dodona, and Delos; after Cepheus, Herakles, Alexander, and Caesar also came to consult it.

An author writing in the first century B.C. suggests a more complex political intrigue at the origin of these events: "Andromeda had been sought in marriage by her uncle Phineus, and also by Phoenix, a Phoenician prince [as his name indicates]. Cepheus, who wanted to make an alliance with Phoenicia [in order to consolidate Egyptian influence there], favored Phoenix, but he did not want this to be known, so he told Phoenix to abduct Andromeda. Phoenix did so when Andromeda was on a little desert island, where she had gone to offer prayers to Aphrodite."

Aphrodite being the goddess of love, and Phoenix being in love with the girl, the site of the abduction was a tacitly appointed trysting place, not a mere coincidence.

But Perseus had also guessed what was happening: "He was close by when the Phoenician brought Andromeda on board his ship, which was named the *Cetos* [cetacean], perhaps for no reason, or because of its shape [or that of its figurehead]."

Drawing his sword of bronze, Perseus fell upon his rival's craft: "He killed those who were boarding the *Cetos* and took Andromeda back with him to Greece."

The story is not much different from that of Europe.

The Cyclops

Since there were no regular winds from Africa, the hero had to take the long route back to Seriphos by way of Syria.[13] It was on the coast of Phoenician territory that he met and hired the Cyclops. The first home of the "Round-Eyes" would appear to have been Lycia (the seaward side of the Taurus Mountains), which is not far from Tyre.

The Cyclops were "lawless and immoral brutes who had such faith in the Immortals that they neither planted nor tilled the soil . . ." However, they were wonderfully skilled at "lifting stones" and would hire themselves out to anyone for pay, either as builders of "Cyclopean" walls or as mercenary soldiers. And redoubtable

[13] According to Herodotus, Strabo, and Pliny, the abduction of Andromeda took place in Phoenicia, not in Egypt, in which case she was already in Phoenix's power when the Greek hero arrived on the scene.

mercenaries they were, too, with only "one eye" between them—in other words, one mind; they "moved as a single man."

Perseus took a regiment of them home with him.

Back to Seriphos

With its numbers thus increased, the expeditionary force sailed home to Seriphos through the Cyclades, the route followed by all navigators at that time.

According to Apollodorus, "when Perseus reached the island, he found that his mother and Diktys [who had remained her protector] had taken refuge in the shrine, to escape from the violence of King Polydectes [the tenacious aspirant]."

According to Pherecydes, "Perseus then told Polydectes to assemble his subjects, so they could all admire the Gorgon's head. When Polydectes had done so, the son of Danaë took the head out of his pouch and held it up in front of them, taking care to look the other way. Everyone who looked upon it, including Polydectes, was turned to stone . . ."—petrified with horror, fear, and amazement.

Whatever form it assumed, the settling of accounts between the companions of Perseus and the supporters of the king could not fail to be dramatic. Perseus liquidated Polydectes and ensured his own supremacy before pausing to divide up the loot.

The "pouch" went, quite properly, to Hermes (that is, the contents of the ships' holds went to their outfitters and to the merchants), and the trophy (the Phorcid shields) went to the mastermind of the expedition: "Perseus gave the emblem of the Medusa to Pallas Athena." (Apollodorus.)

Hanging in the temple like a flag from a cathedral vault, the "Gorgon's head" thereafter formed part of the coat of arms of the Attic goddess. Sculptors place it in the center of her shield, the Aegis. Thus immortalized, Medusa has remained eternally inseparable from Athena, even on today's stamps and picture postcards.

To Thoosa and Scylla, the nymphs, "Perseus gave back the winged sandals they had lent him, and the helmet of Hades."

(Apollodorus.) That is, "removing his mask," he sent back their fleet, whose camouflage he no longer needed.

Perseus' Revenge

With the business of the expedition settled, and having no further obligations, Perseus now turned to claim his inheritance. "Appointing Diktys to act as governor over the island's remaining inhabitants [survivors of the carnage], he sailed to Argos, taking Danaë, Andromeda and the Cyclops with him. He did not find Acrisios." (Apollodorus.)

Terrified by the "conquering hero's return" of his prodigal grandson, the grandfather had gone into hiding on the acropolis of Larissa, where Perseus let him sit and quake to his heart's content while he disposed of Danaë's cowardly seducer, his great-uncle Proetos: "He showed him Medusa's head . . . The throne of Tiryns passed directly to its lawful heir Megapenthes, son of Proetos and his [legitimate] wife Stheneboea."

Supposing Acrisios' terror to have abated by this time, "Perseus, leaving Danaë, Andromeda and the Cyclops with Stheneboea, went to Larissa, where he showed himself to Acrisios and besought him to return to Argos."

The Oracle of Hera Is Fulfilled

At length persuaded of his grandson's good intentions, the king agreed to return to the city. The gods, however, decided that their moment had come.

"As they were preparing to leave, Perseus came upon a group of young men competing for an athletic prize. He removed his clothes, seized a discus [the pentathlon did not yet exist, and there were individual competitions for each event], and hurled it; as it rolled, the discus struck Acrisios on the foot and injured him. Acrisios died at Larissa of the after-effects of this wound [of infection]."

Apollodorus concludes: "Seeing how the Oracle's prophecy had been fulfilled, Perseus gave Acrisios a burial outside the town. Not daring to return to Argos and claim the throne of the man he had killed, he went to Tiryns and agreed upon an exchange with

Megapenthes, the son of Proetos [and his own half-brother]. He gave Megapenthes the kingdom of Argos and took Tiryns for himself, which he fortified, together with Midea and Mycenae."

Great-walled Tiryns

Pausanias compares these great fortifications to the Pyramids of Egypt. The stones raised by the Cyclops weigh many tons; today steel scaffolding and cranes are required to replace any that happen to fall. On the road from Argos to Nauplia, the mass suddenly appears on the left, emerging from a forest of orange trees.

The walls, twenty-nine feet thick in places, are the color of scorched bread, hidden among golden thistles. There are massive corridors a hundred feet long and six and one-half feet wide, casemates suggesting troglodytes' caves, their gaping openings looking out onto the plain. In olden days, they were also used as storehouses and shelter for flocks, and the stones look as though they had been varnished from the contact of their fleece (tallow having the effect of wax); their ancient patina is now being preserved by the fingers of thousands of tourists. "Nothing in Greece communicates the impression of a military people more powerfully than these gloomy corridors."[14]

The ceiling, thirteen feet high, is in the form of an ogive vault, and irresistibly calls to mind another Dark Ages period, similarly feudal in structure and also a builder of castles and towers. Some of the blocks of the Tiryns casemates weigh thirteen tons, however, and there are none like them in any wall built since.

The tower over the entrance ramp stands almost intact, red and ominous. A triumphal drive encircles it. The grooves of bolts as big as a man's arm mark the gray stone outline of a mammoth door.

At the top was the palace, the megaron of Proetos, Megapenthes, and Perseus. Little of it remains, but "the bare foundations of the inner court, portico and colonnaded hall are still impressive in their spacious and orderly arrangement."

The view from the terrace is admirable: to the north, Argolis and its luscious orchards enclosed by arid mountains; to the south,

[14] L. Cottrell, *La Porte des lions.*

the blue gulf lying like a lake, and the towering cape of pink Nauplia; to the west, Argos, under the ocher-hued cone of the acropolis.

In this setting, Perseus rested from his labors.

Mycenae the Golden

It was at Mycenae, however, that the Cyclops showed their talents to the fullest.

Why is it, turning off the main road from Argos to Corinth, down the eucalyptus-lined drive leading to the queenly city, with the peaceful olive groves and white houses of the village of Phikia spreading out before the eyes, that the heartbeat begins to quicken?

At first, the citadel is not even visible; its copper-tinted stones blend into the hills behind it.

"But suddenly, the angle of the light changes, throwing a sharper relief and picking Mycenae out from the mountains. It resembles a recumbent lion, indolent, resting snugly in the hollow between the two hills.

"Its head is the highest point of the citadel; its back follows the curve of the Cyclopean ramparts, assembled without mortar, each stone weighing several tons; and the tail, curling in behind the flank, is the Lion Gate, where the great watchful cats look out over the plain to the sea, backed firmly into their impregnable mountains, their claws protecting all the wealth of Argolis."[15]

Outside, at their feet, are the tholos tombs, huge man-made caverns shaped like miters, colossal and awesome as the temples of ancient Egypt. A second ring of tombs begins just inside the Lion Gate; in these shaft graves, Schliemann thought he had uncovered the remains of the Atreidae, descendants of Pelops (in reality, they were the bones of more ancient, "Perseid" princes).

Then the steep path climbs up inside the citadel, between the vestiges of the close-crowding Mycenaeans' dwellings.

As at Tiryns, the foundations of a palace have been uncovered on the summit: a courtyard, then a portico, leading to the heart of Mycenaean power: a room measuring 13.5×12 meters, with a

[15] L. Cottrell, *La Porte des lions.*

circular hearth in the center, surrounded by four columns; the smoke escaped through a vent in the roof.

Beneath the walls a precipice, where the mad, torrent roars in winter like a "sinister monster," witness to so many wars and crimes that it is impossible to look down into the tormented gorge without feeling a shudder of death.

This is Mycenae the Golden,[16] rival of Crete, amassing wealth throughout the Mediterranean; this is the seat of the throne of Perseus.

The Reign of Perseus

Not content with building walls and palaces, the hero also concerned himself with the welfare of his subjects; under him Argolis prospered, and Mycenae became a great center, the "city of broad roads."

Two of them led southward to Argos and Tiryns, and three more went across Nemea to Corinth in the north.

Never swerving, scaling every hill, the roads were laid on foundations of massive stones and crossed streams on top of walls covered by a single slab—like the "oldest bridge in the world," thirty or forty yards off the road in a gorge halfway between Nauplia and Epidaurus.[17]

Epidaurus

Thousands of automobiles drive down this road every year, when the Greek National Theater revives the great tragedies of Sophocles and Euripides in the setting in which they were first performed, at Epidaurus. An audience of fourteen thousand clambers over the stone tiers of the ancient theater, and it holds them easily.

Those fourteen thousand seats give some idea of the crowds drawn by the sanctuary of Aesculapius in the fourth century B.C. Of course, the theater itself, with its wonderfully harmonious pro-

[16] In funerary masks and breastplates alone, its tombs yielded over thirty-three pounds of gold.

[17] Restored, using the original stones, by Roman engineers in the fifth century A.D.

portions, did not exist in the age of Perseus, but the sanctuary did and was thronged with patients seeking relief at the spring of Tholos; that was why the roads were kept in such good repair—for chariots.

The chariots were first imported from Phoenicia; they were extremely light vehicles, mounted between two four-spoked wheels, and carried travelers or hoplites through the countryside behind a pair of horses. There is one, decorated with bronze bas-reliefs, in the Carapanos Room of the Athens Museum.

But although Perseus filled Argolis with his peacetime achievements, his destiny was written in strife: toward the end of his reign, the Bacchantes arrived on the scene.

Dionysos

Dionysos was another "son of Zeus," and his mother was Semele ("daughter" of Cadmos, a Theban woman who, like Danaë, had occasional moments of weakness); Apollodorus writes that "Zeus sewed him up inside his own thigh." "Of unknown father" would be another way of putting it.

"He spent his childhood in Corinth, and later in Thrace; he wandered throughout the country, and especially in Thebes and Argos, where he drove the women to frenzy."

They held orgies, screaming and leaping crazily about, their eyes hag-ridden, their voices menacing, their hair lashing their naked shoulders. This constituted a definite threat to the established order, so Perseus opposed the Dionysians. Later, when Pausanias toured that part of the country, the tombs of the Bacchantes slain in the ensuing battle were still being shown.

Dionysos is known to have gone to Asia Minor, and perhaps he met a troop of the warlike Amazons along the Thermodon, who became his escort; or perhaps, on the contrary, these were Argive women, intoxicated by "the wine which the god poured out in floods."

For, wherever he went, Dionysos planted the vine. "He gave it to Oeneos, King of Calydon [in Aetolia, near modern Mesolonghion] . . . He became enamored of the king's wife, Althaea." (Apollodorus.)

He made the husband drunk in order to possess the wife, and several authors say he fathered Althaea's daughter Deianeira, who later married Herakles.

Dionysos also gave the vine to Icarios—that is, to Icaria and Attica, where Dionysian rites were officially celebrated for centuries, with greater pomp than in any other part of Hellas.

Thus his history is that of the propagation of the vine cuttings brought to Greece from Asia Minor, and the names of those to whom the "god" taught the art of cultivating the new plant have become part of the Greek language: *oinos,* wine, is derived from King Oeneos, and one of the "sons" of Dionysos was "Staphylos," the grape.

It is also said that this "god" helped bring about the downfall of the Giants (by making them lose their wits through drunkenness). In any case, the first Helladic wines must be attributed to him, as well as the inhabitants' fits of ethylic delirium, for, as soon as they discovered this new form of madness, they promptly began to drink themselves into a state of frenzy, and often.

According to Diodorus Siculus (L. III), Dionysos also invented beer.

Death of Perseus

Pausanias (L. II) says that Perseus and Dionysos were eventually reconciled. "Perseus even paid him great honors . . ." because of the added source of income which his vines brought to the Argive plain. Regarded as a benefactor by the people, this propagator of a form of agriculture hitherto unknown in Greece was transformed, with the passing of time, into a god (as Athena, who brought the olive to Attica).

Tradition has little to say of the end of the reign of Perseus—happy peoples have no tales to tell. He undoubtedly retained to the last the prerogatives attaching to his position as senior descendant of Danaos.

In the first century B.C., Hyginus wrote, "Megapenthes killed Perseus to avenge his father Proetos [actually, Proetos was the father of both men]" (Fab. 244).

His epitaph was written by Homer in the *Iliad* (XIV, 320),

where he pays tribute to the son of Danaë as "the greatest hero of all."

The first Greek to fight the "Atlantids," he "raised the trophy" (Plato) and conquered the Gorgon; and "Athena held his hand." (Apollodorus.)

He became so great that his name was written among the stars, along with those of Cassiopeia and Andromeda.

But while this "god of the sword of bronze" was earning his immortality and his descendants were dividing up his kingdom of Argolis, another hero was growing up in Corinth and preparing to carry on his war against the same enemy, under the aegis of Athena.

Pegasus, the "winged horse," had just been born of the "blood" of Medusa, and Bellerophon was coming to "bridle" him and earn the right to follow Perseus into the starry heavens.

Chapter III
BELLEROPHON OF CORINTH

"While he was in the land where the Xanthos flows,
The king enjoined him to slay the Chimaera . . .

Then his native city claimed his aid,
For Pegasus was drinking at the Peirene spring;

Bellerophon caught, bridled, tamed him."

after PINDAR

Corinth, Queen of the Isthmus

A small, bright town with wide, straight streets, the main thoroughfare adorned with flower gardens—such is Corinth today, at the back of its azure gulf.

The houses are almost all built on one floor, because of the earthquakes which periodically destroy them: the inhabitants are accustomed to having their roof fall on their heads, so they make it light.

Their chief resources are the vine (source of the famous Corinth raisins), their beautiful orchards, and the glories of their past, which attract tourists by the thousands.

The only surviving wonders of ancient Corinth, however, are the Pillars of Apollo and the façade of the Peirene fountain house. Of the Peribolae, the baths, the merchants' arcades, nothing remains but a field of shapeless ruins, and the opulent city of old lies buried beneath the vines, probably forever.

The Acrocorinthus, however, is indestructible. The monolithic sheer rock face dominates both isthmus and city with its 564 meters, at the top of which stands a triple-walled fortress crowned by massive towers, in which Byzantines, Franks, Venetians, and Turks have each had a hand, though all they did was restore more ancient ramparts, for lengths of Cyclopean wall can still be seen in places.

The view from the top of the yellowish, thistle-infested walls explains why Corinth waxed until it became queen of Greek commerce, and also why it waned and died, with no hope of rebirth.

The reason in both cases is the isthmus itself, a stony hyphen scarcely four miles across, uniting (or dividing, as the case may be) the Peloponnesus and the mainland. In the past all overland traffic from north to south had to pass this barrier, and all ships sailing from west to east encountered it.

For thousands of years, Corinth sat at the very center of the compass.

The Isthmus

Argive merchants en route for Attica were compelled to pass that way, and ships from the Adriatic were forced either to send their cargo overland across the isthmus or sail around the whole Peloponnesus.

Hence there was unlimited scope for the levying of tolls, which Ephyra, "daughter" of Phoroneos, realized nineteen hundred years before Christ. She soon became the wealthiest "heiress" in the Greek world, and in the classical period a million people lived in the twin ports on either side of the tongue of land. Soon the ships themselves were being hauled over it, as well as their cargoes—rolled from one sea to the other across the four miles of the ridge (highest point: 80 meters). The groove their keels gouged out of the earth can still be seen, running along beside the modern canal at the bottom of a broad trench of yellow earth. It is most clearly visible at either end of the crossing, where quaint ferries propelled by hand-cranked winches join the two sides of the canal and the cool open-air restaurants frequented by the Corinthians.[1]

In the fourteenth century B.C., when the city was already more than six hundred years old, and shops and warehouses and inns

[1] The very wealth of Corinth, by attracting invaders, was one cause of its downfall; another was earthquake—there have been tremors as recently as 1858, and again in 1928. The canal and the railroad dealt the city its deathblow; now it is by-passed, nobody stops any more, and that is what has ruined it.

and taverns were springing up beside the temples, there was only one cloud in the sky of this burgeoning prosperity: the Phorcid pirates from the Echinades, who were ruthlessly plundering every ship that sailed westward out of the gulf.

Now they were even daring to enter the gulf itself, "proud and threatening." Their confidence was the result of the massive reinforcements they had just received in the form of the fleets of their "sister" Gorgons, coming in pursuit of Perseus and the Greeks.

Born of the Blood of Medusa: Chrysaor and Typhon

First-born of the "blood of the decapitated Gorgon" was a chief named Chrysaor (*chrysos,* gold)—"born" in the sense that the destruction of Medusa precipitated his appearance. He landed at Erytheia, where the people finally learned how Perseus had foiled the vigilant Phorcids by sailing past them in Scylla's ships.

After settling on the island, Chrysaor engendered a "giant" named Geryon, and Geryon's son was a "dog" called Orthrus. Standing guard over the straits, he might fairly be called a "watchdog."

But then this dog "united with Echidne" (sent his fleet to the Echinades, that is) and it was not long afterward that *their* "son" Typhon first appeared in Greek waters. His name soon came to be synonymous with bad weather among the Hellenes, so closely was the thought of the pirate associated in their minds with the unleashing of the elements.

Later, Typhon and Echidne "gave birth" to a second "monster," a "daughter"—Chimaera, who patrolled the coast of Lycia, to the chagrin of the Greek colonists in Asia Minor.[2]

[2] The "blood" of Medusa produced the following:

•	•
The fleet of winged Pegasus, with bases on the islands of Erytheia and the Echinades	A chief, Chrysaor (island of Erytheia) • A giant, Ceryton (island of Erytheia) • An admiral, Orthrus (island of Erytheia) • A pirate, Typhon (Echinades) • A new clan, the Chimaera (coast of Lycia)

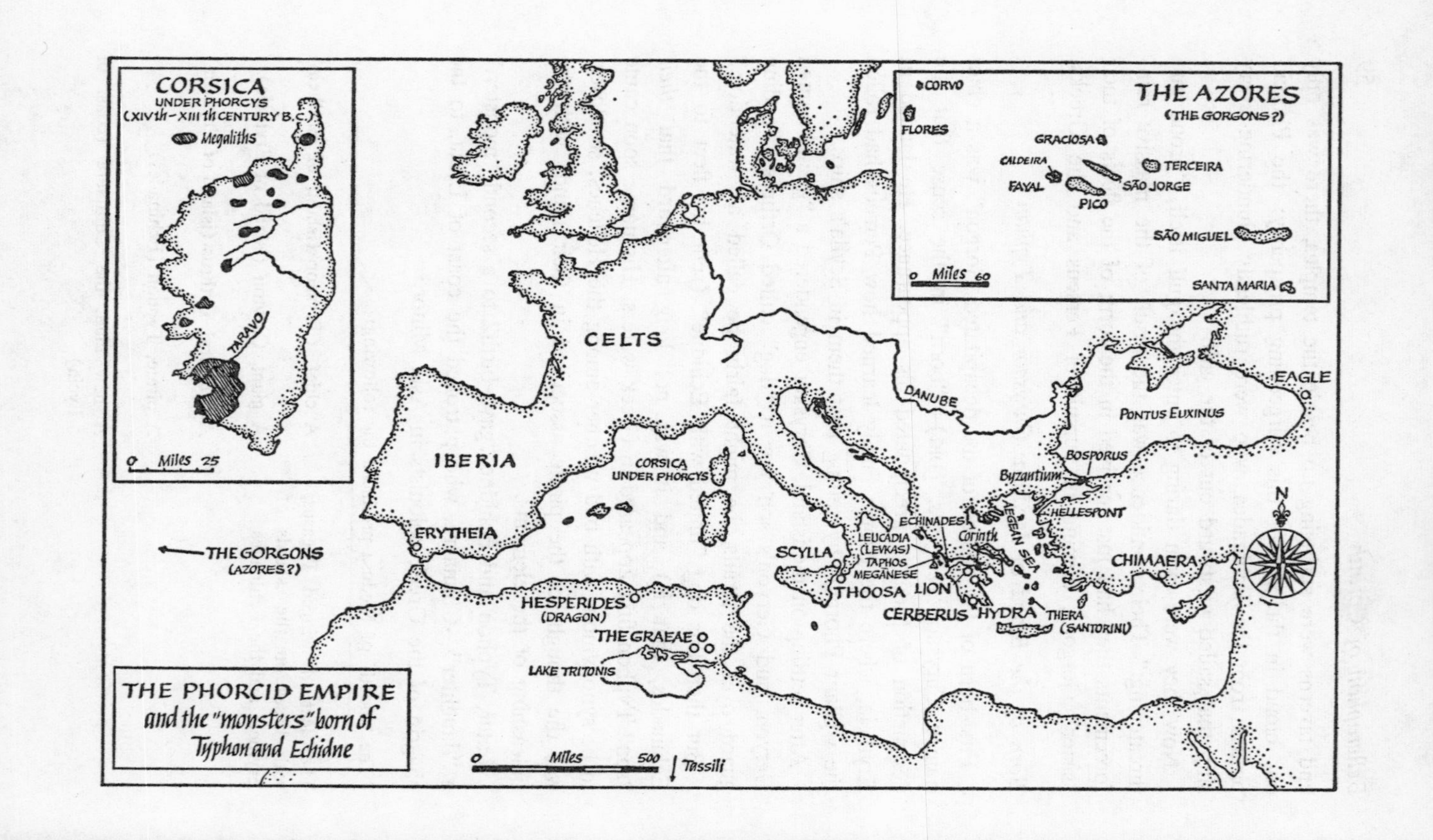

THE PHORCID EMPIRE
and the "monsters" born of
Typhon and Echidne

. . . and Winged Pegasus

No less redoubtable was Pegasus, the "brother" of Chrysaor—in the sense that he too was "born" from the "blood" of the decapitated Medusa.

Pegasus—not one "winged horse" but (here again, wings being a symbol for sails) the "fleet of the winged horse." As "son of Medusa," his eastern headquarters would naturally be the Echinadian archipelago, and so it is not surprising that he should be seen in the very center of the nearby gulf—to the Corinthians an intolerable impertinence.

Bellerophon

It was high time for the gods to find a liberating hero for the city. "In Ephyrus, in the remotest part of Argolis, lived Sisyphus, most cunning of men. His son was Glaucos, and he too became a father in due course." (*Iliad,* VI.)

This is the pedigree of the young Aesclepiades, "to whom the gods gave features of great and manly beauty."

He grew up in Corinth in the reign of one Belleros and, apparently by accident, killed the king one day, for which he was nicknamed Bellerophon (*phonos,* murder).

After this misdeed, he "fled Corinth and went to Proetos, King of Tiryns, who purified him."[3]

Fate was decidedly against him, however: a woman now saw and lusted for him. "Divine Anteia [Stheneboea, Proetos' wife] burned with mad passion for the hero and longed to lie with him secretly. As the loyal and clearheaded warrior would not be seduced by her, she invented a lie, telling King Proetos, 'Ah, Proetos, may you die if you do not destroy Bellerophon, who tried to embrace me against my will.'" (*Iliad,* VI.)

Bellerophon was not the last bachelor to emerge the loser from a similar contest: the husband of a would-be adulterous wife tends to vent his spleen on the man pointed out to him as the culprit,

[3] Some say the correct reading is "fled Proetos," on the ground that the name does not here refer to the King of Tiryns, but to a homonym who succeeded Belleros as King of Corinth.

rather than on his erring spouse (especially if she is shrewd enough to make the first accusation).

Stheneboea's assertions "inflamed the king, but he could not bring himself to kill the hero; his heart restrained him." In the Greece of the Danaans it was an unpardonable offense to murder a guest. But Bellerophon was under obligation to Proetos, for purifying him after the murder of Belleros, so he dutifully obeyed when Proetos sent him to visit his father-in-law Iobates (Stheneboea's father and King of Lycia), "not forgetting to give him a fatal message, a sealed tablet engraved with many murderous signs.[4] Proetos ordered him to give it to his father-in-law [so that he should be killed]. So Bellerophon set out for Lycia. . . . When he reached the land where the Xanthos flows, the king of vast Lycia received him with great ceremony, treating him as a guest for nine consecutive days, and killing nine oxen. But when rosy-fingered dawn arrived for the tenth time, he questioned him and asked for his message from his son-in-law Proetos. As soon as he beheld the fatal missive, he ordered the hero to slay the invincible Chimaera."

According to the custom, Bellerophon, after being "purified," was obliged to perform what were then called "labors"—that is, battles,[5] most often involving "monsters"—on behalf of the person who had "redeemed" him.

The Chimaera

"With the forequarters of a lion, the hindquarters of a serpent and the body of a goat, the Chimaera exhaled the fearful breath of an all-consuming fire." (Hesiod, *Theogony,* 321.)

The author adds that it "had three heads: the first, that of a terrifying lion; the second, that of a goat; and the third, that of a dreadful dragon."

[4] The alphabet, invented to meet the needs of Sumerian commerce in about 6000 B.C., had been brought to Greece by the Phoenicians.

[5] So it was later for Herakles, who, in order to be "redeemed" for the murder of his sons, had to perform the labors imposed upon him by Eurystheus. In more recent times, convicts could have their sentences commuted by enlisting the armed forces.

Apollodorus says that it "possessed in one body the strength of three animals."

Hesiod says that its parents were Typhon and Echidne, its grandparents accordingly being the "watchdog" Orthrus and (again) Echidne, and its great-grandfather, Geryon, the son of Chrysaor, who was the "brother" of Pegasus. In other words, they were all "born of the blood of Medusa."

There is nothing surprising in the clan's choice for one part of its insignia: the dragon, belching fire and sulfur like the volcanoes of its Atlantid ancestor. As for the remaining figures the chief would adopt the lion as a symbol of his courage; and since it is a shepherd custom to tie a goatskin across their backs, the Chimaera possessed "the body" of that animal. Even today, goats are virtually the only domestic animal found on the coast of Asia Minor.

Another possibility is that the tribe was subdivided into three clans (three "heads," says Hesiod; "the strength of three animals," says Apollodorus)—one, of pastoral people (the goat), a second, of warriors (the lion) and a third, of navigators of Gorgonian origin (the dragon).

The Labors of Bellerophon

Assisted by the soldiers of Iobates, who were finding their new neighbors a distinct nuisance, Bellerophon polished off this "monster" with his bow and arrow.

"When this was done, Iobates sent the hero to fight the illustrious Solymians [a people of the Taurus region, often at war with the Lycians]. He thought this was the fiercest battle he had ever waged on earth with humans." (*Iliad,* VI.)

Nevertheless, according to Homer, he emerged from it unscathed. Iobates tried again: "Every time he returned, the king devised some new scheme . . ."

Apollodorus writes, "Bellerophon having defeated the Solymians, the king next ordered him to make war upon the Amazons," the matriarchal people with the famous female warriors, who lived "in Phrygia of the beautiful vines." (*Iliad,* III.)

Once again, the hero triumphed and Iobates, despairing of ever getting rid of him by indirect means, resorted to open warfare: "He chose the best men in all of huge Lycia and him them in ambush one day, but not one of them came back alive; great Bellerophon had massacred the lot."

The sovereign gave up. "Iobates, marveling at Bellerophon's prowess, showed him Proetos' letter. Wishing to keep such a hero by his side, the king also offered him his daughter in marriage, and half of his royal prerogatives." (Apollodorus.)

The Ride of the Winged Pegasus

His native city, however, was demanding its hero back. According to Suidas (tenth-century commentator), Bellerophon returned immediately after his release from his Asian servitude.

The reason for this call for help was that Pegasus, decidedly overstepping the limits, "was drinking at the Peirene well." (Strabo, VII.) In other words the Echinadian fleet, not content with plaguing traffic in the gulf, had sailed up to Corinth itself.

Pindar adds, "Bellerophon did not know how to go about capturing [Pegasus], so Polyeides, a renowned seer, advised him to sleep in the temple of Athena . . ."

In this instance, Polyeides sounds very much like an Athenian negotiator, for as soon as the hero began to follow his advice, by "resting [relying] on the goddess," the scene at Seriphos was repeated: "Athena came to him in a dream," ready to "advise" him and "guide his arm" as she had done for Perseus. The goddess had initiated the raid on the far-distant Gorgon; was she now going to tolerate the presence of a fleet "born of the blood of Medusa" at her very doorstep? Everything pointed to Bellerophon as the successor to the Danaan hero; moreover, he had just conquered the Chimaera—"great-grand niece" of the winged horse, through the "monster" side of the family.

The objective was nothing less than to drive the Phorcids out of the Echinades; as long as the pirates from the west could find a safe harbor there, any Greek victory would have to be won all over again. But only the pilots of Pegasus could find their way through the channels.

The Echinades

The situation has hardly changed since then. The Echinades are approached by way of Leucadia (now called Levkas), one of the Ionian Islands (but so close to the mainland that a causeway connects them). For this part of the trip, one can choose between the sea route, via Patras, and the road turning off the main Epirus highway at Amphilochia.

The next part of the land journey is most picturesque, running for thirty magic miles along the edge of the Gulf of Preveza: limpid miniature bays, blue mountains, gloomy ravines, deserted beaches and solitary fig trees. Suddenly the road dives into a coastal valley covered by luxuriant orchards. On the edge of a fairy-tale bay lies a picture-postcard (but very real) town: Vonitsa, dominated by a fortified castle where the Lion of St. Mark still stands guard, shouldering off an invasion of cactus plants and caperbushes.

Then the road crosses a barren cape, where the only living figures are those of the eucalyptus and pine. At last, at the very end of the headland stands a long, fortified, crenelated jetty, flanked by a redoubt whose stones have been devoured by the rusty grass—the work of Franks and Venetians.

The ferry is at the end, worked by women. The steel cable shrieks as they struggle with the winch, and the ferry inches across.

On the shore of the peaceful silt-choked lagoon of old Leucadia, nothing remains but the phantom of a once patrician city. In 1948 an earthquake destroyed the rest. Jerry-built structures have replaced the handsome homes of noble Ionians and wealthy merchants, and only the frosted façade of an occasional church recalls the splendor of Venice: encrusted with frescoes, crazed, but still standing, "miraculously preserved by the saints."

In the port, oddly shaped caiques with sails like wings are moored near the salt pans; their masters are eagle-beaked, dark as Hades, supple as cats. Surviving every war and cataclysm, the remote descendants of Phorcys are still here.

After clambering on board, the boatman casts off and the craft turns south along the channel dredged out in the shallows. It passes the site of the ancient city, the capital of Homer's Leukas Petre ("white rock") and finally reaches an enclosed sea, cut off by Leucadia itself and Ithaca on the west, and by the mainland on the east.

Here is the Echinadian archipelago, the most secret of all—dozens of islets, of all shapes and sizes, some covered with pine, others arid and barren, some inhabited, others desert, a few inviting, the remainder stern and forbidding. Reefs, rocks, cliffs—a scene of unbelievable beauty.

In calm weather the islands float in a silver bath, emerald- or opal-hued, unreal; but when Meltheme blows they are tossed and rumpled, surrounded by foaming peaks through which the boats pitch and sway, plowing up the waves with their "wings" beating the wind.

Meganese

The largest island, Meganese, is, as its name indicates, a sixty-mile ridge facing the mainland. Suddenly an inlet appears in front of the boat, completely hidden behind its cape. The boat slips around the end, and a white village shines on the crest of the spine. Perched high above the cave-studded cliff, it stands out against a sky only one shade paler than the indigo sea. A rocky path writhes up to it, its hairpin bends so close that they look like the tangled coils of a serpent.

At sea level, narrow-throated wells of brackish water have been sunk in the shade of venerable olive trees; leaning over their curious stonework rims, black-garbed peasant women draw water for the donkeys who stand swishing at the wasps with their tails (the wasps, too, are parched with thirst). Those who have no donkeys trudge up the path in silence, balancing their jars on their heads, carrying water to the village in its eagle's nest.

The houses are poor, whitewashed, austere, and immaculate. There is no hotel or tavern, only a few primitive cafés frequented by rough, steel-eyed men. Visitors are lodged in the home, according to the ancient custom. Hospitality is total or not at all; there is no question of paying for bed or board. No running water, much less electricity: lighting is by oil or acetylene lamp, of the lanterns which the men use to fish at night—along with dynamite: many of the hands you shake do not have all their fingers.

These are the Echinadian sailors: stern, taciturn; above all, proud as kings.

On the inland slopes olive trees grow in the stony fields. Sometimes the hoe lays bare large slabs set in a rectangle: ancient wells and tombs that nobody has yet dreamed of robbing.

Pegasus' Hideout

Inlets like this one beneath the village are scattered all along the jagged coast, each one lurking behind its headland—a paradise for pirates in any age. To the west, even more spectacular, gapes a vast marine cavern, blackening the face of the sheer russet cliff. Its ceiling arches twenty or thirty yards overhead, the floor is a gravel beach rhythmically lapped by the waves. This deep-water port is Pegasus' subterranean stable. A small fleet might easily shelter in it. Looking down through fifty feet of crystal-clear shadow, one can count the smooth stones. Only gulls and swallows nest there now, their young chattering among the stalactites. Sometimes, looking like the shades of the "long ships" as they glide past, fishing boats come in for shelter when the sea outside grows too rough.

The outline of Ithaca (which the thirteenth-century Phorcids may also have occupied) is visible on the horizon to the southwest, along with Arkoudion, "bear island." Due west, the peaks of Levkas rise (over three thousand feet); Skorpios, "scorpion island," lies to the north, and Atokos, "the barren," to the south.

To the east lies a whole constellation of low islets, gradually being joined together by the alluvial deposits of the Achelous.

A labyrinth of channels, bristling with shoals and choked by mudbanks—a treacherous bottom if ever there was one; sheltered ports, hidden caves, and cliffs to be used as acropolises by the pirate race: this was where the Phorcid Spider lurked, and Bellerophon's task was to dislodge winged Pegasus from her lair.

Death of Echidne

Such an ambitious project demanded preparation, and no one knew this better than Pallas Athena, the goddess who never left anything to chance.

"Inspired by Athena," as Pindar writes, the hero entered into a series of carefully chosen alliances. He paid a visit to Oeneos, the Aetolian king who had received the vine from the hands of Dionysos. This sovereign's domain extended to the coast nearest the Echinades (region around Mesolonghion), which meant that he suffered more than anyone else from the Phorcid raids and was therefore particularly eager to hear Bellerophon's plans: "Oeneos kept him twenty days in his palace. They gave each other superb presents: Oeneos gave Bellerophon a dazzling purple belt, and received a two-handled goblet in exchange." (*Iliad,* VI.)

This suggests a pact between the two kingdoms most closely concerned (Corinth and Aetolia), directed against their common enemy. And after "Athena gave Bellerophon a curb, which he used to master Pegasus" (Pindar), the hero was able "to carry out his project brilliantly." He overpowered the winged horse, "bridled" him, and "mounted" his ships.

The Spider was permanently crippled; without her fleet, she languished and could no longer spin the web in which so many Greek ships had been trapped.

The Echinades changed hands, but not vocations[6]; they were soon occupied by the descendants of Mestor, King of Mycenae and son of Perseus. When his time came to die (with no male issue), his daughter Hippothoea was forced to flee. She gave birth to a boy, Pterelaos, who sired other sons: Taphos, Teleboas, Ithacos, Neritos, and Everes.

Taphos, who lived with Pterelaos on Meganese, gave his own name to the island, which subsequently became the home of the "Taphians"; Teleboas fathered generations of Teleboans; and Ithacos colonized Ithaca, which adopted his name and, a little while later, became the kingdom of Ulysses.

[6] They were used for the same purpose by Hellenistic, Roman, and Byzantine pirates, and later by Greek sailors fighting the Turks. Today Skorpios is the home port of the *Christina,* the yacht of the millionaire Onassis, who has bought the island.

Bellerophon Strikes Back, but So Do the Gods

His mission accomplished, Bellerophon, like Perseus, moved on to settle his personal accounts. Suidas says that, "to get even with Stheneboea [who had unjustly accused him], he led her to believe he was going to marry her, invited her to mount [the ships of] Pegasus, and dashed her into the sea."

Hailed as a hero throughout Greece, Bellerophon then returned to Lycia, where Iobates' daughter, who had cost him so many hard-won victories, was still waiting. Her name was Philonoë, and their children were called Isander, Hippolachos, and Laodamia.

But, says Homer, "at the end of his life, he incurred the hatred of the gods" for presuming to aim too high, "imagining he could reach Olympus on the back of Pegasus." His head turned by the success of his labors, the tamer of the Echinadian fleet and emulator of Perseus began to aspire to the rank of demigod.

The gods, greatly annoyed by his insolence, proceeded to teach him a lesson: "Isander, one of his sons, was killed fighting the Solymians, and Artemis caused the death of his daughter."[7]

Disheartened and embittered, the hero "wandered all alone through the Aelian plain [Cilicia], fleeing the haunts of men."

When he died, his son Hippolachos succeeded him and begat more sons. Among them was the warrior Glauchos, who, when he reached manhood, fought with the Achaean forces beneath the walls of Troy.

[7] The illness and sudden death of a woman were attributed to the "arrows of Artemis"; in men the cause was said to be "the arrows of Apollo."

Chapter IV
AMPHITRYON

"Sthenelaos had prevailed over his brothers and nephews,
So the banished Amphitryon sought refuge in Thebes;

Then he went warring in the Taphians' land,
And while he was away his wife Alcmene
Conceived twins, one of them sired by Zeus."

after APOLLODORUS

While Bellerophon was marching into legend, the sons of Perseus were still governing the old kingdom of Danaos. Their names were Alcaeus, Sthenelaos, Helios, Electryon, and Mestor (his offspring were aleady kings in the Echinades). A sixth son, called Perses, lived with his grandfather Cepheus in the land of Phoenix.[1]

But a new strain was now beginning to take root in Argolis—that of the Asian "Achaean" race of Tantalos.

Tantalos and His Torment

This fourteenth-century king of Phrygia (in Asia Minor) suffered all the torments of insatiable ambition. Whatever he did, "even when he stole nectar and ambrosia from the gods," he was never contented, and the "object of his thirst and hunger [for power] seemed to move away every time he reached out to grasp it."

[1] During the Wars with the Medes, Persian diplomats called themselves the "sons" of Perses, hoping to beguile the Greeks by alluding to their common ancestry.

His torment still bears his name; and with such a personality he could hardly fail to make himself unpopular with his neighbors.

Pelops the Emigrant

One day, toward the end of the fourteenth century, his son Pelops decided how he, at least, was going to deal with the obsessive paternal appetite. "Scalded" (the "mythological" texts say "boiled"), that is, frustrated in his desire to share in the government of the country, and seeing clearly that the greedy miser would never relinquish one sliver of his kingdom to his son during his lifetime, Pelops concluded that he had let himself be "eaten alive" long enough.

Determined to carve out a kingdom for himself, he accordingly demanded his share of his inheritance in cash. Tantalos, who was greedy for power rather than money, agreed to this arrangement, which would divest him of his cumbersome heir apparent. With well-lined pockets, the prince then crossed the Aegean and began prospecting for a kingdom in southern Greece.

Now, it happened that there was a princess to be married off in Aetolia: Hippodameia, daughter of King Oenomaos of Pisa, a city near Olympia. Applying for the damsel's hand, however, was no mere formality. She was the prize of a harrowing contest: her father, "told by an oracle that he would be slain by his son-in-law," had made his consent to her marriage conditional upon the outcome of a chariot race against himself, with the loser forfeiting his life.

Doped Horses and a Rigged Race

This "judgment of God," in the manner of the second Middle Ages, was in no danger of being won by anyone other than the king, for his cunning servant "Myrtilos" doped his horses with some kind of fermented juice to obtain extraordinary bursts of speed.

When Pelops came forward, thirteen competitors had already paid for their foolhardiness with their lives.

The Race

In the museum at Olympia the preparations for the race may still be seen: they are the subject of one of the pediments of the Temple of Zeus, reconstructed from fragments according to Pausanias' description, so that both the words and the figures themselves, immortalized by the gifted chisel of Paeonios (fifth century B.C.), can speak to us.

"In the center stands the tallest figure of all, the arbiter of the match—Zeus, bare-chested, his himation falling to his ankles. On his left is Oenomaos, bearded, with one hand on his hip; a servant holds his lance. Then come Sterope, his wife, and Myrtilos, kneeling in front of the horses. To the right of Zeus is Pelops, wearing a pointed cap, smooth-shaven and naked, except for a bronze breastplate. In his left arm he holds a shield[2] and in the other a lance. Beside him stands Hippodameia, in the talar peplos, looking pensive; then Sphaeros [or Cillas], Pelops' charioteer, in front of his four horses."

In one corner reclines the allegorical figure of the river Alpheus, and in the other that of its tributary, the Kladeos; they define the limits of the racecourse.

At stake were the Alpheus and its valley. If Pelops emerged victorious, he would win Hippodameia and the kingdom, too, but there seemed no reason why he should not suffer the same fate as his predecessors and fall a victim to foul play.

But the gods, as it happened, had other intentions, and the prince was probably not entirely ignorant of their projects. Tradition tells how he bribed the not very upright Myrtilos with some of his Phrygian gold.

Some authors say that "Myrtilos contrived to make one of the wheels of his master's chariot fall off during the race"; others maintain that "with evil charms he bewitched the horses of Oenomaos and made them bolt into a ravine."

This version is the more likely, for unless the king were a complete idiot he could scarcely have failed to make certain that his

[2] It was about this time that the shield was coming into general use among the Greeks.

team had been given their drug—only this time Myrtilos had increased the dose so that the horses would run away with him.

Pelops, the winner, pierced the loser's side with his lance, married Hippodameia, and proclaimed himself king.

The "Father" of the Peloponnesus

Thereupon, his ambition began to equal his father's (it is only in adulthood that blood really begins to tell): Pelops decided he must have Argolis, if not for himself, then for his descendants.

"The most reliable compilers of the Peloponnesian traditions affirm that it was Pelops, bringing a considerable fortune with him from Asia, who gradually gained ascendancy over the land and, although not a native, had the honor of giving it his name." (Thucydides.)

As there were no more chariot races in the offing, the Asian had recourse to another method—one that has since met with some success. In exchange for a substantial dowry, he introduced his daughters into the beds of the kings whose states he wished to possess, thereby gaining entry to their courts.

The Perseids became the more or less willing victims of this matrimonial invasion. Following the division of Perseus' empire into five portions, each king had found himself with a bare subsistence, and this made the wealth of Pelops all the more welcome.

To regild the tarnished ancestral coat of arms, Alcaeus (Tiryns) married Hipponomaea, Sthenelaos (Argos) married Eurydice, Electryon (Midea) married his niece Anaxo, the daughter of Alcaeus and Hipponomaea (who was thus 50 per cent Pelopid); and Alcmene, a quarter-bred Asian, was their daughter.

In the next generation there was further inbreeding. Alcmene—25 per cent Pelopid—married Amphitryon, another son of Alcaeus (and hence, both uncle and cousin of his own wife), himself already 50 per cent Pelopid. Therefore, their children Iphicles and Herakles had a very high percentage of Asian blood in their veins.

Eurystheus, the son of Sthenelaos and Amphibia who was to become Herakles' suzerain and taskmaster, was only half Asian.

These family trees, which can be reconstructed from Apollodorus (II, IV) and Apollonius of Rhodes (L. I), give a clear picture of the infiltration of Perseid blood by the Pelopid strain. For the four kings concerned the process was as follows:[3]

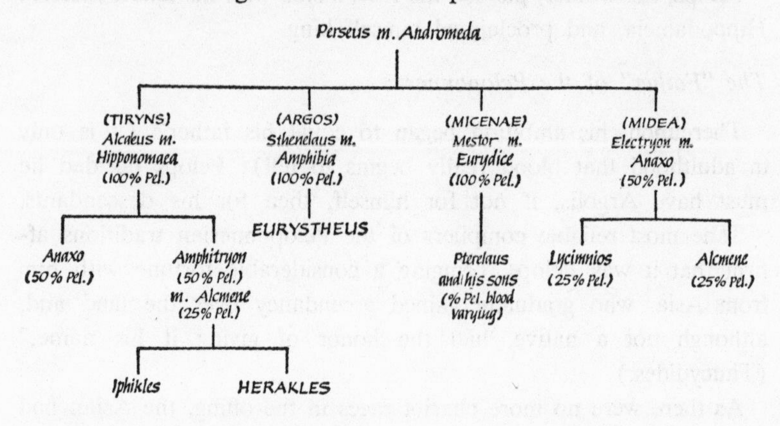

The Wars Between the Brothers

The Pelopid influence continued to increase, assisted by the wars between the sons of Perseus. Mestor had just died and left no male heirs, so his brother Electryon seized Mycenae and annexed that fortress to his own kingdom of Midea. This left Pterelaos and his sons (Taphos, Teleboas, Ithacos, Neritos)—the dead man's heirs through the female line—without an inheritance. From the depths of their Echinadian stronghold, they retaliated by declaring war.

They landed in Argolis, and carnage ensued: "The only survivors were one son of the usurper Electryon, and, on the side of the attacking forces, a son of Pterelaos who had stayed behind to guard the boats." (Apollodorus.)

But since, as Homer writes, he came of a race of "great pirates," this boy proceeded to load Electryon's livestock onto his own ships, providing Pterelaos' side with a hostage.

As nephew of Electryon and cousin of Pterelaos, Amphitryon of Tiryns now decided to step in and arbitrate. He repurchased the

[3] Perseus' two other sons, Helios (King of Helos) and Perses (in Phoenicia), were not affected.

livestock, but just as it was being returned to Electryon, "one animal escaped and Amphitryon threw a club at it, which bounced off its horns and hit Electryon on the head." (Apollodorus.)

This left both Midea and Mycenae kingless. The remaining son of Perseus—Sthenelaos, King of Argos—was not going to miss this golden opportunity. He expelled Amphitryon from Tiryns on the ground that he "had to be purified," and gave himself all the unclaimed crowns: Midea, Mycenae, and Tiryns, in addition to his own (Argos).

Thus the four cities of Perseus were united under the scepter of Sthenelaos, as the result of a coup whose success was due, at least in part, to his in-laws.

In recognition of their contribution, Sthenelaos decided to reward his Pelopid brothers-in-law: "Summoning Atreus and Thyestes, the sons of Pelops, he gave them Midea." (Apollodorus.)

In doing so, he committed a fatal political error, often repeated by kings of later ages: he should never have enlisted the help of outsiders against his own kin. By handing over Midea, he was bringing the Asian wolf into the Perseid fold—a wolf that would like nothing better than to depose the reigning dynasty.

This did not happen, however, until after the time of Herakles, but because of Amphitryon's exile, it was the sky of Thebes that became the great hero's cradle.

Amphitryon in Exile

"Amphitryon went to Thebes with Lycimnios and Alcmene," children of Electryon who had also been dispossessed by Sthenelaos.

The city's origin had some bearing upon its choice as his place of exile. It was founded by Cadmos, the brother of Danaos—in a sense, it was a "sister" of Argos; and the Perseids were most at ease in Phoenician surroundings.

Creon was King of Thebes at that time, and he "purified" Amphitryon of the accidental death which had prompted his exile. "Alcmene said she would marry any man who avenged the deaths of her brothers, slain in the battle with the Teleboans, so Amphitryon promised to make war upon them." (Apollodorus.)

Marriage with his cousin would be a first step toward possession of Midea, in addition to the ancestral throne of Tiryns (Midea having belonged to Alcmene's father, Electryon). "Next, he sought an alliance with Creon [of Thebes]. Being in exile, he did not have enough resources, on his own, to raise an army against the Teleboans."

Creon, who had complete power over Amphitryon after "purifying" him (like Iobates over Bellerophon before him), "promised to help if he would first rid Thebes of a fox that was plaguing the countryside."

The "fox"

According to Antoninus Liberalis (Fab. 41), "this fox lived hidden in the mountains, and captured only male children."

And, adds Apollodorus, "as it was causing such havoc, the Thebans gave it a child every month. If they failed to do so, it stole even more than usual."

This "cunning beast," the source of so much local grief, was apparently demanding hostages, and, if they were not delivered on time, retaliating energetically; he sounds very much like a highway robber who had resolved to obtain a maximum of "understanding" from his victims.

To get himself out of this predicament, Creon would have to think of something ingenious, for Amphitryon could no more hunt the bandit than fight the Teleboans in his present circumstances. He bethought himself of Athens (Athens—through Cecrops, a "Phoenician cousin" of Argos and Thebes), the city that was always ready to take part in any policing operations to be carried out.

And so, says Apollodorus, "he went to see Cephalus, the son-in-law of King Erechtheus of Athens, who was living at Thorea."[4]

Athens, Thirteenth Century B.C.

Thucydides explains the sudden expansion of the city of Cecrops and Erechtheus in the following terms: "Because of the aridity of its soil, Attica had long been inhabited by the same people, for

[4] According to Ovid, Cephalus was a great-grandson of Deucalion (the dates would correspond, as far as the number of generations is concerned), and therefore, an Achaean.

fertile soil and many resources increase the likelihood of attack from without. It was to Athens that the chiefs expelled from other parts of Greece by wars and revolution came for refuge, thinking they would be safer there than anywhere else; and it was they, by coming in such large numbers, who helped to make the city great."

For the same reason, it was in Athens that the civilization then developing was least bellicose: "The Athenians were the first to cease wearing armor [for their everyday dress] and adopt a more peaceful and refined style of life."[5]

Apollodorus writes that after welcoming Amphitryon, "and in exchange for part of the spoils he would take from the Teleboans," Cephalus, son-in-law of Erechtheus—pursuing the policy that had led to the campaigns of Perseus and Bellerophon—promised to help the suppliant, both to drive out the "fox" that was devastating Boeotia (region adjoining Attica) and to cripple the Teleboan pirates.

But to invade the Echinades, a fleet was necessary.

Apollodorus: "Cephalus commanded Amphitryon to hunt the fox with a hound which Procris [his wife, daughter of King Erechtheus] had brought from Crete: Minos had given it to her."[6]

The second period of Cretan naval power (the Cretans, to whom Athens was "bound" in the literal sense of the word) dates from this time.

Minos II, the Oppressor

Following its collapse after the dreadful explosion of Santorini, the island with the warlike emblem of the double ax had managed to rebuild its naval empire.

In Minos II, there was certainly nothing of the son of Phoenician Europe, the wise lawmaker and first of the name. His fleet "protected" maritime cities in return for payment of substantial "con-

[5] *Peloponnesian War,* L. I, II, and IV.

[6] The reign of Minos II corresponded to the period when Seti I and Rameses II were re-establishing Egyptian supremacy in the eastern Mediterranean, on both land and sea, and hence to renewed activity among the Phoenicians, who were once again sailing for great Thebes of the Nile.

tributions"—not unlike the way in which modern gangs extort money from shopkeepers as payment for refraining from demolishing their shops. His "watchdogs"—ships sailing behind the figurehead of the bull—ruthlessly enforced his demands.

This explains the "guardian" given to Athenian Procris—to "protect" her, willy-nilly, and also to look after the interests of the Cretan ruler.[7]

This "Molossos," then, helped (with assistance from Zeus, of course) to rid the Boeotian countryside of the fox which had been such a menace on the public thoroughfare.

Down with the Teleboans

As soon as Thebes was freed of its bandits, Amphitryon returned to his original objective—the Echinadian Teleboans, who were not to be sneezed at. Although some of their princes had perished (in the battle in which Alcmene's brothers were also killed), Pterelaos, the clan chieftain, was still very much alive and had fortified his island of Meganese, now renamed Taphos. It would require a coalition to dislodge him, like the one from Seriphos that went out after the Gorgons, or the one Bellerophon led against Pegasus.

Apollodorus: "Amphitryon and his allies—Cephalus of Thorea in Attica, Panopeus of Phocis ["son" of Phocis, "son" of Sisyphus], Helios, son of Perseus, and Creon of Thebes—set out to destroy Taphos, but as long as Pterelaos was alive, they were unable to take the island."

Treachery, however, finally overcame this tenacious foe: "Comaetho, daughter of Pterelaos, had fallen in love with Amphitryon . . ." We can guess the rest. And "with Pterelaos dead, all the islands were soon subdued."

Amphitryon was not at all grateful to Comaetho for her "cooperation"; his thoughts were riveted on Alcmene. "After killing Comaetho and taking much loot, he returned to Thebes, giving the

[7] This is another version of Phorcid Orthrus, Geryon's "watchdog."

Echinades to Helios [his uncle] and Cephalus, who settled there and founded towns named after themselves."[8]

It was then that a certain world-famous event took place, embroidered upon by Molière three thousand years later: "Amphitryon was about to return to Thebes when Zeus [him again], disguised as the hero, went to Alcmene and told her everything that had happened at Telebos. He slept with her for one whole night, which he made last as long as three."

It is tempting to imagine some advance messenger from the expedition, to whom Alcmene, who had been left by herself for far too long and was, moreover, in a transport of joy (her brothers being avenged at last), refused nothing.

Amphitryon, upon his return, did not fail to observe that something was amiss: "Seeing that his wife did not greet him with much enthusiasm, he asked her the reason, and she replied that he had already come, and spent the whole night with her; then he learned from Tiresias what had transpired with Zeus."

Tiresias, the renowned seer and priest of Zeus at Thebes, confirmed the faithless wife's version of her adultery.

Amphitryon naturally believed no more of this tale than Acrisios had of the story of Danaë's pregnancy.

Alcmene gave birth to twins; the first was called Iphicles, and his brother, in the beginning, was merely Alcaeos—"the strong," like his grandfather.

Later, he abandoned that name and acquired another, under which he became somewhat better known: Herakles, Hercules, son of Zeus, and most famous of all the gods of the sword of bronze.

[8] Cephalus later killed his wife in a fit of jealous rage and was banished from Attica for life. From the Echinades, he extended his dominion to include the modern Ionian Islands, where the Athenians were founding colonies—in particular Cephallenia (which still bears his name) and Ithaca; Ulysses was his grandson.

Chapter V
THE BIRTH OF HERAKLES

"Two choruses of Salians, divided in two rows,
Sang; they sang of Herakles' young strength,
His glorious birth, the strangled serpents . . ."

VIRGIL

"I am fully aware that the history of classical myths, and especially those relating to Herakles, offers serious difficulties: in the greatness of his deeds this god surpassed everything memorable ever accomplished by man, and so it is not easy to give a sober account of the individual acts that made him immortal." The quotation is from Book IV of Diodorus Siculus.

The enigma of the hero's birth, at least, is only apparent; we have seen how, in the absence of her husband, Amphitryon, Alcmene contrived to have him sired by "Zeus."

The ensuing saga was, from first to last, the result of a coincidence: it so happened that the wife of Sthenelaos, the king of Argolis who had dispossessed Amphitryon, was also awaiting a blessed event. Under the Perseid rule of succession, the throne hung in the balance.

The Perseid Law of Succession

This law, laid down by Zeus himself as founder of the family,[1] stipulated that "the empire would be ruled by the first-born descendant of Perseus in every generation."

If the just heavens would only send Amphitryon a male child, that boy would be king—even if he were born in exile, as long

[1] It was "Zeus" who impregnated Perseus' mother Danaë.

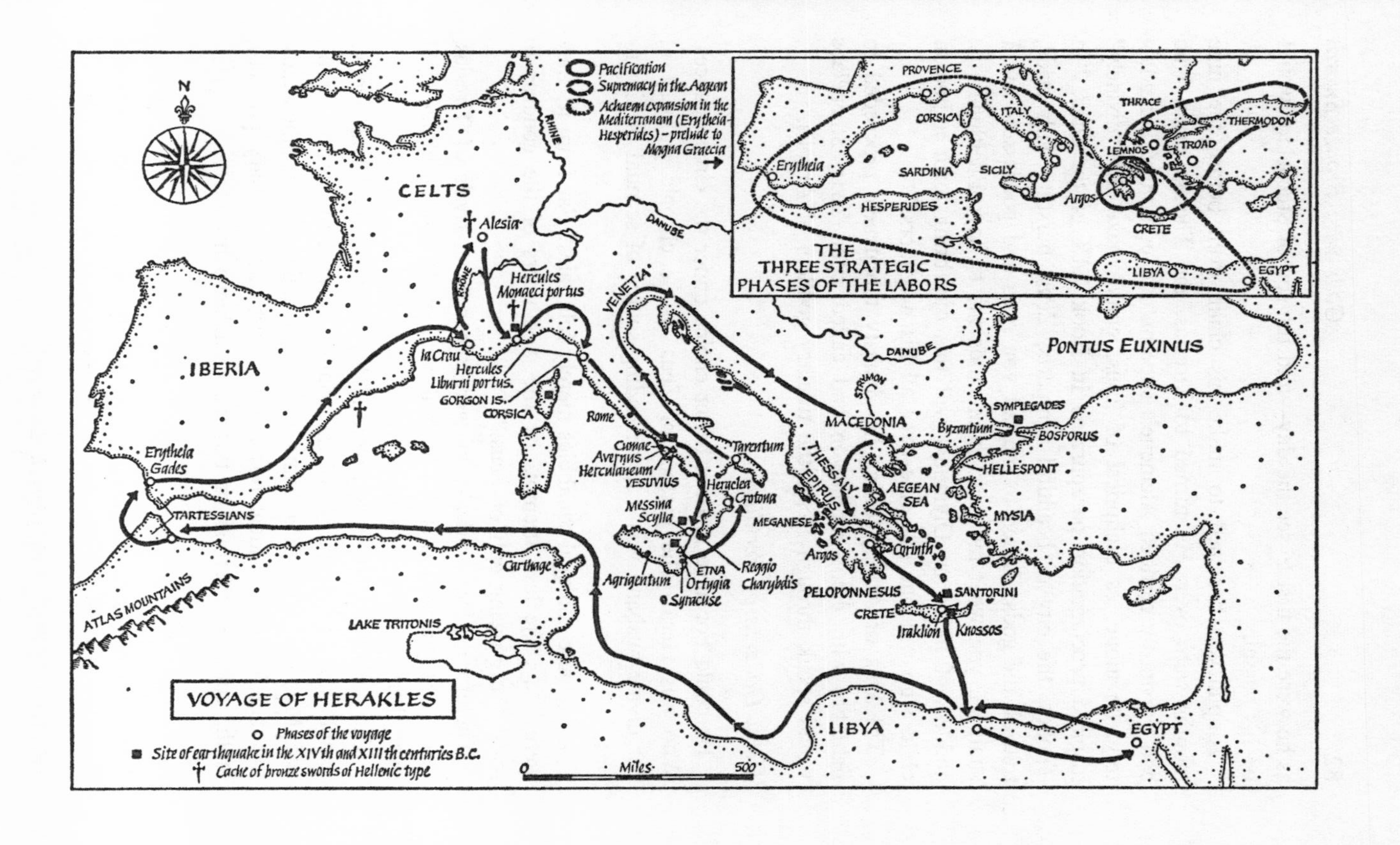
VOYAGE OF HERAKLES
Phases of the voyage
Site of earthquake in the XIVth and XIIIth centuries B.C.
Cache of bronze swords of Hellenic type
0 Miles 500
Pacification
Supremacy in the Aegean
Achaean expansion in the Mediterranean (Erytheia-Hesperides) – prelude to Magna Graecia
THE THREE STRATEGIC PHASES OF THE LABORS
PROVENCE
CORSICA
ITALY
SARDINIA
SICILY
Erytheia
HESPERIDES
THRACE
THERMODON
LEMNOS
TROAD
Argos
CRETE
LIBYA
EGYPT
N
CELTS
IBERIA
Alesia
RHINE
RHONE
DANUBE
Hercules Monaeci portus
la Crau
Hercules Liburni portus.
GORGON IS.
CORSICA
Erythela
Gades
TARTESSIANS
ATLAS MOUNTAINS
Carthage
LAKE TRITONIS
VENETIA
Rome
Cumae
Avernus
Herculaneum
VESUVIUS
Tarentum
Heraclea
Crotona
Messina
Scylla
ETNA
Agrigentum
Ortygia
Syracuse
Reggio
Charybdis
STRYMON
MACEDONIA
THESSALY
EPIRUS
MEGANESE
Argos
Corinth
PELOPONNESUS
AEGEAN SEA
SANTORINI
CRETE
Iraklion
Knossos
Byzantium
SYMPLEGADES
BOSPORUS
HELLESPONT
MYSIA
PONTUS EUXINUS
LIBYA
EGYPT

as he were the first to see the day—and the son of Sthenelaos would be his vassal.

Amphitryon hastened to make his claim even before the nine months were over. He turned to Tiresias, the Theban priest who had previously certified Alcmene's supernatural edition of her adultery; he alone, as archpriest of Zeus, could make the "divinely" inspired proclamation paraphrased in Book XIX of the *Iliad:* "In Thebes, the city of beautiful ramparts, Zeus, bursting with pride, told all the gods: Listen to me, all you gods and goddesses, and I shall tell you what my heart commands me to say: Eileithyia [the goddess of births on Olympus] will this day bring forth a human child who will one day rule over all his neighbors."

The king of Argos, feeling his dynasty threatened, proceeded to fight fire with fire. Amphitryon had called upon Zeus; Sthenelaos would speak through Hera, the tutelary goddess of Argolis.

Hera, Goddess of Fertility

He could not have made a better choice under the circumstances. Who was Hera? The partner of Zeus whose chronic jealousy of her divine husband was a never-ending source of scandal on Olympus.

Were these conjugal squabbles merely folk tales? Far from it: they were ". . . the last attempts by the worshipers of the goddess to resist the growing cult of Zeus."[2]

Therefore, Hera's priestesses were the natural rivals of Tiresias, just as Amphitryon was the natural rival of Sthenelaos in the fight over their thrones.

The priestesses, moreover, were highly ingenious tacticians. Hera's temple stood at the center of the triangle formed by Argos, Tiryns, and Mycenae, and thus came under the influence of Sthenelaos; this put him in an ideal position to exert any necessary pressure, in the form of offerings or threats, to achieve his ends.

The Argive Heraeum

Established as a religious center for the Perseid kingdom, the Heraeum was linked to the three main cities by roads, like the

[2] F. Guiraud (*Mythologie générale Larousse*).

radii of a spider's web leading into the lair of the carnivorous monster.

From Mycenae, for example, a rutted road leads to it along the base of the Euboean hill; this is the Sacred Way, used by the contemporaries of Perseus and Sthenelaos (as may be seen from traces in the rock).

The scene is depressing except in the springtime, when the hollows that still cradle a few clods of soil fill with fresh green grass and daisies; in any other season the earth is barren, showing only tormented boulders and the raw, open flanks of the hill. The road goes through the little village of Monastiraki ("little monastery"), whose simple whitewashed houses are probably very like the dwellings of the humble Bronze Age peasants of the region. Then there is the Eleutherios, a stream whose name means "free torrent."

"Stream" is an exaggeration: the bed is dry except during its brief winter outbursts. Once, though, the hillside was covered with vegetation and the Eleutherios flowed the year round; the priestesses used to purify themselves in its waters.

The terraces of the Heraeum rise beyond its banks. The ruins have all been leveled to the ground, but they are mammoth. The first steps of a monumental staircase lie parallel to the rock—each step is 80 meters long. It is flanked by a second, lateral stairway.

The ruins of the "new temple" are on the first level; it was built by Eupolemos, the architect responsible for the great Argive works of the fifth century B.C. The stylobate (40 by 20 meters) is composed of blocks of rough-hewn tufa. There were six Doric columns along the façade of the peristyle and twelve down each side. The cella (cell) contained the chryselephantine statue of the goddess Hera, sculpted by Polykleitos in ivory and gold.

A host of lesser buildings crowded around the lofty temple over whose remains we now crawl and stumble. Then comes a second staircase, 45 meters wide, leading to the foundations of the portico—a double colonnade, 22 and 63 meters long, respectively; this gives some idea of the size of the congregation that came to worship.

Above this, on the topmost level, is the site of the "old temple—

the oldest known sanctuary of the Greek world (eighth century B.C.). Like those of Mycenae and Tiryns, its foundations are of Cyclopean dimensions—stones of 5.30 by 3.0 meters! They supported a platform, paved with huge slabs, that covered an area larger than the Parthenon. The base of the primitive idol can still be identified: Hera, more powerful here than Zeus.

But even the "old temple" was certainly not the first. In the days of Amphitryon and Sthenelaos, fertility worship was already older than time, as old as the race, dating from the first harvest and the first child.

It was on this terrace—the magnet of Argive religion, overlooking the whole kingdom of Argolis—that the battle of the births was waged, upon which depended Herakles' entire life and labors.

Birth of the Master of the Labors

At Thebes, Amphitryon and Tiresias thought they had won; what could prevent this baby, the embodiment of all their hopes and dreams, from being the first to see the day? After all, Alcmene's pregnancy was two months further advanced than that of her rival, Nicippe.

The answer is contained in a single name: Hera.

"Hera, a goddess, then cunningly took advantage of Zeus. She knew the brave wife of Sthenelaos the Perseid [Nicippe] was seven months pregnant. So then, before the infant came to term, she caused it to be born." (*Iliad,* XIX.)

Was this a ruse? Is Homer alluding to some secret skill of the priestesses of fertility, who were expert obstetricians? Did they know how to accelerate childbirth?

"On the fetus in the seventh month" (Hippocrates)

Summarizing the ancients' knowledge of obstetrics, Hippocrates (fifth century B.C.) writes: "The fetus enters the seventh month at the end of one hundred eighty-two days and a fraction . . . The fetus now gains strength faster than at any other time . . . Thus the strongest and most highly developed of these embyros, by forcing and tearing the membranes, inevitably precipitate labor. Most die, but some survive, undoubtedly because of the relationship and length of time they were nourished in the womb, which, in their case, has given them everything a more fully developed and better-prepared fetus would possess. Furthermore, they leave their mother's womb before the sicknesses of the critical eighth month."

There are certain preparations capable of hastening delivery: "Take some roots or sprouts of oleander: scrape one demioxy-baphon and give in a hot potion . . . Or: dittany, two obols: crush and drink in hot water . . . Or, take abrotanum (one drachma), cedar berries and anise, grind up in one kyathos (0.045 liter) of sweet wine, add one kyathos of stale water, and give as a potion . . . Lastly, one part turpentine, one part honey, and two parts oil, sweet-smelling wine—the most pleasant that can be found—mix all, warm and give to drink in several doses. This will also heal the womb, should it be inflamed . . ."

In addition to the recipes, there are certain magical practices: "Take the fruit of the wild cucumber after it has gone white; coat it with wax, roll it in a piece of red wool, and attach it around the loins."

Parturition could also be precipitated by mechanical means: "A cloth should be placed beneath the woman while she is lying on her back, and another cloth should be put over her to hide the vulva. Both legs and both arms are wrapped in cloths; two women then grasp the legs, and two more women take hold of the arms. Then, holding firmly, they are to give not less than ten wrenches.

"Then they lay the woman on the bed, head down and legs up, and, letting go of her arms, all four take hold of the legs and give several jerks to roll her onto her shoulders, each time throwing the patient back onto the bed so that the fetus, thus shaken, will move into the main channel and can progress properly. If you have some Cretan dittany, give a portion of it to drink afterward, or else boil some castoreum in Chios wine . . ."—tonics which the mother could scarcely fail to need after such treatment.

Was Amphibia (Nicippe) subjected to this ordeal?

Herakles, Vassal of Eurystheus

All we know for certain is that the future of the Argive throne was at stake, and that Eurystheus was born first, at seven months.

The law of succession then turned against the man who had counted his chicken before it was hatched. Sthenelaos had outwitted Amphitryon, and Hera's priestesses gave Tiresias tit for tat: in a counter-proclamation, the goddess taunts her husband, victim of her stratagem: "Zeus, father of white lightning, I want you to engrave these words upon your brain: he is born, *now,* the hero who will reign over the Argive people. He is Eurystheus, son of Sthenelaos." (*Iliad,* XIX.)

Consternation at Thebes: "Zeus felt a great pain in the very core of his heart . . ." The pain of duped Amphitryon and humiliated Tiresias.

A midwife's skill or a stroke of luck? In any case, it is Eurystheus who would reign one day, and Herakles who would be his vassal; and not the other way around.

Herakles and the Serpents

Now came Alcmene's turn to give birth. According to Apollodorus: "She was delivered of two sons, Herakles, son of Zeus, and Iphicles, son of Amphitryon."

Pherecydes writes that, in order to tell which was the god's son and which his own, Amphitryon "placed two serpents in their cradle, to find out which child was his:[3] one baby tried to get away, but the other showed no fear of the serpents, and thus he knew that Iphicles was his own son."

The snakes were probably only garter snakes, for the king did not wish the babies any harm.

There is another version of this story, which would suggest an attempt on the part of the Argive Heraeum (or of Sthenelaos) to eliminate the babies permanently without further ado: "One time Alcmene, daughter of Midea, took her two sons, Herakles, who was ten months old, and Iphicles, who was one night younger, and, after bathing them and giving them their fill of nourishing milk, laid them in a bronze shield which Amphitryon had taken from Pterelaos after killing him. She rocked the shield and the children fell asleep.

[3] At that time it was believed that twins could have different fathers.

"In the middle of the night the insidious Hera brought two serpents into the palace of Amphitryon, horrible monsters intended to devour the infant Herakles . . ." (Theocritus, Id. XXIV.)

Were Sthenelaos and the Argive Heraeum trying to make assurance doubly sure by poisoning the babies (in this case the snakes would be vipers)? If any such attempt were made, however, it did not succeed: "When he saw the monsters in the hollow of the shield, Iphicles uttered piercing screams and, with his foot, pushed away the cloak that covered him. With his two hands, Herakles seized the serpents by the throat, They coiled about him, trying to escape the tiny hands that were choking them . . ."

This is not actually impossible. For one thing, there are snakes in Greece larger than garter snakes or adders; and, for another, the prehensile grasp of a ten-month child is one-fourth that of an adult, quite equal to the task of holding small reptiles away from his face.

Theocritus continues: "Alcmene was first to hear Iphicles' cries and awaken. 'Amphitryon,' she said, 'get up!' Half asleep, he dawdled, reaching out to lace his sandals."

Alcmene insisted: "Don't you hear our youngest child crying? Go on, hurry, I tell you!' "

It was dark. The "palace," like every megaron built in that period, was nothing but a series of rather small rooms, their walls partly decorated with frescoes, half open to wind and weather, summarily furnished with a few rudimentary chests and chairs. Grain, oil, and wine were stored in amphoras.

The night was usually divided into three watches, but just then the country was at peace, and everyone seems to have been asleep.

"Amphitryon woke the snoring slaves: 'Run to the hearth, take fire.' " They scurried off, brought light, cried out when they saw the little Herakles, "crushing the snakes in his two hands and rubbing them together; he laughed and threw them down at Amphitryon's feet."

He obviously thought they were toys, as would many a husky baby at that age. Theocritus says the serpents lying on the ground were "struck with the sleep of death," but this is undoubtedly an exaggeration, added subsequently, when the strength of Herakles had become legendary—as it was in Theocritus' day. But what realism! "Alcmene hugged Iphicles, who was pale as death, to her breast." After all, siblings often do react very differently to the same situation. At dawn she went to question Tiresias (him again), who answered, in the name of Zeus, "More than once the daughters of Greece will weave the name of Alcmene into their song . . . Your son, when he grows older, will mount up into the starry heavens. Nothing, whatever its nature, human or monster, will resist him."

Which was quite the right thing for a tactful courtier to say. Tiresias was subsequently made to predict the twelve labors, too, and the pyre of Oeta, but this is a temptation to which poets might easily yield, since it was into the mouth of a seer they were putting their words.

Chapter VI
HERAKLES AS A YOUTH

"He was instructed in letters and war,
Grew skilled at wrestling, a good charioteer . . ."
after THEOCRITUS

The Education of Herakles

After this incident, the childhood of Iphicles and Herakles passed uneventfully at Thebes, where special care seems to have been taken with the hero's education.

Amphitryon found the best instructors for him, as though he were the prince destined to reign. First, he was taught the savage pancratium practiced in that day. At the Louvre alone, there are a multitude of amphoras and painted pottery objects depicting "the wrestler's skill, the art of overthrowing an adversary by seizing his legs, and the tricks employed by athletes when fighting the buffalo [tauromachy had been introduced by the Cretans] and bending its body to the ground: Herakles learned these from Autolycos,[1] son of Hermes; Autolycos, who struck fear into all who saw him in the arena, even at a distance . . . so great was the terror inspired by his countenance beneath his black brows."

Then he was taught how to drive: "His father Amphitryon [a master charioteer] taught him to drive a team of racers and pivot around the marker without breaking his axle." (Theocritus.)

The wide and fertile Theban plain and the shores of Lake Copais offered an excellent training ground for such maneuvers.

[1] Autolycos was Ulysses' materal grandfather, as Cephalos was his paternal grandfather.

He also learned archery. Apollodorus: "Eurythos taught him to shoot with bow and arrow"; or perhaps it was Teutaros, the Scythian who looked after Amphitryon's flocks (Herodorus). "Peristhenes taught him armed combat." (Apollodorus.) Peristhenes was another exile, a descendant of Nauplius (like Polydectes and Diktys, the kings of Seriphos by whom Perseus had been reared).

"He also knew how to hurl the javelin, avoid the keen edge of a sword, deploy a phalanx, size up an enemy battalion at a glance, command a squadron . . ."

Meanwhile, literature and the arts were not neglected. Apollodorus: "Linos, brother of Orpheus, taught him music." Theocritus, however, says this office was performed by Eumolpus, son of Philammon the Egyptian (*philos,* friend of; Amon, the Egyptian sun god). One of them, in any event, taught him to sing and play the lyre; both were famous in their day.

First Sign of His Fatal Flaw

It was about this time that Herakles suffered his first attack of the homicidal fury that was to overshadow his whole life and shape the course of his destiny. "Herakles, having been struck by Linos, killed him with one blow of his lyre."[2] Then, "when summoned to appear before the court to account for his crime, he quoted the law of Rhadamanthys in his self-defense, which says that a man who commits murder when returning violence for violence shall be acquitted."

This is probably the law mentioned by Aristotle in Book V: "It is just to suffer what one has caused another to suffer."

In short, the law of talion, which dominated classical legislation until the time of Christianity (after first being propounded by the Rhadamanthys referred to above, learned brother of Minos I).

"Under this law Herakles was acquitted, but Amphitryon feared he would commit some further violence and sent him to live with his oxen, where he soon acquired prodigious strength." (Apollodorus.)

[2] Another reference to this murder, in a fragment from an ancient writer paraphrased by Suidas, states that Herakles killed his music teacher with a stone. (*Commentaires sur Apollodore,* by Clavier.)

Physical Appearance

Pindar: "He was four cubits tall." (*Isthm.* IV, 89.) That is, 5′2″—"small and stocky." Herodorus, quoted by the scholiast on Pindar, makes him "over six feet tall," which was exceptional by the standards of that day.

Alus Gellius (I, 1; second century A.D.) explains how Pythagoras calculated Herakles' height.[3]

In addition, "his eyes glanced fire, and he never missed his mark, whether shooting with bow and arrow or hurling the javelin."

Herakles' First "Lion"

"When he was only eighteen years old and still living with the cattle, he killed the lion of Mount Cithaeron [on the border between Attica and Megara]. This lion used to come down from the mountain and wreak havoc among the herds of Amphitryon and Thestios [a neighboring prince]."

This was his first lion, and since no one says it was the offspring of anything other than a lioness, it is just conceivable that he was actually dealing with a quadruped on this occasion. But this animal was unknown in Greece in its natural state. The only lions of which thirteenth-century Greeks had any knowledge were in the form of hides or drawings on vases; Cretan or Phoenician sailors imported their effigies from Egypt.

It is more likely, therefore, that Herakles killed a "lion" of the two-footed species like the "fox" hunted by Amphitryon—particularly since the animal engaged in a similar occupation, i.e., piracy (in this instance, cattle thieving). This first lion, as the scholiast on Theocritus observes (XIII, 6), was later supplemented by two others: the lion of Lesbos and, most famous of all, the Nemean lion.

Early Prowess in Love

This hunt provided the hero with an opportunity to accomplish a feat of a very different sort. Thestios, king of the Thespians,

[3] See the chapter on Olympia.

whose herds were pastured with those of Amphitryon, "had fifty daughters . . ."

Fifty daughters—like the never-sleeping sovereign Argos (founder of the city), who had fifty eyes, and the ships of Cadmos and Danaos, propelled by fifty oars. In the Greek language, both ancient and modern, "fifty" is the customary way of saying "many" and it is not possible to understand anything else by it unless one has no knowledge of the present-day demotic.[4]

"Thestios was anxious for his daughters to have children by Herakles [a son of Amphitryon, after all, was a good prospect]. Every evening when Herakles returned from the hunt [for his "lion"], the king sent one of them to sleep with him. Herakles, thinking it was always the same"—which suggests that, provided there was a girl in his bed, he little cared which it was—"had relations with them all."

Pausanias (IX, 27) and Hesiod say he got them all with child in one night. Herodorus, quoted by Athenaeus (L. XIII), says seven nights. The object of this exercise is to impress us with Herakles' virility, but we have no knowledge of his actual accomplishments, for, as I have said before, in Greek "fifty" simply means "several."

In all likelihood it was about this time that Herakles, wearing the lion's skin which he had stripped off the dead pirate, paid a visit, according to the legend, to his great-uncle (by Alcmene, through her sister Lysidice), the king-seer of Troezen.

Troezen

In the northeast corner of the Peloponnesus, facing Attica, Pittheus' city stands abandoned, far from modern roads. It can be reached only by one of the quaint Gulf of Athens trawlers from Piraeus, or by the "flying boat"—one that really does have wings—that lands on the popular Greek resort of Paros.

Leaving this charming holiday center, the next stage of the

[4] In modern Greek one says, "Thank you fifty times," "I tried fifty times to get him on the phone," "I'm telling you for the fiftieth time," "He owns fifty cars," etc., in French it would be, "I've told you a hundred times," as in English.

voyage is by boat, to the little port of Vidhi—an afternoon's row. From there one can see the village of Damala, which has replaced Troezen on the mountainside.

To the right of the hamlet two bald ravines, wild and forbidding as all those of the Peloponnesus, plunge into the blue gulf. The one on the left—the Devil's Door—is dominated by a Frankish castle, its rust-encrusted walls devoured by dry brush; from it one can watch the distant ships entering and leaving the Corinth Canal. The acropolis was here; all that remains are the ruins of a sanctuary of Pan.

Troezen itself lies on the far side of the Devil's Bridge, boldly spanning the Chrysoroas ravine. There is not much left of it: traces of a sanctuary of Hippolyte (the Amazon queen who loved Theseus), and even they are insignificant.

But a square structure standing nearby (31 meters on a side) has been identified as a sacred refectory, the walls and flagstones of the floor showing the grooves that held the H-shaped couches upon which the guests reclined. They were reached by steps or benches. In the center of each horseshoe, buffets or carving tables rested on marble bases level with the ground; there were places for fifty guests. The scene evokes the banquet given by Pittheus in honor of his great-nephew Herakles.

A Chance Encounter: the Boy Theseus

Herakles removed his Cithaerean lion skin before sitting down to the feast. A group of village children came running to the palace to catch a glimpse of the idol whose exploits were firing the imagination of Hellenic youth. One of them was a grandson of Pittheus, conceived by his daughter Aethra after an encounter with a visitor of note who had passed through Troezen eight years before—Aegeus, ninth king of Athens.

All the children were frightened by the trophy[5] except this boy, who mistook it for a live animal, snatched an ax from the hands of a slave, and whirled to attack it.

Not far from the palace, the royal insignia lay buried beneath a

[5] Others say this meeting took place later and that the skin was that of the Nemean "lion."

stone. Aegeus had put them there, with Aethra as sole witness, so that their son should one day be able to identify himself (when he became strong enough to move the stone). Because of this, Aethra had named him after the verb *tithemai,* "to set" (stone), and this became deformed as Theseus.

Until the time came for him to confront the Minotaur, the young prince was willing to try his hand on a lion.

Jason Is Born

According to Pindar (*Pyth.* IV), Thessaly was the scene of a conspiracy about this time. A king named Cretheus was ruling over Iolcos. Today known as Volos, it lies at the back of the deep gulf bordered by the road that branches off from the Athens-Thessaloniki highway just past Thermopylae. It used to be called the Gulf of Pegasus, because the winged vessels of the Echinades or Chimaera once plied their trade there.

The object of the conspiracy was the rich coastal plain between the sea and Mounts Othrys and Pelion, its income augmented, then as now, by tolls from ships passing through the Euboean Gulf, still a busy seaway.

Cretheus had several sons, two of whom were called Pelias and Aeson. "Pelias seized Cretheus' states, dispossessing Aeson." (Apollodorus.) "He and his vast flocks dwelled in Iolcos and its spacious plain." (*Odyssey,* XI.)

He tracked down all his brothers; Aeson's son was saved only by being passed off as dead, and sent secretly to the centaur Chiron, who undertook his education, chiefly in the art of horsemanship.

The boy was fair-haired, a pure product of the "Achaean" stock of Deucalion, and he, too, was to gain fame by performing deeds of heroism. His name was Jason, and he would one day become the leader of the Argonauts.

Chapter VII
EARLY ACHIEVEMENTS

"He conquered the warriors of great Orchomenos;
But then his fuddled brain led him astray . . .

—Come, look more closely at these children's corpses.
—What are you saying? What have I done? O, messenger
of woe! Then I am Megara's murderer!"

EURIPIDES

Orchomenos

In those days Thebes, the home of Herakles, was obliged to pay a heavy tribute to the powerful neighboring town of Orchomenos. The shores of Lake Copais, which divided the cities, formed a sort of no man's land patrolled by hostile horsemen.

Today the place is an oasis in the heart of sun-stricken Boeotia. The lake has been drained, its floor is dotted with cypress and willow, and fields of cotton and corn blanket it as far as the eye can see. Only the naked mountains shielding the depression have remained as untamed and aggressive as on the day of their creation.

The main road from Thebes to Delphi skirts this idyllic scene and, at the far end of Lake Copais, passes through the little town of Levadia, where a smaller road branches off to the east, as though to complete the tour of the former lake.

After a few miles, this road crosses a little stream, going peacefully along to water the irrigation canals—Boeotian Cephises. A rugged, red-streaked mound is already visible: the Orchomenian acropolis.

At its foot stands a little white convent with a merry campanile and the Church of Leon the Protospathairean; the engraving on a stone set into the masonry dates its construction from "the year 6382 after the creation of the world," or A.D. 874.[1]

Naïve, perhaps but Orchomenos is a very ancient city. Beyond the animated modern village—its main street lined with pepper trees, a thoroughfare for the farmers' clanking tractors—there lies a Neolithic cemetery at the foot of the acropolis, and it is almost eight thousand years old.

The outline is broken by a Mycenaean tholos-tomb, excavated by the indefatigable Schliemann. The pyramid-shaped door is topped by a lintel formed by a single slab of blue schist; it is a monument in itself, over twenty feet long.

Pausanias calls this tholos the Treasury of the Orchomenians. It may have been the tomb of Clymenus, the king of the city, who was killed by a Theban charioteer—a subject of King Creon, Amphitryon's host. Clymenus' son Erginus naturally demanded immediate retribution. Creon refused to pay the price of blood, so they went to war. Orchomenos won and demanded one hundred oxen a year for twenty years as compensation. Thebes paid for a time. . . .

Herakles, Theban Strategist

Then came the incident.

Erginus' heralds were on the way to collect their tribute, when Herakles, still flushed with pride at his first heroic and amatory adventures, "met and mutilated them, cutting off their noses and ears and, after tying their hands behind their necks, told them *that* was the only tribute Erginus and the Orchomenians would ever get from him." (Apollodorus.)

Diodorus Siculus tells the sequel: "Erginus insisted that the malefactor be surrendered to him, and King Creon of Thebes, who was afraid of him, prepared to comply. But Herakles aroused the young men, urging them to free their homeland, and gave them the weapons that were hanging in the temples—the trophies of war which their ancestors had hung there and dedicated to the gods."[2]

[1] In the Middle Ages, the Christian era was said to have begun 5508 years after the creation, so 6382—5509=874.

[2] Just as enemy flags are preserved as national keepsakes in the Invalides in Paris.

This is easily explained, since it was obviously "impossible to find weapons in private hands in the city, the Orchomenians having disarmed the Thebans [after their victory] to prevent them from carrying out any plan of revolt."

Herakles' action was sound psychology: the patriotism of youth is readily mobilized by appeals to the glory of the past.

Apollodorus: "Erginus, incensed at this insult, marched on Thebes. Athena gave Herakles some armor," which probably means he received undercover aid from Athens, anxious to see the Orchomenians weakened.[3]

"Herakles, leading his troops, was informed that Erginus and his men were nearing the town, so he attacked them in a narrow pass and put a great number of them out of commission . . ." (Diodorus Siculus.) Cavalry formed the major part of the enemy forces, so (to put them "out of commission") Herakles dammed up the outlet of the Cephises with boulders—not a very difficult task, as the stream, although deep, is extremely narrow—and flooded the plain, making it impracticable for cavalry maneuvers.[4]

Diodorus ends his tale of the battle as follows: "Herakles killed Erginus and nearly all his soldiers. Then he stormed Orchomenos by surprise, burned the king's palace and razed the town."

In addition, "he forced the Orchomenians to pay tribute to Thebes, twice the size of that they had previously exacted from it." (Apollodorus.)

Diodorus remarks how "news of this exploit spread throughout Greece, where it was thought admirable and prodigious by all. King Creon himself, much impressed by the young man's bravery, gave him his daughter Megara in marriage . . ."

And perhaps the town of that name (on the frontier of Attica) as his fief. Then, "treating him like a son, he made him protector of his state." Whether he did so by choice or by force we do not know (after all, at one point Creon had been prepared to surrender his guest to the Orchomenians). But Herakles, at the head of a

[3] For a long time, Athens pursued a policy in Greece similar to that followed by England in dealing with the Continent, i.e., it supported the weaker state—France or Germany, depending upon the issue—against the stronger.

[4] Polyen I, cf. 3; Pausanias, IX, ch. 29; and the inscription known as the Apotheosis of Herakles.

young and victorious army, re-entered Thebes, having made the city independent again, as its master. He had paid off his and Amphitryon's debt for the hospitality given them during their exile, and at the same time gained control of the city—*de facto* if not *de jure.*

Creon quickly gave his second daughter to Iphicles, who already had a son, Iolas—a favorite nephew of Herakles—by his first wife (Automedusa).

The hero had three children by Megara: Theimacus, Croöntiades, and Deicoön, and their fate was soon sealed, for they were slain by their own father in one of his fits of madness.

A Fit of Madness

Apollodorus: "Hera [his enemy from birth], jealous of Herakles because of the fame he had acquired by his victory over the Orchomenians, drove him into a frenzy, and he threw the children he had had by Megara into the fire, along with two of Iphicles' . . ."

What could this strange affliction be, which had now assumed homicidal form on two occasions (Linos being the first)?

Was it epilepsy, as Diodorus says? Or delirium tremens (since the war between Perseus and Dionysos, the vine had been flourishing in Attica and Boeotia)?

The great Hippocrates, first physician of antiquity, describes the symptoms of alcoholic madness as follows: "The liver swells up and, as a result of the swelling, presses against the diaphragm . . . The patient becomes delirious, he believes he is seeing reptiles and all kinds of beasts and fighting hoplites. He himself is fighting with them, and he talks as though he were witnessing wild combats and pitched battles. He starts up out of his sleep, awakened by dreadful scenes. We know that it is his dreams that cause him to wake in such terror, because the dreams he relates upon awakening correspond to the movements of his body and the words coming out of his mouth." (A. Souques, "Connaissances neurologiques d'Hippocrate," *Revue de Neurologie,* vol. I, no. 2, February 1934).

The hero's symptoms are very similar to those of acute intoxication. The question whether it was epilepsy or alcoholism he suffered from is still unanswered, nor do any two opinions agree as to the names and number of his victims. They range from two to eight, depending on the source—Pindar, scholiast on Hyginus, Apollodorus, etc. The authors cannot even decide at what point in Herakles' career these fits occurred (Diodorus says it was before the "descent into Hades"; Euripides and Asclepiades place it afterward).

But hell it must have been for the man, whatever his age, when he returned to his senses, and saw what he had done. Thestios, who owed him a favor in return for killing the Cithaerean "lion," "purified" him, but even so, "while everyone was discussing his misfortunes, he shut himself up in his house for a long time, shunning all society and human intercourse . . ."

Tormented by remorse, driven by a need to atone for his crime, he finally condemned himself to exile, and went to consult the Delphic oracle to find out where he should go. It was there that he was first called Hera-kles, the name given to him by the Pythoness.

Delphi

Visitors to Delphi usually arrive by the road from Athens, after passing Eleusis, Thebes, Levadia, and the majestic foothills of Parnassus, whose summit, girdled by dizzying precipices, towers among the eagles—and that is no metaphor, for the great birds of prey, their wings spreading over six feet, wheel endlessly in the sky.

After Arachova, on the final turn in the road before the ruins come into view, travelers often stop to look out to the mouth of the valley and exclaim, "There's the sea!"

But they are wrong: it is the sacred forest, not the Gulf of Corinth: 400,000 blue-glazed olive trees, flowing across the gorges and onto the plain of Itea. That is the first wonder.

The second is the great pile of ruins beneath the towering red fangs of the Phedriades rocks. Shaken by earthquakes, battered by the rocks that break off and rebound among the fallen temples, the site is the very image of chaos.

Three great buildings still rise from the ruins—spared by the cataclysms or rebuilt by archaeologists. Half drowned in the olive groves below stands the harmonious circular colonnade of the tholos (fifth century),[5] said to be the temple of the muses of Parnassus. Halfway up the slope above the road is the Treasury of the Athenians (fifth century), a miniature Parthenon glittering in the sun with all the sparkle of its white marble. Lastly, there is the temple of Apollo, the master of Delphi, its truncated columns embedded in colossal foundations: eroded, ponderous, their colors softened by the patina of millenniums, they blend smoothly into the ocher background of the setting.

The visitor clambers up stone tiers of the theater (fourth century, capacity five thousand) and crosses the playing field of the lofty stadium (108 meters long, capacity seven thousand) to look out over the gaping valley to the shimmering gulf of Itea—the port, with a scattering of low houses weaving a white hem at the blue seashore beyond the great expanse of the sacred forest.

There is also the Sacred Way. From Tarento in Italy to Rhodes in the archipelago, and including Argos, Athens, and Arcadia, every city of antiquity was represented on it by a treasury—they would be called chapels today (i.e., a receptacle for ex-votos). Sometimes the Te Deums of warring kingdoms could be heard only a few yards apart, imploring the same divinity to lead them both to victory. This was a source of considerable embarrassment to the god—not to mention the diplomacy it required of the profit-minded clergy. Today nothing remains but shapeless ruins, sacked a score of times (chiefly, after Christ, by Nero, who carried off thousands of statues, and by the Huns and Galations).[6]

Although the museum is too neat and new for its setting, it is worth a visit: it contains the twin sphinxes of the Naxions (island of Naxos), hieratic and mysterious, the work of Egyptian artists; and, above all, it contains the wonder of wonders, the tarnished bronze statue of the *Charioteer,* winner of the Delphic games,

[5] All dates are B.C. unless otherwise indicated.

[6] The Galatians were Gauls; they transported their golden plunder all the way to Toulouse, in France, and then, their numbers decimated by a plague which they attributed to their sacrilege, they threw it all into a lake to propitiate Jupiter.

his hand still grasping the reins—a masterpiece so perfect that no film can convey the indescribable expression on his face.

That is all: near the Castalian fountain, which was to the ancients what the pool of Lourdes is to us, the buses stand waiting under the plane trees. . . .

The greatest Helladic sanctuary has been "recognized" as even more important than Dodona in the north and Delos in the Cyclades. But as for penetrating its mysteries: that is another matter.

The Secret of Delphi

The origins of Delphi are legendary: Zeus, the father of the gods, sent out two eagles to fly toward each other from opposite ends of the earth, and it is above the Phedriades that they are alleged to have met, at the exact spot marked by the umbilical stone, the navel of the ancient world.[7]

The stone is preserved at the top of the main staircase in the museum, and the eagles of east and west are still circling above it.

But the true story is to be read in the earth beneath: the Castalian spring has been a watering place since Neolithic days. In the Bronze Age a notorious metropolis had already been built in the vicinity: Pytho ("the stinking"). In those days volcanic gases issued from the foothills of Parnassus, as confirmed by geological analysis. In particular, these mephitic vapors emanated from the Castalian gorge, and this may be the source of the miraculous (we would say "thermal") properties of its water, which have vanished along with all trace of volcanic activity in the region.

Whenever a goat came near the edge of the gorge, it would utter strange noises and leap about as though possessed. A goatherd named Corytas decided to investigate: peering down into the cleft, he became drugged and began to speak incoherently, in words that were thought to be inspired by the breath of prophecy. Others followed suit, hoping that they too might experience the divine intoxication.

"But, after several persons had fallen into the abyss, the inhabitants thought they would prevent any further accidents by appointing

[7] A similar stone in the basilica of the Holy Sepulcher in Jerusalem marks the center of the Christian world.

one woman to be sole prophetess and pronounce the oracles. A contrivance was built so that she could climb up and receive the inspiration without falling. It was a tripod." (Diodorus Siculus.)

This was the first Pythoness. Others followed; and Dionysos, after being made a god and the "son" of Ghea, or Mother Earth (as the vine is "daughter" of the earth), initially inspired their ravings. For "it is through *mania* [whence "mania" and "maniac"] that the god gives divinatory powers to humans, although only when they are mad, for no one in possession of his senses can be illuminated by divine inspiration."

The site was soon appropriated by an even more potent lord, however: Apollo, the sun. There is an obvious reason for the change, to be found in that same fissure of the Castalian spring, between the twin Phedriades.

Above the spring, the gorge narrows to a mere slit. A thicket of barbed wire has been planted across it, but the mystery of mysteries lies beyond. There, only a few rays of light filter down between the walls of the ravine, and a few yards farther on the passage is completely blocked by a boulder. But that too must be passed. How? On the right, an alarmingly narrow ledge, scarcely eight inches wide, creeps along the face of the rock, polished to glassy smoothness by the bare feet of the many who have inched along it in the past, their backs to the wall, choosing their toeholds with care. This brought them past the first barrier.

Then a second natural wall rose up before them, but it too could be surmounted, and on the far side, at last, was the end of the ravine: Apollo's trysting place.

Forty meters above, the edge of the gorge, where Corytas first leaned over to investigate, is outlined against the sky: the lips of the rock close to form a gigantic womb, its shape so realistic that it could have been copied from an anatomy book. "Delphos," one is reminded, means womb, the function of which is to procreate.

Noon is the best time of day to visit the chasm, when the sun, reaching its zenith, plunges into the gorge and lights up a huge phallus (six or eight meters high) that fills the womb; its outline becomes clear, perfect in detail, even to the pink, flesh-colored tone of the sunlit rock. It is Apollo, fecundating Ghea, the earth.

Even the motion is there, for when the sun moves on, the phallus withdraws.

This is the third and least-known wonder of all, not mentioned in any treatise or guidebook. The water of the Castalian spring, flowing out of the gorge, adds a final touch of realism, fertilizing the olive groves below like the seminal fluid.

That is why the biggest temple at Delphi is the temple of Apollo, and why his priests enjoyed such uncontested authority—it proceeded from the very substance of the sun god himself. They dictated peace and war, they decreed innocence and guilt, they made the law.

"Eh, by Zeus! It wasn't just anybody who went to consult the oracle, to ask whether he ought to buy a slave or set up in business. Mighty cities, kings and tyrants sent to seek advice from the god." (Xenophon.)

Such as Agamemnon, when he formed the league of Hellenic cities before besieging Troy; or Olympias, Alexander's mother, when she wanted confirmation of the divine paternity of her son, conceived "by Zeus" (like Herakles) in the absence of Philip; or Herakles himself, seeking purification after the murder of his children.

The Oracle's Decree

Would the oracle relieve the hero's anguish? "Suddenly, in the dim light, the Pythoness appears, dressed in the costume of Apollo Musagetes,[8] with a branch of holy laurel in her hand . . . Moving like an automaton, she approaches the fateful tripod, sits with her legs apart, and waits. She shivers: the god is drawing near. His breath has touched her; he envelops her, penetrating her most secret places; at last, he possesses her wholly, for the Pythoness is the succubus of Apollo. Choking and panting . . . the color ebbs and flows in her face, which passes from fire-red to the pallor of fear . . . Her eyes roll and pitch heavenward, foam comes out of her mouth . . ." (Lucan.)

The convulsions gradually die away, and she begins to utter

[8] From "muse."

inarticulate sounds. "In a hoarse, broken voice, as though they were torn from her, she lets fall fragments of sentences interrupted by sudden halts and long hesitations."

The priests hang upon every syllable; their business is to interpret. And the priests of Delphi were by no means disinterested —in order to sell more of their sacrificial knives (they had a monopoly on the market), they announced that the god himself had decreed that the same knife could not be used more than once!

To Herakles, their orders were "to go to Tiryns, to serve Eurystheus for twelve years, and to perform the twelve labors Eurystheus would set for him. After completing them all, he would become immortal." (Apollodorus.)

Among oracles, those of Argos and Tiryns decidedly had a long arm, for this sentence placed the hero squarely at the mercy of his rival.[9]

"Upon receiving this command, a great sorrow overcame Herakles: on one hand, he considered it demeaning to serve a man who was his inferior. But on the other, it was dangerous, and in fact impossible, to disobey his father, Zeus." (Diodorus.)

And, looking out over the hills from the heights of Delphi, one can still imagine him setting off, full of resentment, down the road that winds along the hillside toward the sacred forest, where the olive groves tumble down the slopes in a silvery rush and spread out on the plain bordered by the winking sea.

Here he was, the valet of Eurystheus. Supreme humiliation, for without the trickery of the inmates of the Heraeum, he himself would have been the one to mount the throne, and not his crab cousin. But in his day the power of superstition was such that he felt compelled to obey.

Beyond Itea and the Gulf of Corinth, behind the mountains of the Peloponnesus: in Argolis, of which he was now king, Eurystheus, the master of the labors, having just succeeded his father on the throne, was waiting to give him his instructions.

[9] The Pythoness was not incorruptible. Pausanias tells how Cleomenes, a king of Lacedaemon who had been dethroned by Demarates, paid a fortune to the Delphic priesthood to convince the Lacedaemonians that he should be restored to his throne; and he was.

Chapter VIII

FROM THE NEMEAN "LION" TO THE AUGEAN STABLES[1]

"First he freed the sacred wood of Zeus
Of the lion infesting it.
Then the bitch of Lerna, bloodthirsty Hydra,
The thousand-headed monster, he burned to death.
Then there were the Centaurs, a fearless tribe,
Brought down and slain by his murderous bow.
There was the Hind with the golden horns and dappled hide
Which Artemis received in the temple of Oeneus,
And other great deeds . . ."

EURIPIDES

Herakles and Eurystheus

As Herakles drew near, Sthenelaos' successor began to feel uneasy, in spite of the oracle (prompted by him or not).

His shivers at the thought of his prodigal cousin's heritage were more than justified: to the king, the subject of Tiersias' announcement that Zeus, his "father," intended him to have the Perseid throne—him, Herakles, the conqueror of the Cithaerean "lion" and the Orchomenians, the idol of Theban youth—could hardly have appeared otherwise than as a rival consumed by ill-suppressed ambition.

His death was Eurystheus' prime object, as is made abundantly clear by his choice of labors—resorting to the method previously adopted by Iobates when he sent Bellerophon to fight the "monsters."

As it happened, there was no shortage of perilous tasks to be performed in the Peloponnesus. First of all, there was the recovery

[1] See the map of the Peloponnesus of the Labors.

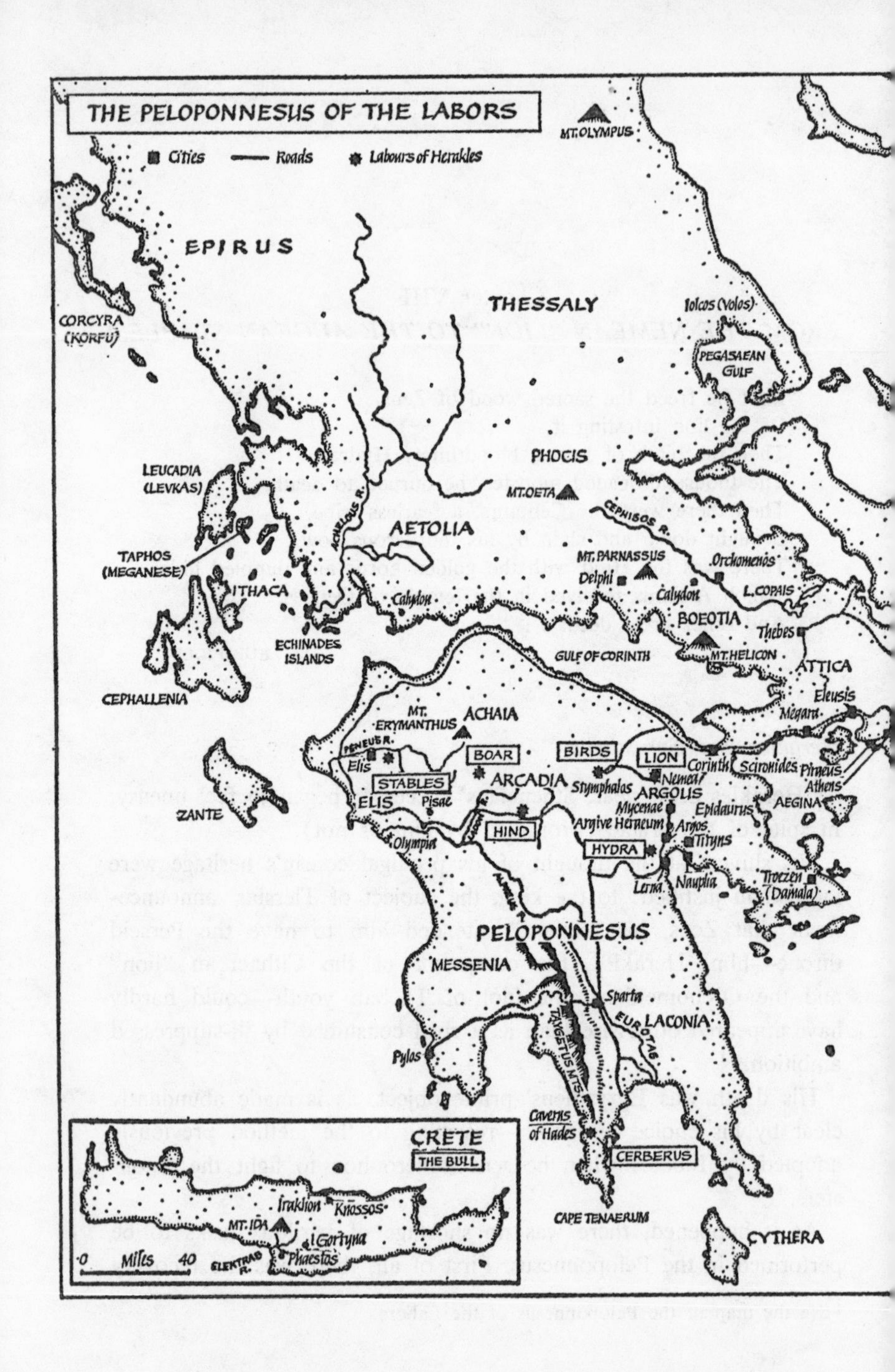

THE PELOPONNESUS OF THE LABORS
Cities
Roads
Labours of Herakles
MT. OLYMPUS
EPIRUS
THESSALY
Iolcos (Volos)
CORCYRA (KORFU)
PEGASAEAN GULF
PHOCIS
LEUCADIA (LEVKAS)
MT. OETA
CEPHISOS R.
AETOLIA
ACHELOUS R.
TAPHOS (MEGANESE)
ITHACA
MT. PARNASSUS
Orchomenos
Delphi
Calydon
L. COPAIS
Calydon
BOEOTIA
Thebes
ECHINADES ISLANDS
GULF OF CORINTH
MT. HELICON
ATTICA
CEPHALLENIA
Eleusis
Megara
MT. ERYMANTHUS
ACHAIA
PENEUS R.
BOAR
BIRDS
LION
Corinth
Scironides
Piraeus
Athens
Elis
STABLES
ARCADIA
Stymphalos
Nemea
ARGOLIS
ELIS
Pisae
Mycenae
Epidaurus
AEGINA
ZANTE
HIND
Argive Heraeum
Argos
Tiryns
Olympia
HYDRA
Lerna
Nauplia
Troezen (Damala)
PELOPONNESUS
MESSENIA
Sparta
LACONIA
EUROTAS
TAYGETUS MTS
Pylos
Caverns of Hades
CERBERUS
CRETE
THE BULL
Iraklion
Knossos
MT. IDA
Gortyna
0 Miles 40
ELEKTRAS R.
Phaestos
CAPE TENAERUM
CYTHERA

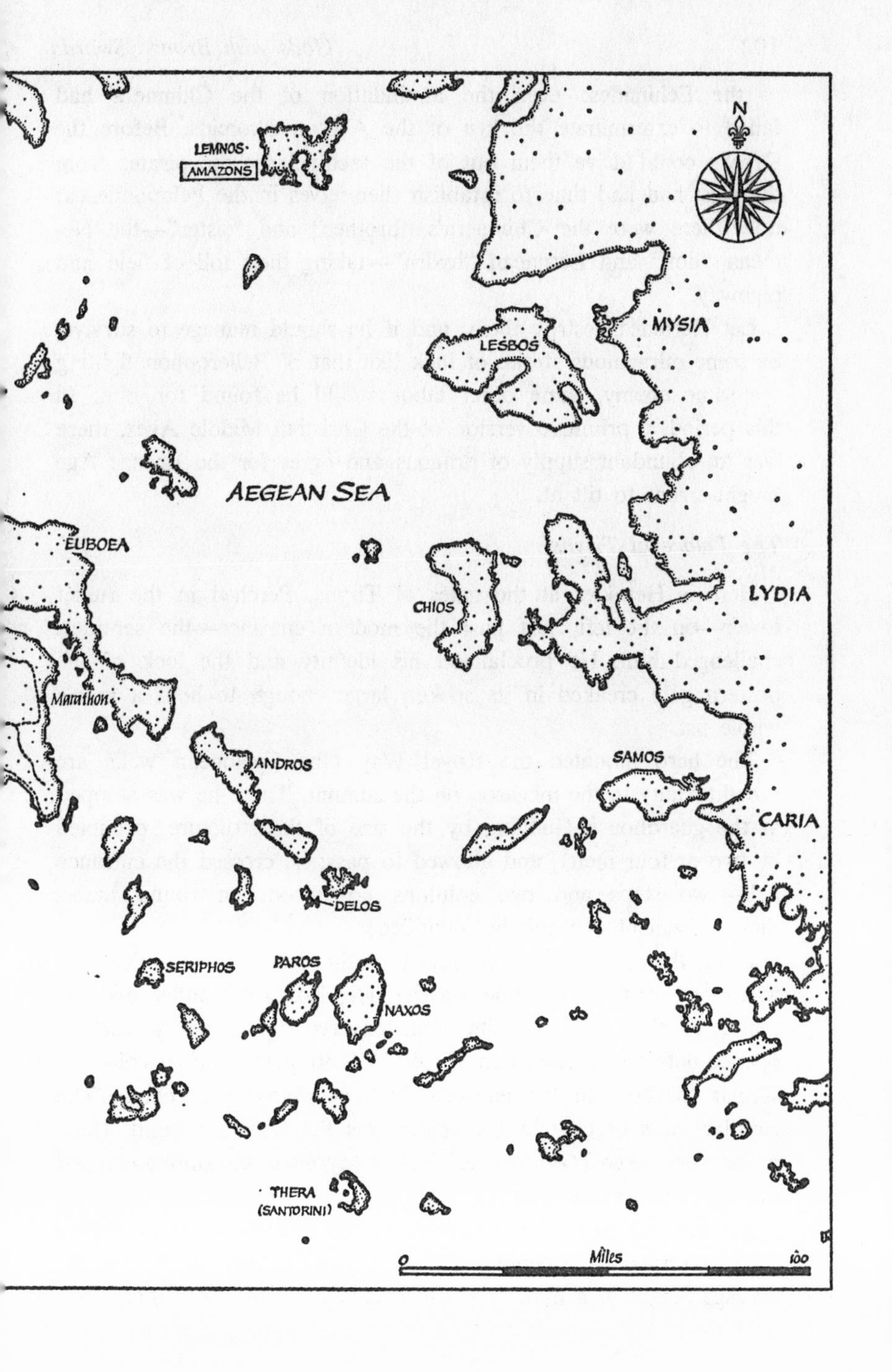

LEMNOS
AMAZONS
N
MYSIA
LESBOS
AEGEAN SEA
EUBOEA
CHIOS
LYDIA
Marathon
ANDROS
SAMOS
CARIA
DELOS
SERIPHOS
PAROS
NAXOS
THERA
(SANTORINI)
Miles
0
100

of the Echinades: even the annihilation of the Chimaera had failed to exterminate the last of the Aegean Phorcids. Before the Greeks could drive them out of the archipelago, the pirates from the west had had time to establish themselves in the Peloponnesus: now there were the Chimaera's "brother" and "sister"—the Nemean "lion" and Lernaean "hydra"—taking their toll of field and highway.

Let Herakles destroy them; and if he should manage to survive, by some miraculous stroke of luck like that of Bellerophon fighting the same enemy, some other labor would be found for him. In this period, a primitive version of the Christian Middle Ages, there was an abundant supply of dragons and ogres for the Bronze Age knight-errant to tilt at.

The Palace at Tiryns

Here is Herakles at the gates of Tiryns. Perched in the russet tower—on the left, just past the modern entrance—the sentinels challenged him. He proclaimed his identity and the lock of the postern gate creaked in its socket, large enough to hold a man's whole fist.

The hero mounted the Royal Way (the Cyclopean walls are breathtaking) to the megaron on the summit. There he was stopped at the guardhouse (judging by the size of the structure, occupied by two or four men), and allowed to pass; he crossed the entrance hall—two steps and two columns (of wood, on round bases; their placement can still be identified).

From there, Herakles proceeded to the antechamber, where he was met by two doors: one, on the side, led to the baths, and the other, in the wall opposite him, covered by a heavy curtain, opened onto the throne room (11.80 by 9.80 meters). Four columns, similar to those in the entrance hall, supported the ceiling. The circular mass of clay in the center was the hearth, around which meals were taken (*Odyssey,* X). As at Mycenae, the smoke escaped through a slit in the roof.

Around this hall were other rooms, their walls made of hollow brick, reserved for sleeping. To us they seem very small, but the average height of a man of those days was hardly more than 5′2″.

The floor of the bath was formed by a single immense slab of gray stone (4 by 3 meters); it is still in place, traversed by a gutter that carries off the rain today.

To the east, two courtyards away from the main building, stood the women's megaron: an entrance hall, a fireplace. Here lived Amphibia (Nicippe), Eurystheus' Pelopid mother.

The Nemean "Lion"

Hoping to send Herakles to his death, his quaking cousin ordered him to go to Nemea and kill the lion.

Apollodorus of Athens says, "This lion was born of Typhon," who, according to Hesiod (*Theog.* v. 329), was himself the offspring of Echidne and Orthrus (the "watchdog" of Geryon); a purebred Phorcid, deposited on the shores of the Peloponnesus by Pegasus' Echinadian fleet, the ships of Orthrus and Typhon.

Like his Cithaerean homonym, he was a "lion" by virtue of his bravery and his coat of arms, and he also wore the big cat's hide across his shoulders, so that no one should fail to recognize him.

"Fallen from the moon into the Peloponnesus," say the scholiast on Apollonius (I. 498) and Hyginus (*Fab.* 30); in other words, a foreigner, unwelcome in a region where he had no business to be. A pirate, like the medieval robber-barons who raided villages and exacted tolls from merchants in the mountain passes.

"As Alpheus in his fury invades the whole Elean countryside, so this monster ranged far afield to plunder." (Theocritus, Id. XXV.)

Diodorus says, "This lion lived in the country between Mycenae and Nemea, near a mountain called 'Tretos,' that is to say, 'bored' or 'pierced through.'"

Mount Tretos

Turning left off the main highway a little after the gorges, halfway between Argos and Corinth, the road crosses a pleasant rolling landscape; after three or four miles of twists and turns, a tall hill comes into view, topped by gray stone palisades resembling a fortress.

There is a grove of poplars on the lower slopes and a clear, cold stream flowing though a deep ravine. Halfway up the hill gapes the entrance to a cave.

A steep white clay path, completely unmarked, leads to the cave; it begins on the left, in the last turning before the road reaches the Nemean plain.

It is little more than a foot-path, climbing rapidly to a fork; the left-hand branch runs along the base of the cliff to the entrance to the cave, which is partly blocked by a low stone wall built by shepherds.

"At the foot of this mountain there was a huge cave where the animal had his lair . . ." (Apollodorus.)

And a well-chosen hideout it was, too; rising a short distance from the gorge crossed by the only North-South road in the Peloponnesus, the Tretos effectively dominates all access to it. Anyone on it must control the traffic between rich Corinth and fertile Argolis; and the Tretos also overlooks the sinuous road that branches off from the highway toward the Nemean plain.

It is like a tower: there is no escape, in any direction, from the sentinel; he can survey every road as far as the horizon.

Apollodorus adds: "It was a cave with two openings." This can be verified on the spot: there is a second cave, overlooking the hills on the opposite side of the mountain. Where is the subterranean passage through the half-mile of rock that separates the two openings? It would be hard to find, for although the first cave (looking southeast) runs some way back into the mountain, the second facing northeast, is stopped by an absolutely impenetrable mass of stone, built up by the earthquakes that are continually thundering through the Peloponnesus.[2]

Herakles' Weapons

Like Perseus at Seriphos and Bellerophon in the Echinades, Herakles was armed by those (the same) who would benefit most directly from the disappearance of the "lion."

First, there were the merchants, from whom the "monster" was

[2] The latest, in 1964, caused whole mountainsides to slip not far from Nemea.

extorting money. Apollodorus: "[Herakles] received a sword from Hermes, god of commerce and travelers . . ."

Then there were the Elean peasants, whose land the pirate was plundering. "[Herakles] received arrows from Apollo [Apollo Agraios, the sun that causes the crops to grow]."

Thirdly, Athena, the deified personification of the Attic city, gave Herakles a "cloak": that is, Athens, eager to wipe out the last traces of the infiltration of her territory by the pirates from the west, "covered" him, we might say—as she had done Perseus before him and Bellerophon in the meantime, when they set out to fight the same tentacular foe.

Tradesmen, travelers, strategists of the embryonic Athenian Empire: all were anxious to restore the safety of the roads, without which there could be no further expansion.

The god of forges and industry himself joined the alliance: "From Hephaestos, Herakles received a golden breastplate."

Then, "on his way to attack [the monster], he stopped at Cleonae,[3] where a certain Molorchos, who lived by the labor of his hands, gave him hospitality."

After a rest, the hero set off in search of his quarry.

The Great Fight

Apollodorus: "The lion had taken shelter inside his two-mouthed cave, so Herakles stopped up one entrance in order to pursue him through the other . . ." This was a wise precaution.

A thousand years later, in the fourth century B.C., Theocritus gives a vivid account of the ensuing battle, from the lips of "Herakles the lion slayer" himself. It offers an excellent example of the process by which legends are formed, for, although the poet's intention is to describe a lion hunt, the traces of the actual event are so persistent that his narrative bristles with telltale clues to the true nature of the combat.

Speaking to Phyleus, the son of Augeias, some time after the event, Herakles says, "I set out, carrying in one hand a supple bow and a quiver of arrows, and in the other a stout club made

[3] A town near Nemea.

from the trunk of a young wild olive tree, still covered with its bark; I found it myself, at the foot of sacred Helicon, and tore it up by the roots. When I reached the place where the lion lived, I took my bow, strung it with the thong around the curved end, lay a sharp-pointed arrow across it and, looking about on all sides, I began to search for the fierce beast, trying to see it before it caught sight of me . . . The day was in the middle of its journey. [However] no herdsman or farmer came down the furrows that lay ready to receive the seed, there was no one I could question. Pale-faced terror kept every man at home . . ."

Even supposing the lion to be a real one (which was impossible in the thirteenth-century Peloponnesus), the inhabitants of Elis would certainly have banded together to hunt it down, since they knew the location of its lair in the Tretos; and they would not have been too frightened of it to venture out in broad daylight, armed with their swords of bronze, their lances, bows, and arrows.

"However, I continued to search the wooded mountain, not stopping until I saw the monster; then I tried my strength against him without delay. He was returning late to his lair, gorged with flesh and blood, stained by his slaughter—his mane soiled, his muzzle dreadful to behold, his chest all spattered with blood. And with his tongue he was licking his beard [not his chops]." His beard, really?

"I quickly hid myself in some thick bushes, waiting for him to come down a path in the forest, and when he was close enough I shot an arrow at his left side but to no avail, for the arrow's point made no impression on his skin and fell back onto the green grass."

The keen arrow, shot at close range by Herakles, pupil of a master marksman of the day, glanced off the lion's side. Perhaps he has a bronze breastplate beneath his hide, like those worn by bandits and warriors.

"Taken by surprise, [the lion] raised its savage head and glared around, showing its voracious teeth. And I loosed another arrow, furious to see that the first had had no effect. I hit him square in the center of his chest, just above his lungs. But even then the arrow, which should have injured him badly, did not pierce his hide, but fell at his feet, as harmless as the first."

A lion in armor?

"In desperation, I was about to shoot a third time when his glittering eye caught sight of me; his neck swelled with rage, his reddish mane rose, he gathered himself and his spine curved like a bow . . . Terrifying, he sprang upon me, but with one hand I pointed an arrow at him, wrapping my cloak around my arm, and with the other I raised my heavy club and struck him over the temple . . ."

One arm bent, protected by the folds of the cape, clutching a dagger for show; the real weapon brandished in the other hand, the side conducting the main offensive. By replacing his club with a Renaissance sword, we find ourselves back in the days of the Three Musketeers.

But then, "the wild olive club split open on the indomitable monster's hairy skull." The trunk of an olive tree? There is no wood tougher or less liable to shatter; beyond any doubt, if this was a real lion, it was clothed in all the invulnerability of legend. But what if it were a bronze-helmeted bandit? Instead of his skull being shattered, he is only half stunned by the blow—that is what helmets are made for.

Death of the Lion

"Stopped in his tracks, he stood there swaying from side to side, his head hanging, for his senses had been befuddled by the violence of the blow, and the shadows swam before his eyes. Seeing him thus dazed by pain, I did not wait for him to collect his wits, I threw my bow and quiver to the ground . . ."

And there followed a hand-to-hand contest between two athletes, carried out according to the rules taught to him by Autolycos.

"My first aim was to break his stout neck; I squeezed his throat as hard as I could, taking support behind his forelegs so he could not claw me; and at the same time I trampled on his feet, crushing them under my heels, and I squeezed his flanks between my thighs; at last, I raised his head and shoulders from the ground. He breathed no more. Incommensurable Pluto received his soul."

Theocritus ends his tale: "Such was the death of the beast of Nemea, who had done much evil among flocks and men."

The Pelt

The lion was dead. Herakles now prepared to skin him, as he had done his Cithaerean predecessor. According to Theocritus and Diodorus, the skin resisted his iron. (It may be observed at this point that unless some item has been omitted from the inventory of the hero's weapons, the only "iron" he had about him was on the tips of his arrows.) This should remove any lingering doubts, for there is no hide so tough that it can withstand a metal edge.

Herakles also tried "stones" (to flay an animal?). Again, one is tempted to imagine him wrestling with a suit of armor; perhaps his club had twisted it out of shape. If so, the task of stripping it off a dead body "of monstrous size" (Diodorus) might conceivably present some difficulties.

As for the hide itself, the conqueror used "the lion's own claws [weapons]" to cut off its limbs, having forgotten to bring a sword. Then he wrapped the trophy around his body "to protect himself in battle."

It is true that a lion's skin, if properly treated, can provide an effective shield against arrows; until the nineteenth century, soldiers wore a similar form of protection—buffalo hide.

The Terror of Eurystheus

Herakles reappeared, "bearing the lion" (Apollodorus)—or, more simply, clothed in the famous robber's unmistakable insignia. Far from going to his death, Eurystheus' rival had come back with his prestige enhanced by a resounding victory, to add to the already lengthy list of exploits to his credit.

Having thus cleared the region of the supposedly "invulnerable" malefactor (Diodorus) who had been regularly plundering the countryside, his popularity soared. Were he to try to capitalize on it, there would be plenty of frustrated Mycenaeans to remember the rightful rank of Amphitryon's heir—particularly those who were loyal to the Perseids; having been ousted by Sthenelaos, they would turn to him as their natural leader.

Apollodorus: "Seeing his assurance, Eurystheus forbade him ever to enter the city again, and ordered him to display the spoils of his future labors outside the gates."

In addition, Herakles' triumphs probably incited the king to strengthen his alliance with the Pelopids, who were easing their way into the throne by occupying, one after another, the high dignitaries' positions. Apollodorus: "Eurystheus transmitted his orders for the subsequent labors through the herald Copreus, a son of Elean Pelops."[4] From this we begin to see that Herakles, in killing the lion (which was causing such havoc in Elis), had been working chiefly for Pelops and the security of his territory, and that, by commanding him to perform this task before any others, Eurystheus was doing the dirty work of his father-in-law, the Asian of the inexhaustible wealth.

Henceforth the Argolid king would give his orders for the labors through his henchman, who was also responsible for selecting them. Copreus carried out his task with unflagging zeal, moreover; for the Pelopids, with the prospect of a complete takeover of the region before them, were intensely anxious to see Herakles—the only Perseid capable of stopping them—permanently out of the way.

Indeed, Herakles' destiny is a strange one: celebrated throughout Greece by the age of twenty, he was forbidden to set foot inside the city of his forefathers.

Lerna

Contrary to all expectations, Herakles had bested the lion. Through his spokesman Copreus, Eurystheus now commanded the hero to tackle the Lernaean "hydra."

His frustrated vassal obeyed, taking along his nephew Iolas, son of Iphicles and the beautiful Automedusa, to act as his lieutenant.

This "monster" was encamped at the very gates of Argos, five miles south of town on the edge of a swamp, from which a jagged red spur of rock protrudes, providing a few dozen yards of

[4] Homer also writes, "Copreus, son of Pelops." (*Illiad*, XV, 639.)

solid ground to carry the road, and forcing the houses of the modern hamlet up the hillside. A few shabby taverns stand in the shade of the plane trees, looking out toward the swamp: a veritable sponge of moss, with weeping willows drooping here and there, and—a miracle in a hot country—streams winding through the tall reeds full of water all year round: silvery snakes, soon lost in the sapphire gulf.

Due south, on the other side of the spur, to the left of the main highway, stands the site of ancient Lerna: remains of neolithic residences, and an archaic megaron, whose fragments are so fragile that a hanger has been built over them to prevent the rain from washing away their few remaining identifiable details.

The "Hydra"

This is the stronghold of the "hydra," child of Typhon and Echidne (Hesiod, *Theog.*, v. 313; Diodorus, IV, ch. 2; Ovid, *Meta.* VII, v. 658). This "sister" of the Chimaera and the defunct "lion" of Nemea was the last creature of undisputed Phorcid ancestry to withstand the Greek heroes.

The lion had controlled the flow of north-south traffic in the Peloponnesus; the hydra dominated the road that goes across the mountains from Argos to Tripolis and Olympia (the peninsula's diagonal artery).

According to Apollodorus and Alcaeus, the monster had nine heads which "spouted flames"—just like the Chimaera and the "matriarch" Medusa, which confirms the link between them. Eight of the heads were mortal and the ninth immortal, just as Medusa was a mortal ancestor, but Stheno and Euryale were not. However, despite the (natural) similarity between the qualities of the hydra and the Gorgons—although here referring to individuals (clan chieftains) and not geographical entities (the islands)—the concept of immortality does not have the same meaning in both cases. "Immortal head" should be taken here to mean "hereditary leader." The "leader" is "he who is at the head": if he were decapitated, another of the same blood would immediately come to take his place. It was in this sense that the hydra could never die.

The authors do not agree, incidentally, as to the number of clan chieftains. Diodorus (IV, II) refers to a hundred, but whenever the Romans wanted to convey the idea of "many" they said "a hundred," where the Greeks said "fifty." Simonides (*Hesiodii scholii*), being Greek, attributes fifty heads to the hydra; but Hesiod never says that it had more than one, and Pausanias (II, c. 37) claims that it was Pisander of Camirus who was responsible for the exaggeration.

Some authors have probably confused the clan with its leader (as modern historians often identify an army by the name of its general), and they regard the hydra as one individual. Those, on the other hand, who are more impressed by the size of his following, employ whatever phrase is current in their language to suggest a large number.

This monster did not operate alone; highway robbers seldom do, and cattle thieves still less. And, as Apollodorus says, "this hydra, who fed in the swamps, would descend upon the fields, lay the countryside to waste, and destroy the flocks."

The Battle

"Herakles, in his chariot driven by Iolas, came to Lerna and drew rein. Having found the hydra on a little hillock near the source of the river Amymone . . ." Where the terrain is low and swampy, nomads prefer to camp on high ground, especially if there is a source of fresh water nearby. And then their profession is cattle thieving, they must have a corral for the livestock. A mobile corral, one that can be expanded at will, and can also serve as a rampart—which is why thorn is used for the purpose where it is plentiful, and reeds on low, swampy ground. At Lerna and in the immediate vicinity there is an abundance of both plants, and they are still being used for the same purpose today. Protective screens of this type do have one drawback, however; in the torrid summers, they will burn at a touch, as any assailant well knows.

Apollodorus: "Herakles drove the hydra out [of its hiding place] by pelting it with burning arrows."

The foe was multiple: "He laid about him with his club, but

for every head he struck down, two appeared in its place." The hydra's men were using the classic technique of hit-and-run, common to both highwaymen and guerrilla fighters—dashing out of the woods, releasing a volley, ducking back to cover, and repeating the process.

"Herakles had to call Iolas to help him, and Iolas, having set fire to one part of the forest, held a torch to the heads as fast as they grew, and so prevented any more from sprouting."

At last the hero must have come to grips with the hydra, the leader himself, for at this point the account of the battle begins to sound like a hand-to-hand combat. "He seized and immobilized it; but the hydra, wrapping itself around one of his feet, began to pull him off balance . . . And then a monstrous crab came to help the hydra, and bit his foot."

Was this just an overgrown crab? Such creatures may be seen everywhere in the region, in both fresh- and salt-water swamps, scuttling along the ground and over the sand, and large ones have been caught even in wells sunk in the mountains. But crabs are also found on shields, if they have been chosen as insignia by warriors, which was a common custom (the sign of Cancer).

Death of the Hydra

"First, Herakles killed the crab, then he finally disposed of his principal foe by cutting off its head. Next he cut open its body and dipped the tips of his arrows in the gall." (Apollodorus.)

This is a common superstition; the blood of a hated adversary is supposed to be poisonous (enemies are often said to exude venom), so his gall is a most suitable substance, in the canon of black magic, for poisoning arrowheads.

"And lest the hydra should revive, Herakles buried it on the road between Lerna and Eleontes, and placed a huge stone on top of it."

Victorious again, Herakles had liquidated the alien "monsters" in the region of Argos as instructed. But when he got back to Mycenae, where Eurystheus had gone, the perfidious king "would not count this as one of the twelve labors, because he had needed the help of Iolas to defeat the hydra."

And, continues Apollodorus, "he [next] commanded Herakles to capture the Erymanthian boar and bring it back alive."[5]

It was during his next excursion that the hero first met the centaurs.

Medieval Antiquity

The resemblance between the Achaean age and our Christian Middle Ages can never be sufficiently stressed. Both had the same fortified castles,[6] built for identical reasons on hilltops, sheltering the lord of the domain, and protecting him from surprise attack while he ruled his fiefdom. Both have the same feudal hierarchy of kings and great vassals, governing a population of villeins and serfs who would be disposed of and exploited at will. The inheritance laws have points in common, too, and led to the same conflicts between princes and the same plundering, although that has been a feature of every age. The way of life and local customs are analogous. There are pirates sailing the seas, and armed bands ranging the countryside, precursors of the "Grandes Compagnies" of the Hundred Years' War. At the crossroads, highwaymen—or noblemen of scarcely higher repute—patrol the roads, extorting ransom from merchants, levying tolls and exacting tribute from the surrounding countryside, with or without the suzerain's consent.

Thus we see in the Erymanthian "boar" a remote ancestor of the Boar of the Ardennes, Guillaume de la Marck. Moreover, the settings for their piratical activities are virtually the same: the forest of Arcadia, like that of the Ardennes, is composed of shadowy stands of trees scaling the hillsides, with dense copses in the ravines. Boars do live there, too, and are adopted as emblems, enhancing their bearers' claims to strength and bravery.

This "boar," then, in the words of Apollodorus, "had his lair

[5] The order of the remaining labors differs in the writings of Apollodorus and Diodorus, but this is relatively unimportant in the total design, in which the pacification of the Peloponnesus clearly emerges as the underlying goal. I have arbitrarily followed the account of Diodorus, as being the more concise of the two.

[6] The Gothic arch can be traced back to the triangular vaulting of the Cyclopean engineers, visible today in the corridors of Tiryns and the Mycenaean tombs.

in the Erymanthian mountains, and preyed upon the whole of Psophis [a region of Arcadia]. On his way there, Herakles passed through the land of Pholoë and was entertained by Pholos the centaur."

The Centaurs

The centaurs are pictured as half-human and half-horse because they were such fine horsemen that they and their mounts were "as one." They were Asians, who had come with the Achaean migrations, and "sons" of Ixion, himself the son of Pision (although Diodorus, the scholiast on Apollonius, the scholiast on Pindar and Pherecydes differ on this point). All, however, say they first settled on Mount Pelion in Thessaly, where they bred the famous stallions coveted throughout Greece; in response to the demand for them, they then scattered all over the country, but were concentrated in the Peloponnesus, "breeders of horses" (Thucydides)—following the general direction of the Achaean migrations.

"[Pholos] served Herakles roast meat, but Herakles preferred it raw." He also liked to drink; we have seen that drunkenness was a fairly common occurrence in his life, even driving him to fits of insanity. "The hero having called for wine, [Pholos] told him he did not dare broach the communal cask of the centaurs," whose law proclaimed that what belonged to one belonged to all. This was old wine, too: "Dionysos had given that wine to Pholos to thank him for deciding a dispute between him and the Naxians in his favor [a dispute over a consignment of horses, perhaps]."

This is alleged to be the same Dionysos who had stirred up a war of "Bacchantes" in the reign of Perseus, and was now teaching the Greeks to cultivate the vine. "Having set sail for Naxos with some Tyrrhenian pirates who were proposing to sell him as a slave, he got rid of them [taking advantage of the effects of his wine] by changing them into dolphins [throwing them overboard]." Disembarking a free man, he proceeded to become a prominent figure on the island, a mediator—once again, thanks to his wine.

Apollodorus does not say exactly when Dionysos gave the cask to Pholos, but in the lifetime of Perseus he was already old enough to start a war of Bacchantes, so he must have been very, very ancient indeed—if not dead—by now.

The wine was old, and so all the more desirable. Herakles pleaded with his host, and "having won him over, opened the cask."

An orgy of drinking ensued. "But the centaurs, drawn by the smell, soon arrived at Pholos' cave, armed with rocks and cudgels. Herakles repulsed them . . . One of them, Nessos, fled to the river Evenos."

Nessos: with him, Herakles opened a new account, one that was not to be settled until long afterward, with the poisoned tunic on Mount Oeta.

Fate dealt harshly with Pholos for yielding to his guest's importunities: "Returning to the cave, Herakles found him dead, among many others: the centaur had accidentally hurt himself by letting an arrow drop on his foot. [The wound became infected, etc.] Herakles buried him and then went to find the boar."

The Erymanthian "Boar"

The hero was supposed to bring his boar back alive. Was this another pirate whom Eurystheus was hoping to eliminate? Arcadia was not part of his kingdom, nor even in the vicinity of Argos. Or was it a scheme devised by Copreus, acting on behalf of the Pelopids? Pelops, who lived in Elis, might well have been suffering from the constant raids of the Erymanthian. And there is one means, frequently employed in those days, of bringing this type of felon to heel: abduction, with release conditional upon payment of ransom.

The practice has assumed varying disguises through the ages: some kings have turned a blind eye while their ministers robbed them, and then periodically recovered the misappropriated goods by threat or simple execution. It was almost a form of investment.

Herakles' instructions, in any event, were explicit, "and difficult to carry out. If [in the course of the fight] Herakles allowed the animal too much freedom, he was in danger of being gored . . . If he attacked too fiercely, he might kill it." (Diodorus.)

If that happened, Eurystheus, who would seize upon any pretext to cheat in his accounting of the labors, could not fail to record this victory as a loss (as he had done with the hydra).

"With loud cries, Herakles drove [the boar] through deep snowdrifts until he had tired it. Then he captured it. . ." Polyen (I.C. 3) goes into more detail than Apollodorus: "This boar had its lair [its manor] at the bottom of a ravine [moat] buried deep in snow. Herakles climbed to the top of the ravine and began to harry it with stones."

In response, "the boar lunged at him and sank floundering in the snow. Herakles captured it."

Apollodorus: "He tied it up and took it to Mycenae."

This sent Eurystheus into transports of panic: "Seeing Herakles arrive with the boar across his shoulders, the king took fright and hid in a brazen jar." (Diodorus.) And this is how the amphora painters, caricaturists of the day, always represent the King of Argos. One of their works, in the Louvre, portrays him inside his jar, with only his head sticking out, his eyes bulging in terror.

This is probably an exaggeration: the jar was more likely to have been a metal-lined strong room like that in which Acrisios had kept Danaë in the days of the "shower of gold."

It should be said, in Eurystheus' defense, that Herakles must have seemed more of a menace than ever, after his latest triumph; all the more reason, then, to send him out to perform some more labors. Not immediately, however; as the murderer of the centaurs, Herakles had to be "purified" again, before he could embark on any new adventures.

He went to Eleusis, near Athens, to the sanctuary of Demeter, where certain "mysteries" that will never be fully explained were celebrated. The Grand Initiates were sworn to secrecy under pain of death, and they have kept their oath so well that after three thousand years of worship and one hundred twenty generations of neophytes, not one word has ever been written or spoken on the subject that is capable of enlightening history.

Demeter

"Demeter of the magnificent tresses" (*Iliad,* XIV) came to Attica "mounted on a chariot drawn by winged dragons." Wings being a symbol for sails, her winged chariot suggests a ship of the Pegasaean type, particularly if drawn by a "dragon" similar to the Chimaera. In addition, the cultivation of cereals, sacred to Demeter, had developed in the "Fertile Crescent" (Egypt and Mesopotamia), passing through Asia Minor—the home of the Chimaera—before reaching Greece.

It is also possible that the culture of wheat made a detour by way of Sicily, where cereals were grown in antiquity, for "in her hand, Demeter held a torch lighted by the fire of Etna."[7] In that case, it would be the ships of Scylla that had brought her to Greece; like the craft of her "kinswoman" the Chimaera, they bore the ancestral emblem of the dragon (the Atlantid dragon of Phorcys).

If the ship (Chimaera or nymph) had been able to enter the Attic ports without arousing Athena's wrath, it was because this happened before Pallas had begun to promote the wars between Perseus and the Gorgon, and Bellerophon and Pegasus. Triptolemy, to whom Demeter taught the art of agriculture (in return for Athenian hospitality), lived in the middle of the second millennium; by dating "Demeter and the sowing of grain in Attica" in 1409 B.C., the "Paros marble" settles the question admirably.

Like Athena, patroness of the olive tree, and Dionysos, propagator of the vine, the bringer of the culture of cereals—"nurse of the human race"—was deified in gratitude for her priceless gift. The Greeks represented her as a beautiful woman, full-bodied as a rich harvest, with a crown of ears of wheat on her head and two infants at her breasts, each holding a horn of plenty. The animal most often sacrificed to her was the pig, because pigs spoiled the crops by rooting in the fields.

She went first to Eleusis, on the Gulf of Salamis (her landing place?). The port erected a great sanctuary in her honor. At the time Pausanias was writing his account, the stone on which Demeter had sat and the well at which she quenched her thirst were still being exhibited.

[7] Although this symbol is chiefly attached to Ceres (Demeter's Latin name), and may date from the period when Sicily became a supplier of grain to Rome.

Eleusis

A Sacred Way more than twelve miles long soon linked the shrine with the Acropolis in Athens. The modern road, still called the Sacred Way, follows the old one, but today's metropolis offers none of the attractions of the city that preceded it; it is covered by a film of dust deposited by local industries. The hallowed ground where the mysteries were celebrated is separated from a gigantic soap factory near the little mound of the Eleusinian acropolis, and Demeter's ancient terraces are dwarfed by a row of belching smokestacks.

The ruins occupy a broad esplanade; first, there is a spring, of which only the basin remains; then comes the pit in which sacrificial animals were immolated. Next come the ruins of monuments built by the Romans in honor of Ceres: propylaea, towers, triumphal arches.

Farther on, the Sacred Way runs along the rock of the acropolis (topped by a hideous clock mounted on a concrete tripod). Entrances to two caves, one large and the other small, bore into the face of the ocher rock—the first signs of a shadow of secrecy. The first was said to lead to the subterranean world of Hades (hell), and the sanctuary of Pluto was accordingly placed there.

At last the Sacred Way comes to an end within the very precincts of the mysteries, which the uninitiated were forbidden to enter upon pain of death: three thousand square meters, unique in the world, consecrated to the enchantments of Demeter and surrounded by walls so high that only the roofs of the buildings outside could be seen from within (Strabo).

Orpheus, the Lyre-Playing Hierophant

The Athenians taught their children the first cycle of the ritual in early childhood, but only the elite—archons, authors and scholars, artists and strategists—were initiated into the supreme mysteries.

The ceremonies took place at night, in September, and lasted for nine days; thus we know at what time of year Herakles was there and how long he stayed, in 1326 B.C. (according to the Paros marble).

In those days Orpheus,[8] son of Oeagrus, a Thracian by birth, was grand master of the ceremonies; from childhood he had applied himself to the study of (theological) traditions and had gone to Egypt to perfect his knowledge.

". . . And he was the greatest of the Greeks in the science of the Mysteries, as well as in poetry and song. He composed admirable and melodious poems. His reputation became so great that he seemed to charm the wild beasts and trees with his songs . . ." (Diodorus, L. IV.)

It was the task of the "inventor of the lyre" (or possibly of his sons) to initiate the heir of Amphitryon.

The priest-king of Athens presided over the ceremonies; being both priest and king, he personified the ideal form of government. Four ministers officiated: the hierophant—he who reveals sacred things; the daduchos,[9] or leader of the lambadophores (torch-bearers); the hierokeryce, or commander of the sacred heralds; and the assistant of the altar ceremonies, who wore an allegorical costume representing the moon; for, as every peasant knows, that planet exerts a most potent influence upon his crops.

The Mysteries

In what did the ritual consist? Pausanias, an initiate, who has written about absolutely everything else, has nothing to say about this: his oath "sealed his lips."

We are reduced to conjecture. All that is certain is that the ceremony was symbolic, and dealt with the movement of the heavenly bodies, the sequence of the seasons, and the course of the sun (Orpheus had learned astrology from his Egyptian professors). By putting together certain remarks, it may also be hypothesized that the revelations took the form of a sacred drama, acting out the legend of the union of Zeus and Demeter (both "sister" and "concubine" of the king of gods). But above all, "the initiates were shown the journey of the soul through the Underworld, and how to accomplish it successfully."

[8] According to the Paros marble, Orpheus and his sons Eumolpus and Musaeus were at Eleusis as early as 1399.

[9] Literally he who holds the torch.

They were given certain particulars relating to Hades and the obstacles encountered there (its "monster guards"), with mystical incantations to placate them, and others to ensure safe passage into the Elysian Fields. But their actual content has never been revealed.

After the performance of the drama, the initiates followed the hierophant and daduchos in a sort of torchlight procession.

Conducted by Orpheus or Eumolpus, Herakles progressed through the hall, each part of which represented some feature of the topography of the Underworld. Then, he watched while the sacred tokens (hiera) were displayed, and finally he made a visit to the temple of Pluto.

"Happy is the man among earthdwellers who has witnessed these great sights; but he who is not initiated is forever deprived of this bliss, even after death has sent him down into the dark dwelling place." (Homer, *Hymn to the Mysteries.*)

Herakles was still a long way from the "dark dwelling place," but fate had already beckoned: perhaps he passed a pretty child in the forecourt of the temple—Persephone (Proserpina), the "daughter" of Demeter (as others are "children" of Mary). It was thanks to her, in later years, that Theseus became acquainted with the hell of the "living dead" in Hades' Underworld, to which he was sent to atone for his sacrilege and from which Herakles, through his knowledge of the "topography of the Underworld" and the passwords he had learned in the sanctuary at Eleusis, was able to rescue him.

In the meantime, now "purified" of the murder of the centaurs, the hero left the temple of Demeter and went back to the implacable Eurystheus to receive his instructions for the next labor.

The Cerynean "Hind"

Upon his return to Argos, Herakles was told "to bring back alive the Cerynean hind." (Apollodorus.)

Like the boar, the hind had to be captured alive. Perhaps Eurystheus was trying to repeat his latest operation, it having proved profitable.

Wild and independent, the hind had thus far eluded capture.

She roamed, always out of reach, through the forest of Oenoë, a region of Arcadia adjoining the haunts of the boar.

Pindar says (*Olymp.* IV) she was sacred to Artemis, goddess of the hunt and the forest, and he is corroborated by Apollodorus. Was this a clan of woodland huntsmen whose emblem was the hind? The inhabitants of Oenoë have always hunted deer.

The symbol was well chosen: the hind had brazen hoofs, like the Arcadian weapons of that time, and the hoofs of deer are almost as important in their self-defense as their antlers. The antlers of the Cerynean hind were of gold, moreover—the symbol of wealth; and the tribe must have possessed enough of it for it to be an obvious target for a demand for tribute or a ransom for its chieftain.

Furthermore, according to Pindar, the hind, or her clan, "had been dedicated to Artemis by Taygetus," the personification of a mountain range near Sparta and the "daughter of Atlas"—the pillar, familiar to all Greeks, which held up the sky at the western end of the Mediterranean, and at whose foot Perseus had found the Graeae on the first lap of his great expedition. In reverse order, these associations would seem to suggest some connection between the Graeae and the hind, through the symbolic kinship of Atlas and Taygetus, the respective "mother" mountains.

Had the clan of the hind also come from the neighboring Echinades, overpopulated by an influx of colonists from the west? If so, this would give the Greeks another motive for bringing her to bay. It should be observed, however, that the Gorgon family tree, as deduced from the ancient writings, speaks of the Chimaera, the lion, and the hydra, but not of the Cyrenean hind; on this subject the authors are silent.

However that may be, the hind, sacred to Artemis, was in a sense untouchable, for the chief, or queen (this was still the age of matriarchal tribes), also acted as high priest or priestess, which gave him or her relative immunity.

The Hunting of the Hind

Apollodorus: "Wanting neither to kill nor injure her, Herakles pursued her for a whole year; to elude him, the hard-pressed hind fled across the river Ladon. Just as she was about to swim the river, Herakles stopped her with his arrows, captured her and, throwing her across his shoulders, carried her through Arcadia."

This time, there were complaints. Unlike the boar, the hydra, and the lion, these nomads were causing no harm to anyone. Even though they may have been emigrant Echinadians, they were content simply to live as hunters in Arcadia, as they had done on Taygetus before, and as their remote ancestors may have done on Atlas.

Then, seeing themselves as the potential targets for one of these Herculean abductions which Eurystheus (or Pelops acting through him) seemed to be making into a regular habit, other hunters and landed gentry rebelled. On behalf of the former, the priesthood of their tutelary goddess Artemis joined forces with that of agrarian Apollo, spokesman for the latter, to make representations.

The texts show some trace of this: "Artemis and Apollo met Herakles as he was coming along the road, and accused him . . . Herakles excused himself on the ground that he was not a free agent, and said Eurystheus should be held to blame."

The plaintiffs accepted his defense: "Having thus appeased the wrath of Artemis . . ."

As a rule the priests did not directly oppose the secular ruler; they merely warned him. Even if a king persisted in some policy that was intolerable to them, the clergy would never fight on open ground; they would seek some other means of undermining his power. "[Herakles] carried the hind to Mycenae alive" and, was immediately sent back to Arcadia, to disperse a flock of birds of prey with brazen beaks and claws that had invaded the Stymphalian Marsh.

The Stymphalian Marsh

Apollodorus: "There was in Arcadia a place called the Stymphalian Marsh, covered with trees and dense thickets."

To reach it, Herakles could choose between two routes. Coming from gentle Nemea, the first is a dizzying series of hairpin turns, winding up high mountain passes and dropping suddenly into a circus surrounded by lofty peaks (1935 and 2376 meters). Today the road is full of ruts and potholes, impracticable except by jeep.

The second makes a scarcely less rugged ascent from the Corinthian coast. (One is wiser to take it, however, rather than the first, for it is asphalted, at least.)

Stymphalos is an alpine lake, fed by swift mountain streams replenished by the melting snows. The summits, covered by dark forests, are reflected in its surface, except at the eastern end, where peat bogs soak up the water like an immense sponge.

A few fields grow food for the meager villages clinging to the slopes, grazed by sheep and goats: vineyards, a little wheat—the altitude is too high for the money-producing olive. The Stymphalians catch the huge lake tench in open nets, but do not like to eat them; thus they are poor, and as proud as the eagle of the summits, whose profile they seem to have borrowed.

The "Birds"

"Huge birds of prey had retreated to the middle of the lake, fearing that wolves would carry off their prey." (Apollodorus.) Why this need of a retreat? The birds were fierce enough "to attack and devour humans" (Pausanias, I. VIII); it is more likely that they themselves were the thieves.

"As they flew they hurled their arrow-sharp quills at passers-by . . ." (Pausanias, L. II), and when their quivers were empty, they would withdraw out of reach on the high plateau, where no one dared follow them: who would attempt to steal the prey from the talons of a savage bird winging its way back to its eyrie?

In view of the similarity between their ways of life, the Stymphalians' choice of the bird of prey with the hooked talons and beak, their cohabitant of the highlands, as their emblem would be an obvious one. Unless it was the greedy sea gull? Both Apollodorus and Aegios speak of "marine" birds, and the lake is not far from the gulf (twelve miles). Perhaps the Stymphalians were pirates who had happened upon this ideal hiding place during one of their inland raids and decided to settle there; the Echinadian ships patrolled the mouth of the gulf, and those of "winged Pegasus" watered in Corinth itself.

Athena Again

Whether of Pelasgian or some other origin, the Stymphalians looked, at first glance, as though they could not be dislodged from their plateau.

"Herakles could not think how to hunt them. Then Athena gave him some brazen cymbals . . ." (Apollodorus.)

Here she is again, adding another entry to her long record of assistance to punitive expeditions: after Perseus (against the Gorgons), Bellerophon (against the Echinades), Amphitryon (against the fox) and Herakles (against the lion), the first city of Attica was now helping to rid Stymphalos of another band of vandals, employing a trick that was typical of the large corpus of procedures devised by the fertile imaginations of the strategist-priests of Pallas.

Cymbals! According to Apollodorus, "Herakles struck them on a mountain near the marsh, in order to frighten away the birds, who flew off in a panic." Our hero was an expert at such tactics—witness the dam across the Cephises in the campaign against the Orchomenians, the blocking up of the Nemean cave, the burning of the Lernaean barricades, the Erymanthian snowdrifts, the foiling of the Cerynean hind at the ford.

At Stymphalos, he announced his coming "with a flourish." Now, a band of robbers seldom fights except for gain, and when the agents of law and order arrive they scatter, waiting until the police grow tired and go away before they return. But if you know this, you can set up ambushes at carefully chosen points and attack the band when it is dispersed, decimating its ranks as it flees. "Herakles killed them with arrows . . ." The few survivors took refuge on the island of Ares, from which they were expelled by the Argonauts (Apollonius Rhodius).

The Peloponnesus Pacified

With the Stymphalians gone, the whole of the Peloponnesus could breathe again: there wasn't a bandit left anywhere worth bothering about.

Herakles had brought peace to the isthmus. Whatever murderous

1. Ex-voto of Agathon of Zante (*photo by the author*).

2. The wings of Pegasus (*photo Arthaud*).

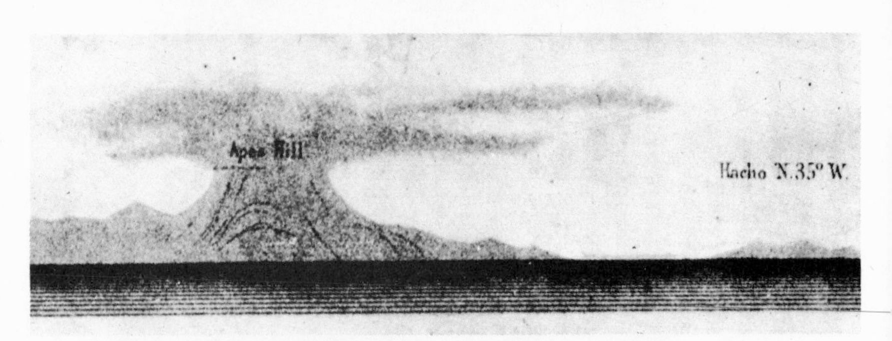

3. Mount Atlas, the "pillar of heaven" (*from V. Bérard,* Les Phéniciens et l'Odyssée).

4. Birth of Pegasus (*sketch by the author*).

5. Menhir of Phorcys (*photo C.N.R.S.*).

6. Crater of Thera (Santorini) (*photo by the author*).

7. Stone slab showing bas-relief swords, found in Corsica (fourteenth–thirteenth century B.C.) (*photo C.N.R.S.*).

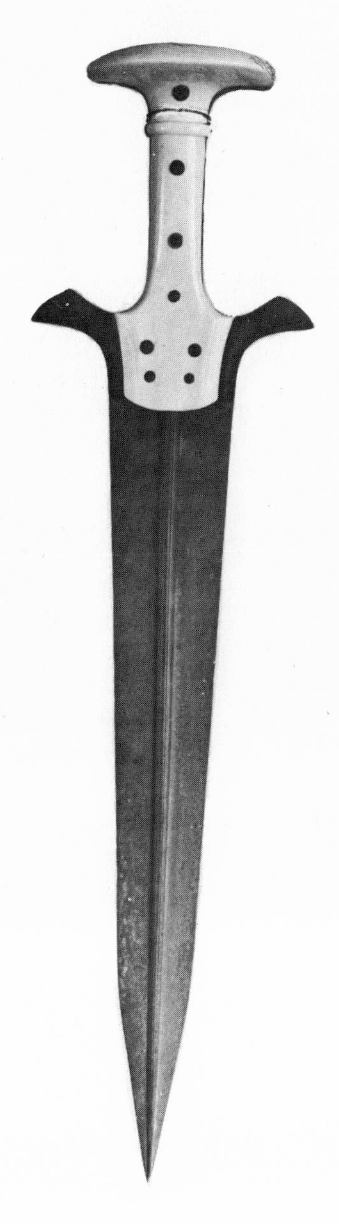

8. Hellenic bronze sword-dagger (fourteenth–thirteenth century B.C.) (*photo by the author*).

9. Gorgon's head (Museum of Sparta) (*photo by the author*).

10. La Caldeira, Azores (*by courtesy of the Portuguese Embassy*).

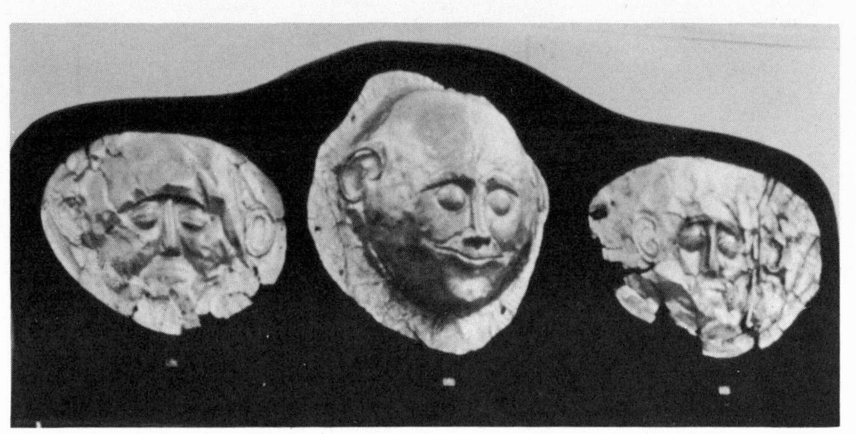

11. Perseid gold funerary masks (Mycenaean tombs) (*photo by the author*).

12. Echinadian Gorgon-head buckler (eighth–seventh century B.C.), with the three "wings" (fleets) of Stheno, Euryale, and Medusa (*photo by the author*).

13. The works of Perseus: the oldest bridge in the world (*photo by the author*).

14. Cyclopean ramparts of Mycenae: in the distance the Lion Gate (*photo by the author*).

15. The Peirenian fountain (Corinth), watering place of Pegasus' fleet (*photo by the author*).

16. Pegasus' secret door, in the Echinadian island of Meganese (*photo by the author*).

17. The phallus of Apollo at Delphi (*photo by the author*).

18. The temple of Apollo at Delphi (*photo by the author*).

19. The sanctuary at Epidaurus (*photo by the author*).

20. Casemates at Tiryns (*photo by the author*).

21. Cave of the Nemean "lion" (*photo by the author*).

22. Lake of the Stymphalian "birds" (*photo by the author*).

23. Entrance to the stadium at Olympia, as stepped off by Herakles (giving our estimates of his height) (*photo by the author*).

24. Herakles and the Cretan bull (*Louvre–photo Arthaud*).

25. The Argonauts: an Aegean ship (*photo Arthaud*).

26. Athena dictating the labors to Herakles (*photo by the author*).

27. The old haulage way along the modern canal of Corinth (*photo by the author*).

28. Lion-damascened bronze dagger (Museum of Athens) (*photo by the author*).

29. Detail of 28.

30. Cape Taenarum: the sentry box of Cerberus (*photo by the author*).

31. Cape Taenarum: the central hall. In the background the kiln (*photo by the author*).

32. Theseus: the Scironian Rocks, with the old road below (*photo by the author*).

33. Herakles presenting Cerberus to the terrified Burystheus (*Louvre–photo Arthaud*).

34. Nearing the caverns of Hades (*photo by the author*).

35. Combat of Herakles and the three-bodied Geryon: not a monster, but three warriors (*photo Arthaud*).

36. Athena helping Herakles to carry the globe (*photo by the author*).

37. The labyrinth at Knossos (*photo by the author*).

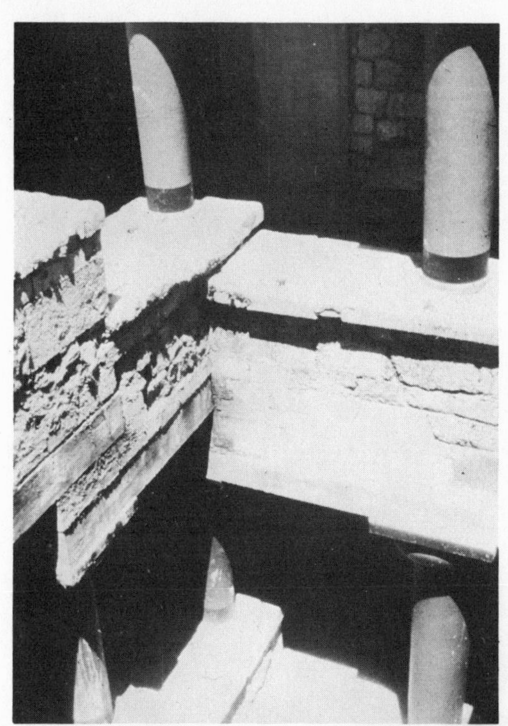

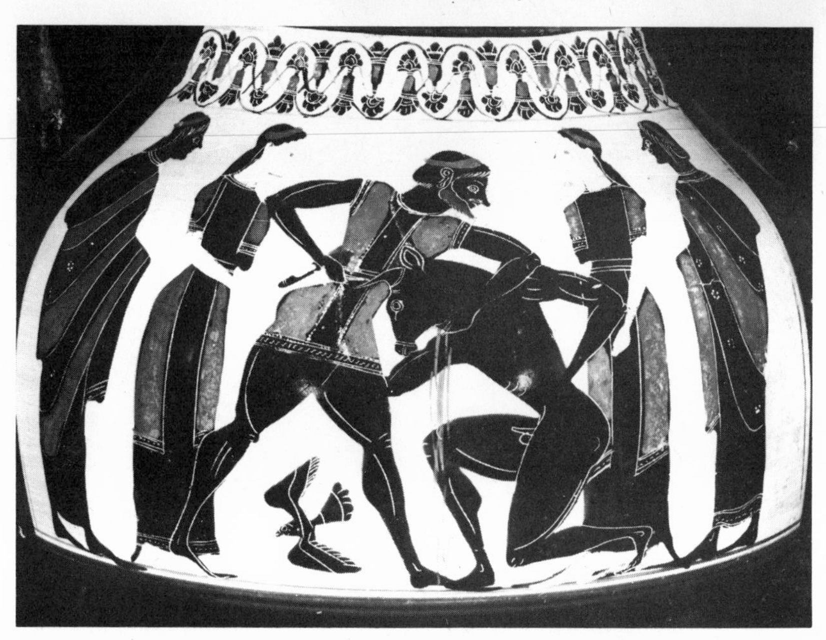

38. Theseus and the Minotaur (*Louvre–photo Arthaud*).

39. Hera and Zeus: man and wife, and rival deities (*photo Boudot-Lamotte*).

impulses Eurystheus may have been indulging, or Pelopid instructions he may have been carrying out, it cannot be denied, in view of the results, that he was a statesman. Unfortunately, there were no more "monsters" for Tiryns to send Herakles to slay, and thus no more chance of his getting himself killed. But his strength and wits might be otherwise exploited: by hiring out his services to fellow monarchs. Herakles seems to have resigned himself to his vassalhood, whether because he sincerely wanted to atone for the crime that had caused him to be saddled with the labors in the first place, or because he was too superstitious to defy the oracle's decree until it had been fulfilled, or for a combination of both reasons.

In any event, when Eurystheus ordered him to cleanse the stables of his ally Augeias,[10] Herakles, with never a murmur, obeyed.

The Wealth of Augeias

The *XXVth Idyll* of Theocritus gives a detailed inventory of the wealth of Augeias[11] and a host of minutiae relating to the life of this flamboyant monarch, his servants, and even his dogs. In the poet's portrait (borrowed from the traditional account) some features of Herakles himself are also revealed.

On his first trip through Elis, shortly after slaying the lion, Herakles questioned an old peasant he met on the road. "And the laborer, stopping his work, spoke to him as follows: 'O stranger, I shall be glad to answer your questions, for I do not want to anger Hermes, god of roads, whose wrath, they say, is worse than that of all other immortals, when any person refuses help to a traveler in need of information to continue his voyage.' "

In the minds of the ancients, the god and his attributes were merged in a single concept.

"First, you must know that the flocks of the king, the prudent Augeias, are not all pastured in the same place; some graze

10 According to the scholiast on Apollonius Rhodius (L. I, 172), Augeias was the son of Phorbas and Hyminia, daughter of Neleus. Pausanias says he was the son of Eleios, "son" of Poseidon (that is, a navigator). Since Eleios sounds like Helios, he was called "son of the sun" in flattery.

11 The subtitle of the *XXVth Idyll* (*Herakles the Lion-Killer*) is "The Splendor of Augeias."

on the banks of the Elisos, others near the sacred waters of the divine Alpheus, others over toward Buprasion of the fertile vineyards, and still others in the pastures where we stand now."

This gives the extent of the prince's lands and main sources of wealth. Livestock was his chief chattel: "The day was drawing to a close. The fat ewes were returning from the pasture to their pens and folds. Innumerable milch cows followed them, marching in single file like the water-loaded clouds which Notos or Thracian Boreas[12] drives with swift breath across the sky, speeding past, countless, with never a pause . . . The whole plain was covered with moving cattle . . . Soon the round-hoofed cows filled the stables, and the ewes lay down in their pens."

A feverish round of activity then began: "Even with as many laborers as there were there, none stood idle. One hobbled the cows' legs with well-cut straps, so they could be safely milked; another brought the thirsty calves to their dams; another held the milk bowl; another made the curdled milk into velvety cheese; another brought the bulls into their special barn and separated them from the heifers. Meanwhile, Augeias walked through his stables measuring the enormity of his wealth. . . .

"Although the heart that beat in Herakles' breast could be neither daunted nor amazed, he marveled at this vast horned population with his whole soul . . .

"After the cows came three hundred bulls with white hoofs and incurved horns, then two hundred more with red coats, all of them young enough to breed. Then came twelve bulls dedicated to the sun: their skins were no less white than the plumage of the swan and they were taller than all other round-hoofed animals . . . The most vigorous and noble of them all was Phaëton, whom the herdsmen called a star of heaven, so brightly did he shine as he paced among the others, his beauty overpowering them all."

Herakles, Toreador

Suddenly the snorting bull scented the skin of the Nemean lion: "And seeing the awesome hide across Herakles' shoulders, the

[12] Notos, the south wind; Boreas, the north wind (hence, coming from Thrace).

dreaded animal charged, trying to gore the hero's flank with his head and powerful muzzle."

Among his other lessons, however, Herakles had been taught the art of bullfighting, which the Cretans, who were the first masters of the sport,[13] popularized wherever they went.

"Stepping forward, Herakles seized the bull's left horn in his powerful hand, until it bent and touched the ground . . ." Theocritus seems to have based this description on one of the numerous Minoan pottery vases of the day, now on view in the glass display cases of museums.

Having thrown the bull off balance, "he drove it backward, leaning against its shoulder, while his rigid muscles rose in knots along his tensed arm."

Augeias, making his tour of his property with his son Phyleus, "for kings, too, may think that the house prospers only when the master is at home, was amazed at the prodigious valor of Amphitryon's son."

The "Stables"

Thus, the King of Elis already knew Herakles other than by reputation, and the hero was a friend of his son Phyleus, to whom, according to Theocritus, he had told the story of the lion whose skin had just provoked the bull's attack.

"Herakles, having [this time] made no mention of his orders from Eurystheus, offered to remove all the dung from Augeias' stables in a single day, in exchange for one-tenth of his livestock."

The manure was indeed becoming a problem in the king's vast pens and stables, and Pliny (L. XVII, c. 9) even says he was the first man to manure his fields in order to increase their fertility, in an attempt to get rid of it. But there was too much—one might say they were bogged down in it.

Here Herakles saw a chance to do a job for his own benefit. It was cheating, of course, but Eurystheus had cheated first by refusing to count the killing of the hydra.

"Not believing the thing possible, Augeias agreed." But he was

[13] Their art combined wrestling and ritual dance, and the bullfighters of the day seem to have performed truly phenomenal feats of audacity and suppleness.

forgetting how Herakles went about his labors, as, for instance, when he dammed up the Cephises to cripple the Orchomenian cavalry. On that occasion, he had had recourse to his Theban army; for this job he would use Augeias' household regiment.

"Having observed that the manure-infested fields were not level, and stood a little higher than the river Peneus, he immediately ordered them to dig deep trenches, some of which were to pass through the stables, forming a sort of dike. Then the water from the river poured down the trenches, transforming them into canals, and the laborers threw all the manure into these canals, which bore it away toward the Ionian Sea.

"When Augeias came to inspect Herakles' work, Herakles told him that he had only to continue dumping his manure into the water, and his land would never again be overrun by it. Great was the king's amazement, and great his delight, too, but he was sorry he had made the promise."[14]

Now, Augeias was not a generous man: Theocritus euphemistically called him "the prudent Augeias," in the speech of the old farm hand. It is also known that he did not trust his tenant farmers, and kept coming out from town "to visit his rich productions." Having learned from Lepreus,[15] a friend of his, that "Herakles was acting under orders from Eurystheus [hence, under obligation], he refused to pay him, denied he had ever promised any payment, and offered to submit the matter to the judges . . ."—those of his own kingdom, of course, of whose loyalty he was certain.

But he had reckoned without the friendship between Phyleus and Herakles. Phyleus was not fond of his miserly sire and was aching to supplant him. To him, the "lion killer" was a potential ally.

Apollodorus: "When the judges assembled, Herakles called Phyleus to testify against his father. Even before the verdict was pronounced, Augeias ordered both Phyleus and Herakles to leave Elis."

[14] Summary by L. R. Lefèvre (*Héraklès,* Gallimard).

[15] Athenaeus (L. X), Pausanias (L. V, c. 5), and Aelian (L., c. 24) even say that Lepreus, a son of Causon, who was a "son" of Poseidon (another navigator, like the father of Augeias), advised Augeias to put Herakles in prison by way of payment.

The two friends were escorted to the coast and forcibly put to sea in a boat. At the mouth of the Peneus, they could see the lumps of manure floating out to sea.

Herakles and Dexamenos

Phyleus went ashore on one of the Echinades and settled there. "Herakles went to Olenus, to see Dexamenos [an Achaean centaur]."

Dexamenos had a daughter, whom he was about to marry off against his will, "compelled by Eurytion, another centaur of the region. Dexamenos begged Herakles to help him, and Herakles killed Eurytion in order to marry the girl himself."

Apollodorus gives her name as Mnesimache, and Diodorus Siculus calls her Hippolyte, but according to Hyginus (*Fab.* 33), "Dexamenos' daughter was named Deianeira, and Herakles later married her."

Deianeira, who is elsewhere claimed by Dionysos; perhaps she was, in a figurative sense, his "daughter," like the Bacchantes in the war between Dionysos and Perseus.

The scholiast on Stace (*Thebais,* 5, 263) writes: "In the course of a previous voyage [Herakles] had seduced her, and promised to marry her when he returned. In his absence, Eurytion the centaur had sued for her hand, and Dexamenos, fearing his violent temper, dared not refuse. He and his brother arrived on the appointed day to celebrate the wedding, but Herakles appeared and killed him."

This incident remains obscure, and in any event Herakles did not linger with Dexamenos. He went back to Eurystheus, who, in another display of deceitfulness, "would not count the cleansing of the Augeian stables as one of the twelve labors, on the ground that the hero had been working for payment."[16]

[16] Apollodorus places the hunting of the Stymphalian birds at this point, whereas Diodorus' account of it occurs earlier.

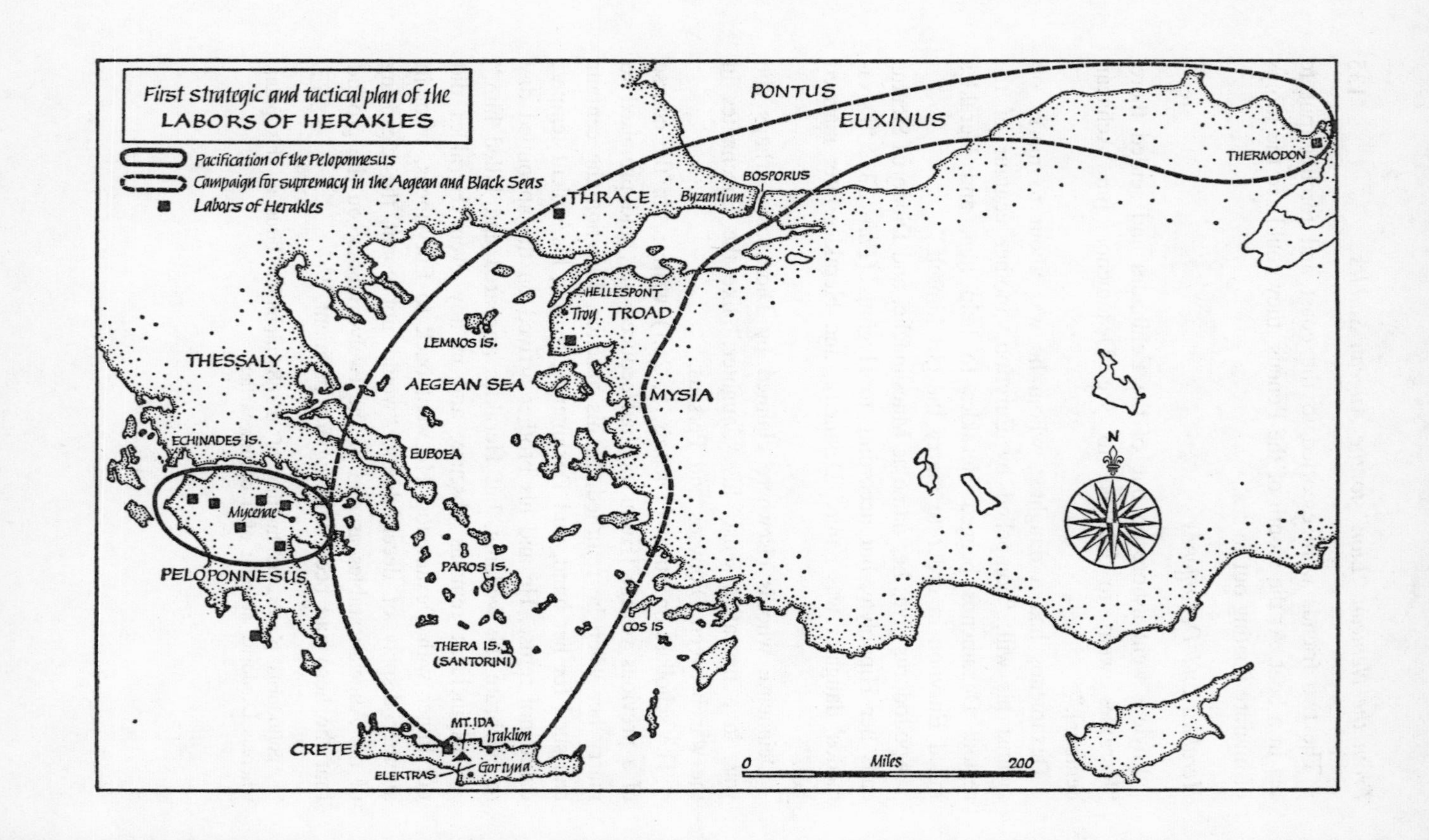
First strategic and tactical plan of the
LABORS OF HERAKLES
Pacification of the Peloponnesus
Campaign for supremacy in the Aegean and Black Seas
Labors of Herakles
PONTUS
EUXINUS
THERMODON
BOSPORUS
Byzantium
THRACE
HELLESPONT
Troy
TROAD
LEMNOS IS.
THESSALY
AEGEAN SEA
MYSIA
ECHINADES IS.
EUBOEA
Mycenae
PELOPONNESUS
PAROS IS.
COS IS
THERA IS.
(SANTORINI)
N
MT. IDA
Iraklion
CRETE
ELEKTRAS
Gortyna
0
Miles
200

Chapter IX
FROM THE CRETAN "BULL" TO THE "GIRDLE" OF HIPPOLYTE[1]

> "The great bull of Crete fell beneath his blows;
> He subdued the mares of fierce Diomedes,
> Whose teeth tore bleeding flesh for food.
> He captured the proud Amazon's girdle—
> Barbarian booty, now safe in Mycenae."
>
> after EURIPIDES

The Cretan "Bull"

About that time, Crete was being devastated by a strange "bull." According to Acusilaus, this was the same bull that carried Europe to Minos. Not exactly the same (the princess's ravisher lived in the reign of Minos I), but a "brother," in the reign of Minos II: like his senior, the master of a bull-prowed ship and, like many Cretan sailors, wearing the bull as his emblem.

Whatever else he may have been, the Tauros of the period of Minos II was a menace on the sea. The exasperated shipbuilders and sailors complained to their tutelary god, and Poseidon's priests immediately demanded that the king rid the sea lanes of the pest.

"Minos promised Poseidon to sacrifice the bull to him . . . but he did not keep his promise." (Apollodorus.)

The truth was that this sovereign, unlike his goodly predecessor, was something of a pirate himself, "exploiting the archipelago, a greedy tax collector, universally detested."

Rather than exterminating Tauros, therefore, he began to wonder how he could make use of him: "Impressed by his beauty, he sent him home to his lands . . ." But he rued the day; emboldened,

[1] See map of the strategic and tactical plan of the labors.

the "fine lord" proved a rebellious handful: "The god [Poseidon] was angered, and drove the bull into a rage." (Apollodorus.)

In fact, Minos could no longer handle him. Taking advantage of the king's illness, the headstrong bull "started an affair with the queen [Pasiphaë]." (Diodorus.) From this union was born a "Minotaur"—the one Theseus was later to fight.

This was too much; the outraged Minos applied to Eurystheus for the services of the knight-errant who had subdued the Nemean lion, the Erymanthian boar, and the Cerynean hind.

Capture of the Bull

"Eurystheus ordered Herakles to bring him the bull from Crete . . . The hero went to the island . . ." (Apollodorus.)

Risen from its ruins, the kingdom of the double ax was not far in those days from equaling Homer's description of it: "Far out in the winy sea lies a land as lovely as it is rich, alone among the waves: this is the land of Crete, with a countless population and ninety cities . . ."

There were houses three stories high; the streets were paved, the roads had hog-backed bridges to facilitate the passage of merchandise being handled in the ports. At Phaestos, Gortyna, and, above all, Knossos, Minos II had superb palaces; he eagerly welcomed Herakles, "and agreed to give him the bull if he could tame it."

The hero immediately set about the task: "Having captured it, Herakles took the bull to Eurystheus and, after showing it to him, set it free." Tauros was released, that is, on condition that he go away and bother somebody else.

"After passing through the regions of Sparta and Arcadia, the bull crossed the isthmus [of Corinth] and went to Marathon in Attica, where he caused much damage."

The task of permanently ridding the Athenian territory of the bull was reserved for Theseus, still only a boy.

Herakles at Olympia

According to Diodorus, the Cretan expedition was followed by a great apotheosis: Herakles went to Olympia, the Elean town sacred to his "father," Zeus. "And there, in gratitude to the god for his good fortune, he dedicated games to him." (Diodorus.)

Although the Greeks did not officially establish the Olympic games until 776 B.C., Olympia was a center of athletic and religious activity long before that. Often, the publicity given to an official "inauguration" is simply a consecration of a long but irregular tradition which has already made a place famous and drawn crowds of people to it.

The site was a gentle valley near the western coast of the Peloponnesus. Cradled in the lap of the hills, the river Alpheus glints above a bed of golden sand. Where it encounters the wooded bulk of Mount Kronos, it circles the base and is joined by a tributary, the Kladeos.

The site was foreordained: by the fourteenth century the worship of Zeus had already supplanted the prehistoric cult of Ghea (Mother Earth), and donations were pouring in from the nearby cities of Pisa and Elis.

At the foot of Mount Kronos, the religious community of Altis was beginning to develop, and alongside the altar of Olympian Zeus rose a Heraeum with columns of wood[2] and, no doubt, the first Theokolion (residence of the clergy).

As there was no real stadium in those days, "Herakles, choosing a field suitable for the solemn rites near the river Alpheus . . ." (Diodorus), created one for the occasion.

The Stadium

It is visible from the road, on the edge of a grove of pines at the very bottom of the hill, surrounded on three sides by earth banks forming the tiers of seats for spectators.

A vaulted passageway (32 meters long) leads into it from Altis—the athletes' entrance, similar to those of modern stadiums.[3]

The gloom of the passageway ends on the playing field itself,

[2] Two more temples of Hera were built on the same site, the second in shell-fossil stone; it may still be visited.

[3] Initially, there was only a trench; the vault was added in the first century, when the embankment had to be raised to increase the stadium's capacity to twenty thousand spectators.

below the grassy tiers stretching away in a long perspective in the form of a graceful horseshoe. Just ahead, the white chalk starting line cuts across the yellow ground. Square holes have been sunk at intervals, to hold the runners' starting posts (a maximum of twenty). When crouching for the start, they braced their feet in triangular grooves hollowed out of the paving stones—the starting blocks of that age.

At the far end of the stadium, the finish line is laid out in the same way, so that it may also be used as a starting line (for relays). There are 192.27 meters between the two lines: the length of the Olympic stadium. It was Herakles who determined its dimensions, for it was he who marked off the distance on the field, "placing his feet one in front of the other six hundred times."

These were footsteps, not strides, giving us the measure of the heroic foot, which later became the Olympic foot: 0.32 meters. And also, by inference, Herakles' height: approximately 1.65 meters.[4] Since the average height of the men of that day was 1.55 meters or less (judging by the lengths of their bathtubs and tombs), and he towered a full ten centimeters (4″) above them, he could fairly be regarded as the giant of the age.

The First Games

But smallness of stature had no adverse effect upon the strength of the Bronze Age athletes, attested to by the weights and dumbbells in the museum at Olympia, the discus of the famous pentathlon champion Asklepiades (241 B.C.), and the stone weighing 143.5 kilograms, which Bybon raised above his head with one hand in the sixth century B.C. (a record that has never been equaled)—tangible evidence of the performances achieved by the Olympionites.

For what reward? "Herakles offered a crown [of scented leaves] to the winner of the games, as he himself had never taken payment for his services." (Diodorus.)

In that he was telling a white lie, at least, for he had tried to obtain some form of remuneration from Augeias. However, the

[4] Herodorus' estimate (six feet) would seem to be an exaggeration.

principle was a good one: instead of gold and silver medals, simple laurel wreaths. The promoters of today's Olympics have not respected this proviso, any more than modern nations at war have observed the truce which was also a rule of the ancient games.

However, they still remember to light the torch at Olympia by the rays of Apollo the Sun, in homage to the pagans, for whom the flame signified purity; sport, the aesthetics of the body; and the body, the receptacle of the soul. Their faith, that the spirit should be influenced through the flesh, is one to which our world is slowly returning.

"Herakles was the uncontested victor in all the games, for no one dared compete against him on account of his remarkable strength . . ."

Afterward the gods, through their agents the priests, presented him with votive offerings. "Athena" gave him a veil, as she had previously given him a "cloak" to "cover" him against the Nemean lion; "Hephaestos" presented him, as before, with a club and a breastplate. "Poseidon" gave him a horse. "Hermes" gave him a sword (he had already done so on another occasion); and "Apollo" gave him a bow (his second from that source).

Thus laden with tokens of esteem from the cities and corporations, Herakles left Olympia and marched back to resume his labors.

Twentieth Century A.D.*: the Ruins*

In the fifth century A.D., during the Byzantine Empire, an earthquake uprooted the temples and buried them under a landslide from Mount Kronion; the Alpheus contributed to their destruction by leaping out of its bed and washing away the Hippodrome. Then time passed: fifteen hundred years.

At last, in the eighteenth century, at the dawn of the age of enlightenment, a French scholar, Montfaucon, became interested in the site. He had read Pausanias. Others followed: Cardinal Quirini, the Archbishop of Corfu, Winckelmann and Richard Chandler, Fauvel, Choiseul-Gouffier, Dodwell and Lord Stanhope—English, French, Germans, a whole constellation of them. Then, in 1829, Blouet and Dubois of the Morea Commission began to excavate. Determined not to be left behind, Frederick III and Kaiser Wilhelm of Germany dug into their pockets and produced nearly a million gold marks. Their archaeologists exhumed thirteen thousand bronzes, six thousand coins, four hundred inscriptions, a thousand terra cotta objects and precious statues, including the Nike of Paeonios and Praxiteles' Hermes (found in the Heraeum, exactly where Pausanias had seen it).

The ruins are grandiose, with the dust of the columns of twenty primitive, Hellenistic, and Roman temples mingling underfoot, but the scene is a melancholy chaos. Once it thronged with hundreds of priests and tens of thousands of proselytes. The only sound to be heard today is the tireless shrill of the cicada fastened to the brown masts of the pines.

They are dead ruins, and yet they are inhabited. Wherever you stand, your eyes are met by such a plethora of stones that you cannot decide where to look first.

There is the portico of the Gymnasium, the rhythmic colonnade of the Palaestra (wrestlers' ring, third century B.C.), the Theokolion (fourth century B.C.)—residence of seers and priests. Next to it, the Heroön, or heroes' altar. Opposite, the Prytaneion (fifth century B.C.), where the administrators of Altis used to meet; and the Philippeion, begun under Philip of Macedonia and completed by Alexander the Great.

Farther on, at the foot of Mount Kronion, lies the most recent of the temples of Hera (seventh century B.C.): six columns across the façade, sixteen on each side, powerful, austere, but they are lying on the ground, and the rains are slowly disintegrating the shell-fossil stone.

There are also the Metroön and the temple of Rhea-Cybele, and there is a sort of architectural anachronism, the Exedra of Herodes Atticus (second century A.D.): a tribune with a coffered demi-cupola, filled with statuary and adorned with a swimming bath by the ostentatious banker (fresh water splashed into it from nine lion's-head orifices).

And then there are the Treasuries—a whole army of them, as at Delphi: altars erected by all the cities of the Greek world: Sicyon,

Epidame, Byzantium, Sybaris, Cyrene, Selinus, Metapontis, Megara—Mediterranean Europe, Asia, and Africa combined.

In the plain circumscribed by the Alpheus stood the Pelopeion, a temple built in honor of Pelops by his descendants from Pisa, with the pit where the Asian's cherished black rams were immolated.

Lastly, the temple of Zeus (fifth century B.C.). It is colossal, 64×28 meters, with six columns across the front and thirteen down the sides; and it was over twenty meters high. A marble cornice ran the entire length, decorated with leonine muzzles. Its celebrated pediments and the friezes of the peristyle have been reconstituted, but the monumental statue of Zeus originally enthroned in the cella has been lost forever. It is possible to obtain some idea of its dimensions, however, by visiting the workroom of Phidias, who sculpted it.

The remains of his studio lie to the right of the portico of the Gymnasium, not far from the Theokolion. Here the clay and wooden model of the colossus was built, in a space whose orientation, dimensions, and arrangement were identical in every particular to those of the cella in which the figure was to be permanently exhibited, so that the artist could gauge the precise effect of every strike of his chisel, in exactly the same conditions of light and proportion as in the statue's future home.

There are other porticoes and altars within the Altis, but there are things to see outside it, too. To the south, beyond the walls, stood the Bouletirion (palace of the Olympic Senate, third century B.C.), Agora (market and forum) and Leonidaion (so called after a Naxion of the fourth century A.D.). There were also a great Hippodrome, Roman fountains, thermal baths, and a house and triumphal arch erected by Nero and dedicated to his own greater glory, when he, like Herakles, was declared winner of the games in the absence of any other contestants (although not, we may suppose, for the same reason).

Lastly, there was and still is the stadium, which used to thunder with the ovations of the Greeks acclaiming the naked athletes. The echo had not died away completely, moreover: one can still imagine it, listening to the roar of the swollen Alpheus in winter.

The Museum

Statues, bronzes, and terra cotta objects from Roman and Hellenistic periods are preserved in the museum, their forms coming to life with the changing light from the cornices.

In the vestibule, Rhea-Cybele presides by the side of Emperor Hadrian, the Greek-loving Roman. (Athena is sculpted on his breastplate, along with the she-wolf who nursed Romulus and Remus.) Next to him is Titus—heir to the symbol of Medusa, borrowed from the arms of Athens. Farther on, Augustus, Claudius (as Jupiter), Faustina—the wife of Marcus Aurelius—and Trajan form his cortege.

Beyond the Roman cohort lies the great hall, inhabited exclusively by the Greeks; its length is equal to the width of the temple of Zeus, in order to accommodate the pediments.

Here, Pausanias has been our stage-manager again. From his account it has been possible to reconstruct the two titanic tableaux which dominated Altis from the top of their colonnade.

The east pediment was sculpted by Paeonios: the "Preparations for the contest between Oenomaos and Pelops" (on which I have based my description of the race). The west pediment shows the "Combat of the Lapiths and Centaurs." Towering above the rest (height: 2.75 meters), Apollo, the founder of both tribes, surveys the melee, a scene of orgy and violence. In the center of the hall, a polychromed terra cotta Zeus strides off with Ganymede, gratifying the protagonists of the marble carnage with an enigmatic smile which some have qualified as facetious. At the far end, the Nike of Paeonios floats unmoved above the writhing throng. She has been placed between the pair of exits leading to the cella of the museum—the shrine of modern Olympia's most priceless treasure: "Among other votive offerings is a marble Hermes carrying the child Dionysos; this is the work of the sculptor Praxiteles." (Pausanias.)

The statue was found in the cella of the Heraeum on May 8, 1898. It had been buried for well over a thousand years, but the Parian marble, most noble material of all, has lost none of its gleam. What young ephebus, his muscles developed to perfection in the palaestra, posed for the Athenian sculptor? For his beauty and his grace, he truly deserved to impersonate the god. Immortalized in the pearly stone in the fourth century B.C., he is bearing the infant Dionysos, child of Zeus and the mortal Semele, to the nymphs, who will protect the fruit of the god's adultery from Hera's vindictive wrath. He carries his small burden lightly as he travels on through eternity, and his veiled gaze seems to be scanning the interminable road of history, his eyes fixed on some far-off horizon.

Lastly, there are the metopes of the temple of Zeus: the twelve labors of Herakles, matchless masterpieces of perspective in bas-relief. They are also invaluable clues to history: Athena is always in the wings. When the hero slays the Nemean lion, a marble Pallas is standing beside him, whispering advice. After killing the Stymphalian birds, he comes to deposit their corpses at her feet. There she is again, helmeted, her hand upon her Aegis, telling him how to cleanse the Augeian stables. And when, later, Herakles must steal the "golden apples" from the Hesperides, Athena will help him to hold up the sky while he briefly relieves the giant Atlas.

Thus the sculptor of these compelling marble friezes confirms the indications of the texts.

The bronzes in their glass-fronted cases give further corroboration: weapons, dented breastplates, staved-in helmets, balls from slingshots, blunted arrowheads, swords chipped by blows as well as by the ravages of time—all tell of the battles, the duels, and murders that were the very fabric of the heroes' hard lives.

Hardest of all, though, was Herakles', when, "for his eighth labor, Eurystheus commanded him to fetch the mares of Diomedes, King of Thrace." (Apollodorus.)

The "Mares" of Diomedes

It began to look as though the king—or his Pelopid counselors—emboldened by the repeated triumphs of the "son" of Zeus, had decided to make him the instrument of a vast Aegean hegemony (after Crete, Thrace—the northern coast). "Diomedes, son of Ares [a warrior] and Cyrene, was king of the Bistones, an extremely warlike people living in Thrace. He owned some mares, which he fed on human flesh."

According to Klearchos, Hesychios says that Diomedes' mares were no more or less than his daughters. This is all the more credible in view of the fact that in Greece women of easy virtue are called "mares" to this day.

Women they were, then, and ugly ones, too. There were no willing suitors for their hands, and so Diomedes, who needed grandchildren to strengthen his hold upon the throne, compelled passing foreigners to sleep with them, after which he killed them. Hence the legend—reminiscent of the habits of the praying mantis—which is revived every time some male perishes through too great intimacy with a woman.

What could Eurystheus' object be this time? The sovereigns of old (like those of the later Middle Ages) went to considerable lengths to attract the sons and daughters of neighboring royal households to their courts—an honor that was not without its practical side (since the "guests" could easily be transformed into hostages).

Apollodorus: "Having set out with a few willing companions, Herakles took these mares despite their keepers' efforts and carried them off to sea. The Bistones took arms and came hurrying to recover them, so he gave the steeds to Abderos—a son of Hermes with whom he was in love—to look after."

This detail is confirmed by Philostratos (Im. L. I, c. 25). The society of that day was less militant in its attitude toward homosexuality.

"The mares devoured Abderos," whose girlishness cannot have been much help to him in defending himself against hellions of their species.

"Herakles fought the Bistones and routed them, after killing their king, Diomedes. And, after founding a city named Abdera near the tomb of his unfortunate friend, he took the mares and gave them to Eurystheus." "Who dedicated them to Hera," if we are to believe Diodorus Siculus (L. IV). Once again, the king was merely anticipating a later custom, whereby large numbers of heiresses of noble lineage were cloistered in convents so that no husband who was not to the monarch's liking could come along and lay claim to their inheritances. The temple of Hera being also that of fertility, the mares' imprisonment brought about no great change in their sexual or reproductive habits.

"Their race endured until the reign of Alexander." (Diodorus.)

The Amazons of the Thermodon

Eurystheus' successes began to go to his head: he gave free rein to his ambition, there was no holding him. Looking beyond the Hellespont, he set his sights on Asia Minor, home of the Amazons, "who lived on the banks of the Thermodon." (Apollodorus.)

These warlike tribes, still subject to matriarchal law, "were a valiant and bellicose people," and their temperament undoubtedly had some bearing upon the term used by the Greeks to designate the Black Sea: "In those days the shores of the Euxinus were inhabited by barbarian peoples who killed any stranger venturing into the area. For that reason the Hellenes had given it the name of Axenos [inhospitable]." (Diodorus.)

The same author adds that the Amazons "excelled in warfare. Only female children were raised to adulthood. They bound [but did not amputate] their right breasts for greater freedom when hurling their darts, and used the left for nursing their babies.

"Hippolyte, their queen, wore the girdle of Ares [god of war], which was the symbol of royal power among them." (Diodorus.)

It was this object, and with it the authority attaching to it that Eurystheus hoped to acquire—not for himself, since a woman was a more likely candidate than a man to bid for the leadership of the Amazons, but for his daughter Admete (whom he had had by the first Admete, priestess of Hera at Argos).[5]

"Admete desired this girdle, so for the ninth labor he ordered Herakles to obtain possession of it." (Apollodorus.)

But Queen Hippolyte was unlikely to relinquish her insignia of Ares without a fight; Herakles would have to organize an expedition.

[5] The record known as the "Farnese inscription" is the source of this genealogy and also bears out the reports from other sources concerning the alliance formed under Eurystheus' father Sthenelaos between his throne and the priesthood of Hera.

Hippolyte's "Girdle"

Apollodorus: "Having assembled a few willing men, Herakles set sail in a single ship and landed on the island of Paros [Cyclades], where the sons of Minos lived—Eurymedon, Chryses, Nephalion and Philolaos ["friend of the people"]. . . ." A Minoan colony; that is, a fief of Crete. His reception was, to say the least, lukewarm: "[The sons of Minos] killed two of his companions. Herakles, grieved by their loss, killed their murderers on the spot and drove the rest of the inhabitants inside their city, which he besieged until they sent ambassadors offering him his choice of their menfolk in exchange for the companions who had been slain."

As his force was a small one (they had set sail in a single boat), it was essential to keep a full complement. "Herakles took Alcaeus because of his strength [Alcaeus means "the strong"; it was also the name of Herakles' grandfather and of the hero himself at his birth]. He also chose Sthenelaos, son of Androgeus, and then raised the siege.

"He next went to Mysia [on the coast of Asia Minor] . . . The Bebrycans had invaded this country, so Herakles marched upon them and, after capturing part of their territory, presented it to the Mysians who had given him hospitality. He then entered the port of Themiscyra [inside Amazonian territory]. Hippolyte came to greet him."

According to Apollodorus, after learning "the object of Herakles' voyage, she promised to give him her girdle. But Hera, disguising herself as an Amazon, excited the crowd . . ."

Small wonder: how could a body of such fierce warriors be unanimously persuaded to capitulate? Hera—feminist *par excellence,* jealous rival of the excessively virile Zeus and an "Amazon" among the gods on Olympus, in the modern sense of the word—assumed human form at Themiscyra, in the person of one of her priestesses, and led the opposition. Once more Herakles, "son" of Zeus, found his path crossed by his lifelong enemy.

Apollodorus: "Armed and on horseback, the warrior-women rushed toward the ship. Believing himself betrayed, Herakles killed Hippolyte . . ."

On the basis of the sources at his disposal, however, Diodorus maintains that the hero stopped short of murder. He says there was "a battle, in which many Amazons were slain and a few taken prisoner, including the queen, who bought her freedom by giving up her girdle—that is, relinquishing her command."

Was Hippolyte living or dead? Which is the true version? Later, when it was the turn of the Argonauts to land in the country of the Amazons, Theseus kidnaped a queen named Hippolyte, who became his concubine and bore his child. Is this the same woman, or a daughter, bearing the title assumed by every leader of the tribe? The son of Theseus and Hippolyte was also called Hippolytus, which adds some weight to this hypothesis.

In any event, "after fighting the rest of the Amazons [to clear a passage], Herakles set sail again and went to Troy [where Laomedon was king]."

Herakles at the Gates of Troy

This sojourn involved him in a quarrel that had no direct bearing on his labors but was of the greatest strategic importance. "At the time Troy was in a sorry plight, owing to the wrath of Apollo and Poseidon, who had disguised themselves as humans and been commissioned to build the walls of Pergamum . . ." (Apollodorus.)

More probably it was some "land dwellers" (worshipers of Apollo) and people living along the coast (sacred to Poseidon) who were building the ramparts. But "when the walls were finished, Laomedon refused to pay, so Apollo sent a plague over the land and Poseidon inflicted a sea monster upon it, which kidnaped the men from the fields."

In other words, the Apollonians and Poseidonians, cheated of their due, were seeking retribution by raiding the countryside, and the leader of the latter group was taking hostages.

"The oracle said their troubles would end when Laomedon exposed his daughter Hesione and left her to be devoured by the monster."

In days gone by a "monster" of the same breed (a pirate)

had claimed Andromeda, and, like her father, Laomedon yielded and "ordered his daughter to be bound to a rock by the sea."

Like Perseus before him, however, Herakles arrived in the nick of time: "Seeing her exposed, he promised to deliver her if Laomedon would give him the horses he had received from Zeus as compensation for the abduction of Ganymede."

This hero was in search of money, not romance, but that is the only difference between the incident and the one involving his ancestor. "Laomedon agreed, and Herakles killed the monster," after a battle described in detail by Valerian Flaccus (L. II). "Afterward, Laomedon refused to keep his promise, so Herakles left, after threatening to return and sack Troy." He did not have enough men to destroy the city then, but this was, effectively, only a rain check, as events subsequently proved.

"He went on to Aenos, where he was well received by Polytos," whose brother Sarpedon was angling for that throne. Herakles accordingly repaid the king who had given him hospitality in a manner befitting his rank. "Sailing along the coast of Aenos, he killed Polytos' brother Sarpedon, on account of his insolence. From there he went to Thasos, subjugated the Thracians living on that island, and presented it to the sons of Androgeus [his companion]. From Thasos he went to Torone." This was the home of one Proteus, a "son of Poseidon" who had come from Egypt to settle at Pollene in Thrace. He had two sons by his wife Corone: Polygonus and Telegonus, and these sons, made bullies by their great strength, challenged all strangers and forced them to wrestle (scholiast on Lycophron, v. 124). They had the effrontery to tackle Herakles, who promptly killed them and set sail again, this time, at last, in the direction of Argos.

"He took Hippolyte's girdle to Mycenae and gave it to Eurystheus."

He had been away a long time and found Greece resounding with the exploits of heroes other than himself.

Chapter X
THE YOUTH OF THESEUS

> "Then it was that Theseus, son of Aegeus, appeared
> To clear the roads of innumerable barbarians—
> Corunetes, Sinis, Pityocamptes;
> Then the Cretan bull that had fled to Attica,
> And afterward, the Minotaur . . ."
>
> after APOLLODORUS

Theseus Sets Forth

When Theseus was sixteen, his mother told him the secret of his birth, and he went out to move the stone near Troezen under which Aegeus had buried the sword and sandal. He took them and set out for Athens.

"The road was infested with bandits" (Apollodorus), for Herakles had dealt only with the major ones assigned to him by Eurystheus.

"Theseus cleared the road. First, at Epidaurus, he killed Periphetes, a son of Hephaestus who was nicknamed Corunetes [cudgel bearer]. He appropriated his club and thereafter carried it himself. Then he killed Sinis, son of Corinth."

This was a cousin of his. "He lived on the isthmus and forced passers-by to hold down the tops of the pines he had bent over. Despite their efforts, they were hurled a great distance into the air when the trees sprang upright, and perished miserably."

Diodorus writes, "Sinis bent down the tops of two pines and tied one arm to each of them; then he released the trees, and the bodies were torn apart."

Because of this habit, he was nicknamed Pityocamptes (pine bender). "Theseus disposed of him, using the bandit's own method," thus freeing the isthmus of the tolls he had been imposing upon it.

"Thirdly, he killed the Crommyonian boar [Crommyon was a town on the Gulf of Corinth], who was tremendously powerful and had gored many men," and, after removing this emulator of the Erymanthian robber baron from the highways, he "also killed Sciron, who dwelled in the territory of Megara among the rocks known as the Scironides."

The Scironian Rocks

The Scironides are located halfway between Corinth and Athens, on the high point of the coast road linking the isthmus to the Attic mainland. In 1963 much of the area was dynamited during the construction of the new highway, but part of the old road remains, narrow and rugged, full of hairpin bends, and suggests how propitious a place it was for ambush. Greeks today still call it the *kakia scala* (evil ladder). The gaping entrances of caves in the cliff face suggest where the robber lay in wait for his prey.

"Sciron used to compel passers-by to wash his feet at the edge of the precipice, and then, with a kick, he would hurl them into the sea in the middle of a bay called the Turtle." These days, an ill-timed twist of the steering wheel would suffice to send a driver plunging after them.

Having now reached the confines of Attica, near Eleusis, "Theseus cut the throat of Cercyon, who would wrestle with passing travelers and kill the losers." After that, he killed Procrustes, who lived at Corydallus.

"Procrustes forced travelers to lie on a bed, then cut off their legs if they were too long and stretched them if they were too short."

One would have to forget the tortures inflicted by other barbarians in more recent times to find anything remarkable in the ability of the human imagination to devise such distractions as these in the thirteenth century B.C.

"After these exploits, Theseus came to Athens." (Diodorus.)

Athens, Twentieth Century A.D.

Athens: a white city bordered by honey-producing Hymettos, Mount Pentelichos, where the blue marble is quarried, and wooded

Parnis. Two hills rise from the middle of the plain: a steep prominence crowned by a white convent, and a temple-crested pile of rock. From the summits the twinkling Bay of Phalerum can be seen, hemmed by a beach of golden sand, and the humpbacked promontory masking Piraeus.

The visitor who, like Theseus, arrives by way of Eleusis will travel along the Sacred Way and pause at Daphni (the laurels)[1] to look at the capital. The modern metropolis (population two million) blends miraculously into its setting. And the size of the Acropolis is in such perfect proportion to the mountains that it immediately becomes clear why the Athenians developed the love of harmony in relationships, artistic order, and clear thinking, to a higher degree than any other culture.

At night it is as though the Milky Way had fallen to earth: millions of lights sparkle in the air—so pure one could believe it made of transparent, glittering crystals. At the center of the galaxy the Acropolis sits enthroned, illuminated, resplendent under the beacons of the projectors, crowned by its diadem, the Parthenon.

No flights of lyricism can equal the sight itself. It is the very image of natural harmony wedded to man-made architectural harmony.

The Acropolis

At the cost of sacrificing part of the picturesque Plaka district, a favorite haunt of tourists in search of local color (and of cats), the approach to the Acropolis is now being cleared. (Greeks may also be seen in the district on occasion, but when they go out to dine in their favorite tavern, they take along a guitar instead of a camera.) But what sacrifice would be too great for the Acropolis?

At the base of its russet walls, the whiteness of the first ruins greets the eye from the shade of cypress and pine. This is the Peripatos esplanade, where the wise men used to stroll. As they walked along, the "peripatetics" would teach their doctrine to anyone willing to listen. Its essence can be stated very simply: above all, let us seek to understand, that is what man was made for. To understand, for the sake of the pure joy of understanding.

[1] The site, incidentally, of one of the finest Byzantine churches in Greece.

Thus barbarism was banished, at last and forever.

Then come the Odeon of Pericles, the theater of Dionysos, and the Odeon of Herodes Atticus; at the foot of its shell-shaped tiers, classical theater was born.

The road, paved with gray stone, turns to the right and mounts between scraggly tamarisks to the foot of the rock.

It is like a sudden, staggering blow: the powerful, harmonious colonnade commanding the entrance. The temple of the Wingless Victory, a miniature Parthenon, peers from the top of the fortifications designed by the priest-strategists so that an approaching enemy must show an unprotected flank.

At the top of the marble staircase lies the platform of the Acropolis. Why did the Greek fail to level the ground outside their temples? Why is the surrounding terrain as rugged and uneven as it was when the first humans settled there, even before the Pelasgians? The Sacred Way itself, as it circles the Parthenon, has to be navigated with care, like the groping search for truth.

The Greeks, more subtle than the Romans, had grasped one essential principle: man emerged from the original chaos, and he must never forget it. The column thrusting upward to scale the sky inhabited by the all-knowing gods is simply a tangible expression of the urge that drives the human mind in its ceaseless effort to decipher the mysteries.[2]

The Parthenon

Therefore, the Parthenon, with all its architectural perfection, and all the sophisticated techniques employed to achieve it, stands on the bare, undressed stone of the hill. History has preserved the names of the men who built it: Pericles, a great administrator; Iktinos, an architect; Phidias, a sculptor; Kallicrates, a master builder. By day the age-old patina on the Pentelic marble of its gigantic colonnade basks in the sun. At night, a huge phantom seems to drift down from the moon, returning to haunt it: the chryselephantine statue of Athena, armed and helmeted, holding

[2] t'Serstevens, one of the great authors of this century, has understood this better than anyone else.

the Aegis in one hand and her lance in the other, its gilded point visible in Piraeus five miles away.

What care was lavished upon this ivory-encrusted effigy! To protect it from the parched atmosphere, the air in the temple was artificially humidified. Pausanias was telling the truth: traces of the evaporating trough are visible between the pillars.

As for the aesthetics of the structure: its foundations, instead of being perfectly level, are slightly convex, so that the curve of the steps and architrave will soften the rigid lines of perspective. And as for its solidity: the axes of the columns are inclined inward, so that the temple can withstand the rages of the "Earthshaker." Air-conditioned and antiseismic was the "Virgin's Chamber" of the fifth century B.C.

Its pediments were a digest of the city's history. On the eastern end, armed Athena stands beside Zeus—her ally, rather than her "father." To the west, Athena again, vying with Poseidon for possession of Attica. He brought the horse, she the olive tree—a source of greater wealth and hence the reason for her ultimate triumph.

Moreover, the olive was present at every ceremony, planted in the calcareous soil of the hill—justification, witness, and symbol all in one. But why speak in the past tense? When the first tree died, later generations planted another in its stead, and then another, so that in a sense, it is still there. Today's tree is growing peacefully near the temple built in memory of the great king Erectheus; it stands guard beside the haughty Caryatids, draped eternally in their dignity—there is something frozen and stiff, and yet so beautiful, about this colonnade. Its foundations hide a host of mysteries, for beneath the temple is another, older structure, both sanctuary and a palace.

Athens, Twelfth Century B.C.

The Polis, the original city of houses built out of hollow brick, lay between the Erechtheion and where the Parthenon was eventually built. The dwellings huddled around a megaron, or palace, much like those of Tiryns and Mycenae; all that remain of it are a terrace on the north side paved with polygonal stones and a conglomerate foundation on the south (measuring 27×17 meters).

In accordance with the prevailing political precepts, which held that those who governed should be both priest and king, the walls of this palace also enclosed altars, sacred to the deities protecting the city ("Polius"): Zeus and his counselor Athena.

There is nothing left of the first sanctuary but its site—although that, at least, is well substantiated: beneath an opening in the pavement of the Erechtheion, three holes bored by lightning (the proper tool of the king of gods) may be seen in the bare surface of the rock.

As for the second (the original shrine of Pallas): traces have been found of the cella containing the primitive idol, said to have been dedicated by Phoenician Cecrops at the beginning of the second millennium, and carved, of course, out of olive wood. After all, the olive did come from Phoenician Asia Minor, and perhaps Cecrops brought it with him.

Mycenaean outer walls (fourteenth century), embedded in the rock, were being built to complete the fortification of the site when Erechtheus' successor Aegeus greeted Theseus, "and recognized him as his son by the marks he bore [sandal and sword]." (Diodorus.)

The "Bull" of Marathon

Restored to his rightful rank, the young man redoubled his heroic activities. When still a child he had seen Herakles at Troezen and flung himself upon his lion's skin, mistaking it for a live animal. Ever since, people had been talking about the glorious deeds of the invincible Theban. The young man now saw an opportunity close at hand (in Attica itself) to perform a deed worthy of his senior and place his own name on a level with that of Herakles.

The place was Marathon (field of fennel), near the spring where a temple was subsequently built and dedicated to the hero Amphiaraos, one of the seven chiefs who fought against Thebes in 1251 B.C. (date recorded on the Paros marble).

The ruins of the shrine comprise a peribole, a theater—as in every "watering place," past and present—and an incubatory portico where the oracle's clientele slept while waiting for their revelation.

The miraculous water was drunk out of shells, large numbers of which have been found. Those who were cured threw gold and silver coins into the wonder-working pool.

The plain extends on all sides, traversed by many streams shaded by plane trees[3] and protected by the swamps that border it. A deep, narrow gorge opens onto it from the north; the sea approach is a crescent-shaped bay, forever blue, edged by beaches offering an ideal landing place for boats.

It was here that the Persian fleet beached in 490 B.C.[4] At night, as Pausanias says, when the wind is blowing in from sea, "the whinnying of horses can [still] be heard, and a sound like fighting soldiers."

The sound of footsteps, too, still echoes in men's memories—those of the wounded hoplite, dragging himself painfully along to announce to the people of Athens that a handful of their sons had just saved European civilization from ruin.

At the end of his journey (the first "marathon") the hero died and became immortal. But before him, Theseus had raced along the same fourteen miles on his way from Athens to meet the monstrous bull that was terrorizing Attica.

To finish the job begun by Eurystheus' vassal, "at Marathon, he attacked the bull which Herakles, in one of his labors, had brought to the Peloponnesus from Crete. He mastered it in the course of a single fight and took it to Athens, where Aegeus offered it as a sacrifice to Apollo" (Apollodorus), to the intense satisfaction of the worshipers of the agrarian god whose crops the brigand had been plundering remorselessly.

The Calydonian "Boar"

This deed made Theseus famous throughout Greece, and so he was one of the guests invited by Oeneus to visit his estate in

[3] The marble-clad dam blocking off the reservoir that supplies water to Athens is near Marathon.

[4] According to Herodotus, the Persian army was composed of 100,000 infantry and 10,000 cavalry; modern writers say 6000 infantry and 800 horse.

Aetolia and hunt "an enormous wild boar with white tusks" (*Iliad,* IX), a monster that was ruining the orchards of Calydon. "Nearby [the town of that name], a war was in process between the Aetolians and [their neighbors] the Curetes. The gallant warriors were outvying each other in slaughter, the former to defend their Calydon and the latter in their furious desire to capture the city." (*Iliad,* IX.)

The site dominates the entrance to the Gulf of Corinth and the valley of the Evenos. Six miles from Missolonghi, near Evenokhorion, the old castle of Kourtaga stands in a landscape of olive groves. Excavations in 1925 revealed a primitive terrace, a temple of Apollo, and the remains of another, larger temple of Artemis Laphria.

The cause of the conflict was that "Oeneus had failed to make his annual harvest offering to the goddess on the hill above his olive groves." (*Iliad,* IX.)

Or, possibly, he had not given the Curetes—hunters and followers of Artemis—their yearly tribute in kind, which purchased the tribe's good humor by providing it with a welcome change from its staple diet of game.

The clan exploded in anger—and especially its chief, a piratic boar, "who hurled all the great trees to earth, tearing them up by the roots with the fruit-bearing blossoms still on them."

This tells us the time of year: spring. Oeneus, who was unable to master the animal singlehanded, invited his noble friends to a battue. The slayer of the Erymanthian boar being otherwise occupied, Castor and Pollux (the Dioscuri—twins "born of Zeus" at Sparta), and Herakles' twin brother Iphicles were among those who answered the call.

Oeneus' son Meleager was naturally one of the party, and the honor of finishing off the animal fell to him, whereupon the followers of Artemis predictably raised "a great tumult of shouting and set the Aetolians and Curetes to fighting over the carcass."

The goddess and her priesthood were mourning the loss of their champion "of the bristled head and hide." (He was probably wearing the hide of the animal he had taken as his emblem.)

Among those in at the kill was a young Thessalian also destined for fame. Did the first meeting between Theseus and Jason take place during the Calydonian hunt? The membership of the party who brought down the boar is almost identical with that of the group who set sail in the *Argo* in quest of the Golden Fleece.

Some authors place Oeneus' war against the Curetes at a later period in the lives of Theseus and Jason. Which of the two expeditions was the prelude to the other?

It is hard to imagine the Athenian prince, already a much-lauded hero, consenting to set sail for Colchis under the orders of the Thessalian unless Jason had already given some proof of his mettle, which he may have been able to do during the hunt of the robber-boar.

Chapter XI
JASON AND THE ARGONAUTS[1]

> "Suspended from an oak in the land of Colchis
> Was the Golden Fleece, guarded by a dragon.
> Jason, with his companions, built the *Argo,*
> And set off in quest of it. He met Medea . . ."
>
> after APOLLODORUS

The Challenge

"Jason lived in Iolcos, where Pelias was king, after the death of Cretheus . . ." (Apollodorus.) Like all usurpers, the monarch lived in a state of uneasy watchfulness; he consulted oracles. "The gods warned him to beware of someone 'shod on only one foot'; at first he did not know what to make of this, but the meaning soon became clear. Planning a sacrifice to Poseidon by the sea, he invited a number of people, including Jason [whom he viewed with suspicion, for having shone at the Calydonian hunt]."

Now, "[Jason], who lived in the country because of his love of farming [shared with many other ousted pretendants], had lost one of his sandals crossing the river Anauros."

But although he may have had "only one foot," as we would say, in the ancestral kingdom, that one was firmly planted. "Pelias, observing this, remembered the oracle," and also, most likely, remembered that in Greek the expression "to bring someone to heel" is rendered "to put both feet in one shoe" (a metaphor in common use today). "He inquired what [Jason] would do if he

[1] See map of the voyage of the Argonauts.

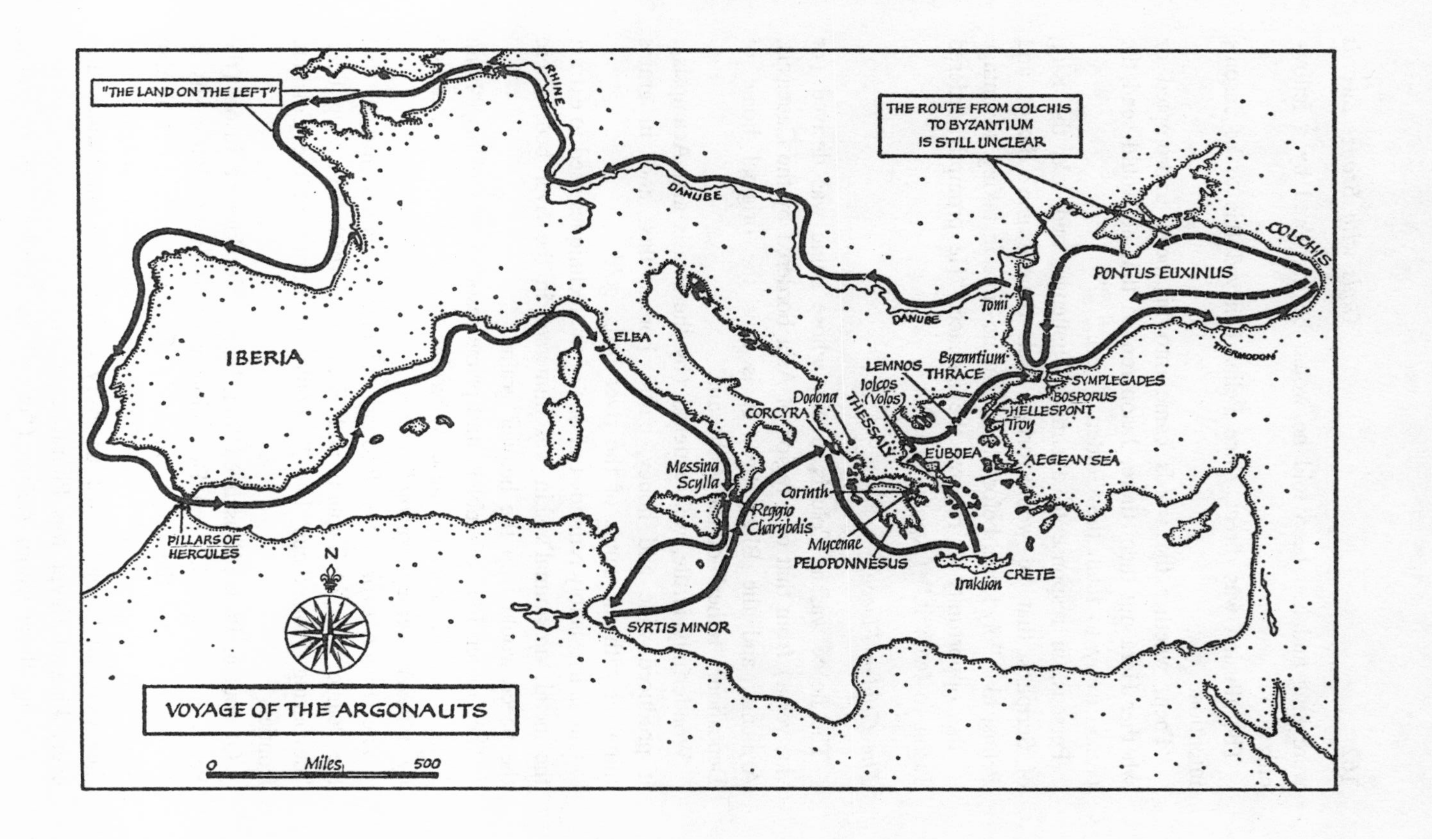

VOYAGE OF THE ARGONAUTS

were king and had been told he would be murdered by a fellow-citizen."

The allusion was direct, since Pelias believed this to be Jason's intention.

"Then, whether the words came into his head unprompted or whether Hera put them there, Jason replied that he would send the person away to fetch the Golden Fleece."

Perseus, in response to a similar challenge, had told the King of Seriphos that he would bring back the Gorgon's head; and Pelias, like Polydectes before him, lost no time in taking advantage of this opportunity to remove the menace. "He promptly ordered Jason to fetch it." (Apollodorus.)

The Golden Fleece

The fleece was at Colchis, a city whose name was derived (or vice versa) from that of a region of Asia bordered by the Caucasus, Armenia, and the Black Sea. It is thus the original home of Deucalion, "father" of the Achaeans.

Wonderfully fertile, well watered (by the Phasis and Acampsis), it produced wine and honey, cattle, horses, flax, and, in grains mingling with the sands of the river beds, gold.

One is irresistibly reminded of one of the techniques used to extract the metal: an animal's skin was immersed in the river bed, where the fleece would trap the heavier grains.

The Golden Fleece, emblem and prime resource of Colchis, "hung from a sacred oak [as these venerable trees often are] guarded by a never-sleeping dragon."

The dragon evokes the Phorcid colonies: it is no miracle that the "eagle born of Typhon and Echidne," which had long been "devouring Prometheus' liver," should be lurking at the Colchian frontier.

Of course, Prometheus lived long before Herakles or Jason (the Paros marble says his son Deucalion came to Mount Parnassus in 1574 B.C.). But the anachronism is only apparent; the Colchian rulers had adopted the bird of prey as their royal insignia, and they were all "eagles," just as every Cretan king was Minos and every king of Egypt was Pharaoh.

Among those whom Aeëtes ("eagle," in Greek) kept in chains

were some of the descendants of the Caucasian emigrants who, at the time of Deucalion, had become Greek. These people had settled in Boeotia, but they still remembered the way to their ancestral Caucasus,[2] and when Phrixos, a Theban prince, was forced to leave the Boeotian city in a hurry, he turned naturally to Colchis, the land of his forefathers, for refuge.

The Hellespont

As Thebans had been enduring for some time a deep famine, the oracle, whether bribed by his enemies or not, stipulated that "he must be sacrificed, before the plague could end."

"Forced to flee Greece with his sister Helle . . . he boarded a ship with a [gilded] ram's head on its prow." (Diodorus.) He took along a few of the "teeth" of the "dragon" slain by Cadmos when the first came to Thebes long before—in other words, some of the weapons of the Phorcids whom the Phoenicians had ousted, which had been hanging in the temple as trophies.

Hesiod, in the *Great Ehoiai,* says that Phineus, a "son of Poseidon" and hence a sailor, lived in Thrace on the coast by the strait, and used to act as a guide to fugitives en route to Colchis.

Just as, in the vocabulary of myth, they were going through the passage "mounted on a golden ram . . . Helle moved to the front of the ship and fell into the waves" (Diodorus), which is how the Dardanelles acquired their first name—Hellespont (Helle's sea).

Phrixos eventually reached the Caucasus and Aeëtes, the eagle, gave him his daughter in marriage in order to keep him there. In exchange, the monarch received the "teeth" of the Theban dragon (as a symbolic homage).

Phineus, the Blind Navigator

But, like Deucalion, this couple's offspring must have yearned for some more civilized place than "savage Scythia." The sons of Phrixos wanted to return to Thebes, but this did not suit the King

[2] At Maikop (in northern Colchis) a tablet has been found covered with inscriptions proving the existence of communications between that region and the Aegean in the thirteenth century B.C. (*UNESCO Courrier,* March 1964).

of Colchis, whose population was melting away to the gentler climes of Greece. Phineus the sailor, who was held responsible for this hemorrhage of "manpower," was Aeëtes' bête noire, for he "broke the chains" of those who wanted to leave by guiding them into the Aegean, flaunting the king's ban on emigration (so like the restrictions enacted by modern countries with manpower shortages).

This is confirmed by the poet Istros: "Having learned that Phineus, by his skill, had enabled the son of Phrixos to escape and return to Greece, Aeëtes implored his father the sun to avenge him, and the god blinded Phineus."

This explains Jason's decision, when preparing his expedition, to "send for Argos, the son of Phrixos" (not to be confused with Argos, the founder of the city, who had, of course, been dead for centuries)—Argos, who had come from Colchis with the aid of Phineus.

For added assurance, Jason also planned a halt in Thrace, to consult Phineus himself as to the best route to follow.

The Good Ship Argo

"Under Athena's guidance Argos built a fifty-oared ship."

In the light of her past behavior, it would have been strange had Athena abstained on this occasion, for her pocket was never empty when there was a foreign pest to be exterminated. Following in the footsteps of Perseus, Bellerophon, and Herakles, it was now Jason's turn to become the instrument of Attic expansion.

"The ship was named the *Argo* on account of the man who built it." (Apollodorus.) "Athena attached to the prow a beam of oracular beech from the forest of Dodona. When the ship was ready, Jason consulted the oracle."

Dodona

The oracle of Dodona, reputed to be the equal of the Delphic Pythoness, held sway in the north of the Epirus, near present-day Joannina. The Pelasgians had probably founded the shrine on their way down from the Balkans. Their god was Zeus, whose worship spread steadily southward as they advanced, competing with more primitive deities (Ghea-Mother Earth; Hera-Fertility, etc.).

The site is reached from the main road south of Joannina. Soon another road branches off to the right and winds up through wooded slopes. There is a magnificent view of the lake of the Epirot capital in the distance, a vast expanse of sea-green water set in a chain of naked mountains.

Then the road drops down into a verdant valley running north-south—the eternal thoroughfare of both tradesmen and invaders, a little like the Sedan gap in France. This explains the choice of the site: the priests were sure of customers, for the nature of the terrain compelled everyone to pass their temple.

The theater of Dodona alone, which had a capacity larger than that of Epidaurus, gives an idea of the crowds attracted by the sanctuary in its days of glory: between sixteen and eighteen thousand pilgrims could be seated on the gray stone tiers leaning against the acropolis. Since the hill was no higher than the tallest of the *kerkides,* however, its shell-like form is shallower and broader than that of its Argolid emulator, and does not seem as large as it actually is.

At the foot of the acropolis, the outer wall of which is five meters thick in places, the archaeologist Carapanos has excavated the sanctuary, producing a sort of skeleton of the structure in stone slabs at ground level. A young beech perpetuates the memory of its prophetic ancestor, like the young olive planted on the Athenian Acropolis in memory of Athena's first olive tree.

The Voice of Zeus

The Pelasgians believed that the wind moaning through its leaves articulated the words of the king of gods; afterward, it was the priests' business to interpret his speech. When the Hellenes learned that at Dodona Zeus would answer the questions of mortals, they began filing past the sacred tree in a never-ending stream.

Excavations have unearthed its massive trunk, protected by the terrain from the weathering of time. Quantities of bronze tablets have also been dug up, on which the questions posed by the worshipers were picked out. There is one in the Athens museum (Carapanos room), next to the famous phallic ex-voto of Agathon of Zante,[3] submitted by a navigator who wanted to know whether he would have a fair wind for his journey. His request is phrased in the very words Jason might have used.

The captain of the *Argo* did not have to wait for a reply: "The oracle urged Jason to set sail as soon as he had assembled a crew of the foremost men of Greece." (Apollodorus.) To be sure, it was no mean task to go to the far end of the Pontus Euxinus, destroy the kingdom of Aeëtes, and seize his treasure. A coalition would be necessary, on the scale of that led by Perseus against Medusa, or by Amphitryon against the Echinades.

The Muster Roll of the Argonauts

Jason accordingly made a tour of the connections he had formed at the Calydonian hunt: Castor and Pollux (the Dioscuri), Meleager, the son of Oeneus; Theseus, and, lastly, Herakles, who had now returned from the Thermodon.

From the four corners of Greece the heroes came running, overjoyed at this opportunity to accompany Herakles and Theseus on a campaign—the fondest dream of any warrior of that age.

In the muster roll of the Argonauts, as given by Apollodorus (supplemented by Apollonius Rhodius and others), almost every region of Greece was represented. There were:

- Tiphys, son of Aeginios (a pilot from the island of Aegina), the helmsman;
- Zetes and Calais, "sons" of Boreas, the north wind;
- Palaemon, "son" of Hephaestos (a smith) and Aetolos (i.e., representing Aetolia);
- Cepheus, son of Aleus;
- Ancaeus, "son" of Poseidon and Astypaleus (a sailor from the island of that name);
- Autolycos, "son of Hermes" and, as such, a traveler and merchant;
- Eurytos, another "son of Hermes."

[3] See Introduction.

Merchants, because pirates always need agents to market their plunder.

Only Apollodorus and Diodorus include Atalanta—"daughter" of Shoeneus—among the crew. Apollonius says the adventuress, who was in every respect a worthy exponent of the age of the Amazons, wanted to come with them, but Jason would not sign her on, "fearing the consequences of the presence of one woman among so many men" (L. I, v. 769), a precaution taken by many sea captains after him.

The following also made the voyage:

- Euphemos, "son" of Poseidon (a mariner whose descendants long governed Cyrene in Libya);
- Actor, son of Hippasos;
- Acastus, son of Pelias;
- Poeas, son of Thaumacos;
- Butes, son of Teleon;
- Phanos and Staphylos, two "sons" of Dionysos (although Ion says the latter was hardly more than a boy);
- Periclymenes, son of Neleus;
- Augeias, "son" of the sun (King Augeias himself, that is);
- Iphitos, Eurystheus' brother;
- Asterion, son of Cometes;
- Idmon, the seer;
- Pirithous, friend of Theseus (who later kidnaped Persephone at Eleusis);
- Telamon, Herakles' companion at arms;
- Hylas, a squire and favorite protégé of the hero.

Lastly, there were:

- *Polyphemos,* "son" of Poseidon and Elatos;
- *Oïleus,* father of Ajax;
- *Peleus,* father of Achilles;
- *Menetios,* son of Actor and father of Patroclus;
- *Laertes,* son of Acrisios and father of Ulysses;
- *Euryalos, Peneleos* and *Leitos* (who commanded the Argive forces at Troy);
- *Ascalaphos* and *Ialmenos* (leaders of the Orchomenians during the siege);

· for it should be observed that the expedition of the Argonauts and the siege immortalized by Homer are separated by only thirty years.[4]

With rare exceptions—anachronisms caused by the occasionally faulty "perspective" of history—the texts follow the natural span of generations so closely that one might as easily deny the existence of Schliemann's Troy or Mycenae while staring at their walls, as doubt the accuracy of this list.

Besides, the errors are easily spotted: some authors, for instance, say that Orpheus was one of the Argonauts. If the name refers to the poet-priest, this is impossible, because the Paros marble says the initiation at Eleusis took place in 1399 B.C., and Orpheus' son was already an old man when Herakles knew him.

The Expedition Sets Sail

There were fifty-four heroes in the company when the campaign began. "Under Jason's orders, they stopped first at Lemnos [outside the Dardanelles], an island completely without men, governed by Hypsipyle, daughter of Thoas." An Amazon; was Lemnos a colony of the tribes of the Thermodon?

"The Argonauts went ashore and slept with the women, and Hypsipyle had two sons by Jason—Euneos and Nebrophonos."

Having seen no women since they left port, the Greeks must not have been hard to please, for legend has it that "Aphrodite, goddess of love, was so vexed with the Lemnian women for refusing to worship her that she caused them to stink, so that their husbands could not bear to come near them."[5]

"After leaving Lemnos, the Argonauts reached the country of the Doliones, whose king, Cyzicus, gave them a most cordial welcome."

Then a tragic error was made. The Greeks set sail again at

[4] Italicized names are those of the future participants in the Trojan War. As for Herakles: he was a contemporary of Atreus, whose son Agamemnon led the Greeks in the attack upon the city, and also of the young Priam—we shall see how it was that Priam, in fact, owed his throne to Herakles.

[5] Whereupon the men "kidnaped" virgins from Thrace and shared their beds with them, and their offended wives killed all the husbands and fathers except Thoas, spared by Hypsipyle.

night, and contrary winds drove them back to shore. The Doliones mistook them for their hereditary enemies, the Pelasgians (from Euboea)[6] and, believing themselves attacked, came out and engaged in battle, and neither side recognized the other.

"After killing a large number, including Cyzicus," whom Jason himself dispatched, according to Apollonius (L. I, v. 1032), "the Argonauts saw their mistake at sunrise."

Cyzicus had only recently married, and his bride Cleite hanged herself in despair. (Apollonius, L. I, v. 1065 Parthenius, narr. 28).

"Deeply grieved by this event, the Argonauts shaved their heads and organized a magnificent funeral for Cyzicus. Then they left and stopped next in Mysia." (Apollodorus.)

A serious quarrel flared up among the crew at this point on the coast of Asia Minor. There were too many heroes on board, coming from too many different backgrounds: the inevitable friction between them now degenerated into open conflict. "In this country they abandoned Polyphemos, and he founded and became king of a city named Cius in Mysia."

Herakles Marooned

Far more serious, they also abandoned Herakles, because "the ship said he was too heavy for it to carry." (Pherecydes.)

Aristotle confirms this (*Politic.* L. III, c. 9): "The *Argo* could no longer carry him too, because he weighed so much more than the others."

One may well ask whether Herakles—triumphant at Nemea and Lerna, tamer of the Erymanthian boar and Cretan bull, conqueror of Diomedes and the Amazons—would long consent to take orders from Jason, whose record at that time consisted solely of his unremarkable performance at the Calydonian boar hunt.

Diodorus Siculus (L. IV, c. 41) and Antoninus Liberalis (C. 26) even maintain that Herakles was the original leader of the Argonauts, who made Jason their captain only after they had abandoned him. Jason was certainly the promoter of the expedition, however, so one is inclined to believe Herakles may simply have tried to

[6] This detail is supplied by Apollonius Rhodius, L. I, v. 1024.

take over the leadership after they had set out. The crew voted ("the ship said") and decided to unload the "heavy man."

According to Theocritus (Id. XIII), they found a pretext for leaving him stranded on shore: "Having beached in the Propontis, they came ashore and were preparing the evening meal . . . Hylas took a jar and went to find water for Herakles and the intrepid Telamon." When the youth failed to return (he had fallen into the water and drowned, "carried away by the nymphs"), Herakles, who loved him (and not only platonically, either, *vide* Abderos), set out in search of him.

"Just then the wind rose, and a navigator called out, 'Man the sail, boys. Ease off the rigging, the wind is freshening!' But Herakles was still far away, looking for Hylas. The warriors boarded the ship and left the sails slack all night long, waiting for him. But he was wandering aimlessly, for a powerful sorrow had gripped his heart.

"Thus the fair Hylas went to the gods. The heroes laughed at Herakles and called him a deserter because he had abandoned the deep-hulled *Argos*—for the love of a cabin boy."

They set sail without him.

"But Herakles continued walking, and came to Colchis and the unhospitable Phasis . . ."

Navigating the Aegean

It is a long way across Asia Minor, and virtually nothing is known of the route followed by the hero from Mysia to the Caucasus; too many texts have been lost (in particular, the last books of Apollodorus and Diodorus).

The amazing voyage of the Argonauts, on the other hand, can be traced: "From Mysia they went to the country of the Bebryces, where Amycos, son of Poseidon and Bithynia [i.e., a Bithynian], was king." (Apollodorus.)

Clement of Alexandria says that Amycos was the inventor of the cestus used by pugilists (*Stromates,* L. I). "He wrestled with Pollux, who killed him with a blow on the neck."

Pisander says Pollux merely hog-tied him, and that is how

Amycos is shown on a funerary urn reproduced by Winckelmann (*Histoire de l'art,* ed. 1789).

Nicephorus Callistus (*Hist.* L. VII, c. 50) reports that upon their arrival in the land of the Bebryces, the Argonauts promptly sacked it—which is likely, since this was a military campaign. Amycos and his men counterattacked, and, after suffering an initial setback, the Argonauts recovered their wind and slaughtered him. "Then they went to Salmydessus in Thrace, where Phineus, son of Poseidon, reigned; he was skilled in foretelling the future."

This was the same old man who had told Phrixos how to get from Greece to Colchis and advised his children how to make the return journey after their escape from the "eagle."

The Harpies

"Phineus was plagued by the Harpies. They had wings [or sails] and would fall upon all the victuals that were served, carrying most of them away . . ."

In other words, they were pirates, scavenging along the coast of Thrace. Contrary to more recent usage, the ancient poets do not describe the Harpies as misshapen monsters. In his *Theogony* (v. 267) Hesiod describes them as having "beautiful hair," and Homer (*Iliad,* XV) says one of them was the bride of Zephyr, gentlest of breezes. That is, the Harpies' "wings" were "married" to Zephyr, the wind.

"The Argonauts wished to know what lay in store for them on their voyage, and Phineus promised to tell them if they would free him from these monsters. To do so, they ordered a table to be dressed [set out plunder on the beach, as a lure]."

The Harpies fell into the trap: "They lunged at the food, screaming loudly. Then Zetes and Calais, the winged sons of Boreas, gave chase to them."

They fled—one to the Peloponnesus and the other to the Echinades, eternal heaven of pirates, "which have been known as the Strophades [circlings] ever since, because when the Harpy Ocypode [or Ocypete; that is, "swift"] fell exhausted on the shore, she was turning in circles with fatigue." (Apollodorus.)

Through the Strait

"Phineus, now being rid of the Harpies, told the Argonauts how to plan their trip and warned them against the Symplegades rocks, which tower high above the sea and are driven together by the wind, closing the passage. Phineus advised them to send a pigeon through ahead of their boat; if the bird got through, they could follow safely; otherwise, they should not attempt to pass."

It was not the wind, of course, that drove the rocks together, but tectonic spasms; geological analysis of the shores of the Bosporus and the volcanic rock on both sides of the strait confirms the ancient tradition. (*Larousse universel.*)

The use of a bird in such circumstances was a common practice among primitive peoples (viz., Noah's dove), for birds, like most animals, possess an uncanny premonitory instinct about earthquakes.

Another tradition relates that before entering the Bosporus the Argonauts were advised by Athena, goddess of wisdom, to send out a heron, which was almost crushed between the rocks, "losing the tip of its tail."

In the Black Sea

"The Argonauts then came to the land of the Mariandynians, and Lycos [in Greek, "wolf"], the king, received them most hospitably."

According to Herodorus (*Apollonoii schol.* II, v. 754), Lycos was a grandson of Tantalos and thus a nephew of Pelops (i.e., related to Herakles and the Argive Argonauts).

In this country, "Idmon the seer was killed by a boar [which may, for once, have been a real one]. Tiphys, the pilot, also died there, and after that Ancaeus, son of Poseidon and Astypaleus, took the helm.[7]

"Then they passed the Thermodon, and it was there that Theseus captured Hippolyte, Queen of the Amazons, in battle; her tribe was still recovering from its war with Herakles."

[7] Herodorus says Tiphys did not die until the homeward journey, and it was Erginios who took the helm.

Continuing their cruise along the coast, they passed the Caucasus and finally reached "the mouth of the Phasis, which is a river in Colchis."

The Land of the Golden Fleece

"Leaving the ship in port, Jason went to find Aeëtes and, after explaining Pelias' orders, asked for the fleece.

"Aeëtes had received two wild bulls as a present from Hephaestos; they were enormous, fire snorted from their nostrils, and they had brazen hoofs." Two champion athletes, "strong as oxen," armed in bronze and originating in the country of the Caucasian volcanoes, the subterranean kingdom of the god of forges.

"Aeëtes promised to give Jason the fleece if he could yoke these bulls singlehanded, and sow [distribute] the teeth of the serpent which Cadmos had killed at Thebes . . ."

The "teeth" were weapons—the Theban booty Phrixos had brought with him into exile in Colchis and given to the king.

Jason was wondering how on earth he could "yoke these bulls [overpower them] when Medea, who had fallen in love with him . . ."

Medea, Authority on Poisons

Aeëtes, "son" of Ocean and the sun (Hesiod, *Theog.* v. 955 ff.),[8] had married Hecate, who had been deified according to the same process as Athena and Dionysos, "because she was the first to study both the beneficial and harmful plants—in particular, wolfsbane [aconite]." (Diodorus, L. IV.)

Two daughters were born of this union: Circe and Medea, both "magicians": graduates in their mother's field of study.[9]

"Fearing that Jason would be killed by the bulls, Medea sent him a secret message, saying she would help him to harness them and give him the fleece if he swore to marry her and take her back to Greece with him."

[8] "Son" also of Typhon and Echidne, of Echinadian and Gorgonian parentage, and therefore able to claim kinship with Ocean.
[9] Circe, who later bewitched Ulysses.

Aeëtes' Colchis was decidedly not an earthly paradise; even his little girl was trying to run away.

"Jason promised, and Medea, who, thanks to her mother, had become learned in the preparation of the deadly poisons manufactured by the earth and water [by plants], gave him a lotion and told him to rub it on his body, so that neither iron nor fire could hurt him . . ." An external anesthetic, to render the hero insensitive to pain from blows?

"She also warned him that armed men would spring up from the teeth of the serpent he had to sow [small wonder, in view of their true nature] and said he must throw stones among them and wait until they began fighting with each other, and then he could kill them."

Jason's Ordeal

He followed his instructions to the letter: "He went into the woods in front of the temple and challenged the bulls. They charged at him, snorting fire." We still use the image, when we speak of someone so angry that he is "spouting fire."

"He managed to yoke them, however; and when he sowed the serpent's teeth, armed men immediately sprang out of the ground."

Now, even assuming that the monster of Thebes had owned several sets of armor, those brought to Colchis could not have equipped more than a small body of soldiers to act as reinforcements for the bulls.

"He made them fight among themselves, killing the survivors."

By forcing him to take on the two champions first, and then a whole body of armed men, Aeëtes thought he had given Jason a task from which he could never emerge alive, and he was infuriated by the Achaean's success.

"Nevertheless, Aeëtes would not give him the fleece, and even threatened to burn the ship and massacre her crew."

Success

"But Medea, having warned Jason, led him to the fleece at night and, after sending the dragon who guarded it to sleep with a potion, she took it."

Diodorus explains: "They say Medea led the Argonauts inside the temple of Ares, seventy stadia [eight miles] from the town. When they reached the temple doors, she spoke to the guards in the Tauric language. They opened the doors in obedience to the king's daughter, whereupon the Argonauts went inside and slew a great many barbarians. Others fled."

Pursuit

The two main historiographers differ as to what happened next. Apollodorus says that "Medea boarded the ship with Jason and her [younger] brother Apsyrtus, and the Argonauts left the same night." According to Apollonius (L. III, v. 242), Apsyrtus was the son of Aeëtes and Asterodeia, one of the "nymphs" of the Caucasus. Pherecydes says (in his fourth book) that Medea stole Apsyrtus from his cradle on Jason's advice, as a hostage for the Argonauts.

Diodorus, however, states that "the Taurians who escaped from the temple told the king what had happened. It is said that Aeëtes led his men in pursuit of the Greeks and caught up with them by the seashore. He immediately engaged them in battle and killed one of the Argonauts—Iphitos, the brother of Eurystheus, who was master of the labors of Herakles.

"But his forces were surrounded and hard-pressed, and fell under the blows of Meleager. The king himself died . . . Jason, Atalanta [Diodorus maintains that she was one of the Argonauts], and the Thespians were wounded, but Medea is said to have healed them all in a few days, using herbs."

This version seems to contain several flaws: Aeëtes survived to continue the pursuit for a long time, and the last Caucasian king to wear the eagle on his coat of arms perished sometime later, at the hands of Herakles.

Apollodorus agrees: "Seeing what Medea had dared to do, Aeëtes set out in pursuit of the ship. When Medea saw him approaching, she killed her brother, cut him into pieces and threw them into the sea."

The site of this murder is hard to determine. In *The Women of Colchis,* Sophocles says that Medea cut Apsyrtus' throat in front of their father's house (*Apol. scholii* IV, 28). Orpheus says Apsyrtus was already a young man, who joined in the pursuit of the *Argo* and was killed in an ambush laid for him by its crew. Arrian claims he was killed at Apsarus, where his tomb was shown to visitors (*Periplus Ponti Euxini*). Ovid (L. III, El. 9) asserts that he was killed at Tomi (in the Danube delta).

Apollodorus: "Aeëtes, who was unable to catch the ship because he had to stop and gather up the limbs of his dismembered son, gave the name Tomi [from *tomei,* which means "severed piece" in Greek] to the place where he buried them."

This account has some features in common with that of Arrian and, in any case, marks the fugitives' passage in the Danube delta, which is confirmed by subsequent events.

"Aeëtes then sent out a great number of Colchians in pursuit of the ship."

Diodorus: "The *Argo* was already in the middle of the Pontus Euxinus when it was caught by a storm." Apollodorus corroborates this: "Zeus, angered by the murder of Apsyrtus, stirred up a tempest that drove them off their course . . ." and slowed their flight, to the advantage of Aeëtes.

Byzantium

"Upon reaching the strait of the Propontis, the Argonauts set foot in a land, the king of which was Byzas, who gave his name to Byzantium." (Diodorus.)

There they learned of the danger threatening them. Diodorus continues: "Many historians, both ancient and modern [Timaeus is one of them] say the Argonauts were informed that Aeëtes' ships were blocking the entrance to the Propontis."

Having lost sight of the Greek ship, the Colchians had resorted to strategy, and were lying in wait for the Argonauts at the entrance to the Bosporus, which they would have to pass in order to re-enter the Aegean.

This was the cause of a new voyage, in itself as astonishing as any performed in antiquity.

The Mouth of the Danube

As asserted by Diodorus, Aeëtes' fleet, patrolling the channel, "gave the Argonauts an opportunity to perform a strange and wonderful deed."

Unable to sail through the strait, "they went up the Tanais [Danube] to its source."

The Greeks' idea of what lay in store for them on this bold venture was undoubtedly much mistaken from the beginning (perhaps, at Tomi). The only source of their knowledge of the geography of the continent were the tales told by travelers, which already possessed a sort of rough accuracy, but also led to some serious miscalculations.

Long before they ever came to Greece, the Achaeans had explored the valley of the Danube from their point of departure in the Caucasus, finding copper and tin for their first swords of bronze. Other Indo-Europeans (the Celts) had pushed as far west as the valley of the Rhine. Still others, after spending some time in Central Europe, were making their way over the mountain passes and down into Italy (the Umbrians).

The River with Two Estuaries

All of them had gone up the Danube and down some other river to return to the sea—the Atlantic, if they came down the Rhine; or the inland sea, if they chose the Rhône. It was this second route that led the ancients to believe in the existence of a river that had its source far inland on the continent and "emptied into both the Black Sea and the Mediterranean."

This was the route opted for by Jason's companions in order to circumvent the Colchian ambush in the Bosporus, taking them on a detour of whose length they could have had no idea. But once they had started, they had no choice but to continue, in a sort of forward flight.

But then they were misled by the direction of a tributary. Diodorus: "When they came to the source of the Danube, they pulled the ship out of the water and hauled it overland to a river which emptied into the ocean [not the Mediterranean]."

Long-distance portages were a common practice in those days. (At Corinth ships were hauled across the isthmus daily.) And the distance between the source of the Danube and that of the Neckar, a tributary of the Rhine, is no more than three times the width of the isthmus, nor is the terrain much more difficult.

Down the Rhine

Apollonius Rhodius (L. IV, 646): "They passed safely through large nations of Celts and Ligurians."

"To substantiate this, historians add that the Celts living on the shores of Ocean worship the Dioscuri[10] . . . and that many places along the coast of Ocean still bear the names of the Argonauts and the Dioscuri." (Diodorus.)

According to Tacitus (*De moribus Germanicorum,* 44), who follows the same version, the Narhavales, a people of Celtic origin, had dedicated a forest to Castor and Pollux.

The Argonauts Reach the Ocean

Thus it was the ocean, and not the Greek sea, that the Argonauts entered: an unexplored region, but only as far as the English Channel, for Phoenician and Cretan vessels had long been visiting the Cassiterides Islands (the Tin Isles), northwest of Great Britain.

It was a hazardous voyage, and must have seemed endless to the Argonauts. Yet the texts are explicit: "After reaching Ocean, with the land on their left, they continued sailing southward and toward the setting sun and, when they came to the straits near Gades, entered the Mediterranean." (Diodorus.)

Return to the Mediterranean

"Inside the straits of Gades, there are also clear signs of their passage. Sailing along the Tyrrhenian coast, the Argonauts came ashore on the island called Athalia [Elba]," whose port was named Argos after their ship, and is still so called to this day. "Similarly, they gave the name of Telamon to a Tyrrhenian port eight hundred stadia from Rome. Lastly, near Formiae in Italy, there is the port of Aeëtes, now called Caieta." (Diodorus.)

[10] That is, Castor and Pollux, twin sons of Zeus and Leda.

Apollodorus: "Then they met Charybdis and Scylla, the wandering rocks on which one sees quantities of flames and smoke."

These were chunks of floating pumice ejected by the erupting Liparian craters (Vulcan Island), which are still in continuous activity.

"In addition, having been driven to Syrtis by the wind, the Argonauts met Triton, then King of Africa, who taught them the special nature of that sea ["Lake" Tritonis, i.e., the Chotts], and after escaping from it, they presented him with a bronze tripod. This tripod bore an inscription in ancient writing: the Hesperides preserved it until very recently." (Diodorus.)

". . . but Thetis and the Nereids [the "peoples of the sea" mentioned in connection with Andromeda] conducted the ship safely through all these hazards, at the behest of Hera [whom they invoked], and [sailing northward] they reached Corcyra [Corfu], the Phaeacian island ruled by Alcinous." (Apollodorus.)

In Sight of Crete

"Then they came in sight of Crete, but Talos held them offshore.[11] He went around the island three times every day to guard it." "Three times a day" is another Greek idiom—still used in popular speech—meaning "incessantly" (as in, "I tell him three times a day," that is, "all the time").

"Medea killed him; some say she drove him to frenzy [from *phrenos,* mind—i.e., insane] with a potion she gave him to drink, but others say that after promising him immortality, she pulled out the bronze nail that closed the vein running from his neck to his heels," or, rather, she drove it in: the proverbs of Zenobius (*Cent.* v. 85) contain the expression "a bronze nail driven into that vein," which might be translated as a sword thrust through the jugular. Apollonius Rhodius says of the skin covering this vein that "the membrane was thin."

Apollodorus: "Others say Poeas the Argonaut killed him by

[11] Some authors equate this Talos with Tauros, the Cretan bull captured by Herakles and killed by Theseus. This is an anachronism of the same type as those mentioned elsewhere in the book; or else Talos, boasting of his strength, said that he too was a "bull" of Crete.

shooting an arrow into his heel. After spending the night there, they went to Aegina to take on water, and had a quarrel with the inhabitants. From there, they sailed between Euboea and Locris to Iolcos."

The great expedition was over, but not its repercussions for "Pelias [usurper of the throne], believing the Argonauts would never return, had resolved to kill Jason's father, Aeson, the true heir to the throne. Aeson asked permission to take his own life, offered a sacrifice, and bravely ended his days by drinking bull's blood." Blood (soured) seems to have been one of the standard poisons of antiquity.

Ovid does not say that Aeson died, and describes him as being on good terms with his daughter-in-law Medea, who rejuvenated him. But Apollodorus insists: "After cursing Pelias, Jason's mother hanged herself, leaving an infant son, Promachos, whom Pelias also killed."

He was trying to exterminate every member of the dispossessed branch of the family, when, incredibly, Jason returned, a famous hero.

"Jason came home, gave him the fleece, and bided his time, waiting for an opportunity for revenge.

"First, he went to the Isthmus of Corinth with the other leaders of the Argonauts and dedicated his ship to Poseidon, god of the sea.

"Then he asked Medea to find some means whereby he could avenge himself upon Pelias. To do this, she went into the prince's palace and commanded his daughters Asterope and Antinoë to cut him into pieces and cook him, promising to rejuvenate him with her drugs . . ."

This may be only a figure of speech: we have seen, in connection with the "boiling" and "eating" of Pelops by Tantalos, that "to cook" someone simply means to cause trouble for him, even in modern Greek.

Apollodorus, however, takes the expression literally: "To prove that it was possible, Medea performed the experiment on an old ram, which she transformed into a lamb . . ." by a trick of substitution or sleight-of-hand, no doubt, and, after drugging the two girls, an easy matter for her. "Then they did as she told them, and so killed their father."

Aeson, Jason's mother, and Promachos were now avenged, their *manes* could rest content. But in ancient Greece this form of murder was not pardoned. (Two generations later, Orestes and Electra were punished by the irate populace for killing Clytemnestra.)

"The inhabitants of Iolcos built a sepulcher for Pelias, and drove Jason and Medea out of the city. They went to Corinth and lived there for ten years in relative peace."

Theseus and the Amazons

Theseus, too, had his share of trouble when he reached home. The jealous gods would not allow him to live happily with his Amazon queen Hippolyte.

"The Amazons of the Thermodon were angry with the Athenians because their queen was being kept in slavery by Theseus. Forming an alliance with the Scythians, they mobilized a large army, which crossed the Cimmerian Bosporus, passed through Thrace, and finally reach Attica, where it camped in a place which is still called the Amazon Field.

"Informed of their approach, Theseus went to meet them with an army from the city. Hippolyte went with him; they had a son called Hippolytus." (Diodorus.)

A battle ensued, from which, by dint of their ferocity, the Athenians emerged victorious: they hacked part of the Amazons to pieces and drove the remainder out of Attica.

"Hippolyte, fighting at the side of her husband Theseus, died heroically. The Amazons who escaped from the massacre, despairing of ever reaching their homeland again, went back to Scythia and settled among the Scythians." There they were "assimilated," and we hear no more of the matriarchal tribes of the Thermodon.

A few years passed. The Athenians adored Theseus, and Aegeus was settling into a contented old age: the future of his throne was assured by his brilliant heir.

And then it was that the hero made one of those mistakes to which young leaders, their heads turned by the adulation of the crowds, are ever prone. At Eleusis, Persephone had now grown up and become a priestess in the sanctuary of Demeter. A friend of Theseus, the ex-Argonaut Pirithous, coveted her, and Theseus agreed to act as an accomplice in this abduction, which was soon to send him, in chains, to the caverns of Hades (the Greek hell).

Chapter XII
FROM THE CAUCASUS TO THE PILLARS OF HERCULES[1]

"In the Caucasus he killed the eagle of lofty peaks,
The offspring of Echidne, Typhon's eldest son."

"Then, after travelling to the ends of the earth,
His bow brought down the cowherd of Erytheia."

EURIPIDES

Death of the "Eagle"

In the meantime, Herakles had somehow made his way to the Caucasus. The texts have left historians in doubt as to the route he followed after being marooned by the Argonauts (according to Diodorus) on the coast of Asia Minor, while out searching for his pretty cabin boy Hylas.

Pherecydes, Apollodorus, and Diodorus place the death of the "eagle" at different periods in Herakles' life.[2] But its logical place is after the passage of the Argonauts: firstly, because Aeëtes was still alive when they left Colchis, and secondly, because Herakles went to the Caucasus "on foot," so the trip must certainly have taken him longer than it did them.

Pherecydes announces him at Porgos, a city of Asia Minor—after making him traverse Egypt, coastal Libya, and the "outer sea," however.

One way or another, he reached his destination, and, "on Mount Caucasus, he shot the eagle born of Typhon and Echidne, which had been eating Prometheus' liver, and set him free." (Apollodorus.)

[1] See map of the voyage of Herakles.

[2] Diodorus: immediately after the institution of the Olympic games; Apollodorus: during the tenth labor.

Once again the anachronism of Prometheus is only apparent: among Colchian sovereigns it was both a tradition and, one might say, a long-standing vocation to enslave the Achaeans and "eat their livers." All the text means is that Herakles freed the descendants of Prometheus from the successor of the first "eagle."

After the king's death, no more is ever heard of an "eagle of the Caucasus," apart from the feathered birds of prey nesting in their mountain eyries.

The Tenth Labor

By whatever road he traveled, Herakles now returned to Argolis after a prolonged absence, and the tenacious Eurystheus, eager to send him still farther away, immediately took him in hand. "For the tenth labor, he ordered him to fetch the cattle of Erytheia . . ."

This meant the hero must go to Gades, on the Atlantic coast, where the men "born of the blood of the Gorgon"—that is, Chrysaor and Pegasus' fleet—had halted during their pursuit of Perseus.

Chrysaor, the superrich Atlantid chief, had settled on the island of Erytheia and was using this forerunner of Gibraltar as a base for the fleet of Pegasus.

He had fortified the island and imposed taxes on ships carrying the tin required by bronzesmiths from the Atlantic Cassiterides to the eastern Mediterranean.

Having established an inexhaustible source of income, he proceeded to adopt the same policy in his own region that had dispersed the earlier Phorcid "monsters" to places as remote as the Caucasus; that is, he attempted to gain mastery of the entire Hispanic peninsula.

"It was rumored everywhere that Chrysaor, so-called because of his wealth, reigned over the whole of Iberia . . ." (Diodorus.)

"Delenda Erytheia"

Two generations (fifty years) had sufficed to put the loathed race of the Gorgons back on its feet, after the expedition in which Perseus thought he had decapitated it.

True, Bellerophon and Herakles had rooted them out of the east, but if Hellas were ever to colonize the Mediterranean basin of the setting sun, it must first clear the ground of its hereditary enemies there. The prerequisite to the Magna Graecia of the Sicilian and Phocaean pioneers was the extermination of their rival, Erytheia; it was as vital to the Achaeans as the destruction of Carthage was to Rome.

Now, Medusa's reanimated heart was beating in the Iberia of Chrysaor; Herakles' job was to silence it forever.

All that would remain then would be Phorcys' Scylla, glowering over the strait of Messina, and the fire-belching dragon at the foot of Mount Atlas in the country of the Graeae, the "garden of the Hesperides." He would deal with them later, and, isolated by the waxing Hellenic power, these last strongholds would also fall.

The "Sons" of Chrysaor

Half a century had passed since Perseus; Chrysaor must have been an old man. But "his companions at arms were three sons, outstanding for their strength and bravery." (Diodorus.) Or rather: one heir and two loyal vassals (as such, also his "sons"). Mythology sometimes transforms the three princes into one: Apollodorus says, "Geryon had three bodies joined into one." Hesiod writes, "three heads."

Chrysaor and his three sons, or Geryon and his three heads; in any event, there were three allied chiefs to reckon with in Erytheia, and they fought "as one man." Their names were Geryon, Eurytion (literally, man of Erytheia), and Orthrus.

Geryon was born of Chrysaor and Callirhoë, a "nymph" of Ocean—a princess, like him, of Atlantid origin—unless the term "born" is used figuratively here, to designate one of Chrysaor's colonies rather than a woman—an Ocean "sister" of the nymph Scylla, for example. In that case, Geryon would simply be a "native" of the land of Callirhoë—but it little matters; what is important, as far as history is concerned, is that he was a general.

Eurytion was Geryon's "shepherd," a term here expanded to mean "responsible for the people," as a priest leading the Lord's flock to pasture. This does not mean that "Geryon's blood-red cattle" (Diodorus) did not exist; the man actually in charge of them, however, was called Manoetes. Hellanicos says that Eurytion was the "son" of Ares (god of war) and Erytheia (his motherland). What better way to define a warrior-patriot?

As for Orthrus, "watchdog" of the sea, it was his duty to guard the coast, patrolling it with the fleet—the "wings" with which the scholiast on Hesiod embellishes his portrait.

Thus the defense of the last stronghold of Erytheia, its government entrusted by the aged Chrysaor to his regent Geryon, was in the hands of Geryon himself, assisted by a priest-strategist (Eurytion, "son" of Ares) and the faithful Orthrus ("father" of Typhon).[3]

The Sacred Cattle of Erytheia

It was from the clutches of this deadly trio that Herakles was supposed to wrest the cattle of the sanctuaries. In later days, other assailants, to complete the destruction of the Hebrews, rent the veil of the Temple; and the downfall of Rome was not certain until the legendary geese of the Capitoline had been sacrificed by the barbarians. A nation's back is broken only when its tutelary gods have been humiliated, for power comes from the gods.

There can be no other explanation for Herakles' expedition, for nobody would travel all the way from the Peloponnesus to the pillars of the setting sun just to capture a herd of common cattle, but those of Geryon were sacred to Hades; that is, to hell (Apollodorus, L. V).

Preparations for the Voyage

"Seeing that this undertaking would demand much preparation and equipment . . . Herakles fitted out a handsome fleet and raised a large body of soldiers." (Diodorus.)

Perseus, Bellerophon, and Jason never set sail without mapping out their campaign in advance; their projects were dangerous, sometimes foolhardy, but there is never any evidence in the texts to suggest that they were embarked upon without forethought. The

[3] See the "genealogy" of the monsters in Chapter I.

heroes armed and equipped themselves properly, they organized supporters and, if necessary, concluded alliances. For their raids upon the far-distant Medusa, the Echinades, and Aeëtes' Caucasus, they formed full-scale coalitions (the Trojan War was a perfect example, in the following generation).

Perseus conquering the Gorgon singlehanded, Herakles cleaning the Augean stables alone or setting off to confront Geryon by himself: these are fairy-tale illustrations resulting from a schematization of the texts—witness the following: "Herakles assembled his troops on the island of Crete, which is advantageously placed as a base from which to launch an army in any direction. The Cretans received him with great pomp and ceremony." (Diodorus.)

After all, he had rid them of their "bull," but in the meanwhile the bull must have had many imitators, for, to thank the islanders for their hospitality, "Herakles cleared their country of all its savage beasts, and since that day there have been no bears, wolves or snakes on the island."

Herakles, General

Diodorus might as well have added "or lions, foxes, and dragons" to his list, for there are both wild quadrupeds and reptiles on Crete today.

These operations were dictated by imperatives very different from those of common courtesy. Herakles was welding his heterogeneous troops into a cohesive body of men, training his companions for the coming campaign: he was "breaking in" his army, as modern generals do today with their local skirmishes, like rehearsals for the universal conflagration.[4]

Herakles, Politician

Ridding Crete of its undesirables was also a means of earning assistance, in the form of more Minoan ships, if necessary, to swell the ranks of his expeditionary force.

Lastly, "the hero announced his determination to render illustrious

[4] The Spanish Civil War served this purpose for Hitler, Stalin, and Mussolini; since then we have had Korea, Indochina, Vietnam.

the land in which his father Zeus had been born and reared." That is, the master politician simultaneously disguised the utilitarian aspect of his pacification campaign, and jogged the public memory with this allusion to his divine ancestry, source of his prestige and popularity. (The founding of Herakleion in Crete is said to date from this occasion.) The process is very much akin to that propounded by Machiavelli in his lessons to the prince: to the great general and the empire builder, a third image is now added, that of the wily statesman.

The Army Sets Sail

Their preparations completed, Herakles and his comrades at arms set out, and, "leaving the island, anchored first in Libya." (The direct north-south route is practicable during only three months of the year, when the persistent puffing of Boreas drives any sails in its path in the direction of Africa.)

Thus Herakles reached the land of the giant Antaeus,[5] "who, notorious for his strength and skill at wrestling, killed every stranger he succeeded in throwing to the ground." Both Herakles and Jason had already encountered this custom at other times during their careers.

"Herakles challenged Antaeus." In the Bronze Age, as in the Middle Ages, the fate of armies was sometimes decided by a wrestling match between two champions (the "judgment of God" replacing the costly hazards of the battlefield). "Antaeus was killed in hand-to-hand combat with Herakles."

Here, as everywhere else he went, the conqueror, having become master of the situation, "proceeded to clear Libya of a great many wild animals infesting it." After expulsing the caravan robbers, he suddenly recalled his bucolic youth in Elis and "put much desert land under cultivation, so that it was soon covered with fruit trees and vineyards, producing olives and other crops."

[5] According to some traditions, Antaeus was the founder of Tangier, around 1400 B.C. If so, it would have to be conceded that Herakles did not meet him until after his visit to Egypt—not, as Apollodorus claims, before. The "Caves of Hercules," containing a collection of bones of very tall warriors and pygmies slain in battle, are located not far from Tangier.

Emulating Athena and Dionysos, and destined like them for deification, the warrior now assumed the role of benefactor of the nation he had just conquered.

Herakles in Egypt

However, our tireless knight-errant soon resumed his journey toward the troubled horizon: "After killing Antaeus, he went to Egypt and slew King Busiris, who used to slaughter every stranger who entered the country"—Pharaoh's hatred of the "people from the sea" was as keen as ever. Once again, Herakles' blood lust was succeeded by more constructive impulses. "Finding the land fertile and well watered, he founded a city of immense size and named it Hecatompylos."

On this occasion, Diodorus would seem to be guilty of exaggeration, confusion, and anachronism all at once. For although Herakles did found a city in the Nile Delta (Heracleum, whose ruins may be seen today), Hecatompylos[6] inevitably evokes "Thebes of the Hundred Gates," the capital of ancient Egypt which existed long before him. What can be the cause of such a misconstruction? It is simply that in antiquity legend attributed the greatest cities to the greatest hero, just as the highest mountain was coupled with the greatest god (Olympus and Zeus); there can be no other explanation.

Also, "the Carthaginians [writes Diodorus] sent out a large force, led by excellent chiefs, who attacked and overran this metropolis." But the imperialist city of Carthage did not yet exist (only its embryo, the Phoenician fortress from which it subsequently developed). And the people who conquered Thebes during the lifetime (approximately) of Herakles were the Hyksos, a pastoral tribe that had come to Egypt by way of Phoenicia—Phoenicia, which gave the impetus to the forthcoming rise of Carthage. Hence Diodorus' mistake; writing a thousand years a posteriori, he attributes to the city that had grown mighty in his day a war it could not have waged when Herakles was alive.

[6] *Hecaton*—hundred; *pyle*—gate.

The "Golden Goblet" of Tartessus

Herakles did not linger to supervise the expansion of Heracleum. Turning westward to meet his designated foe, "he crossed Libya and reached the ocean at Gades." (Diodorus.)

Did he go overland, by the thousand-year-old trail described by Herodotus as being "marked by fresh-water wells at every ten days' march?" Or was his fleet still with him?

Diodorus writes: "Arriving in Iberia with his fleet . . ." But, according to Apollodorus, these were not the ships he had embarked with: "He borrowed a fleet in the land of Tartessus." Now, Tartessus was a powerful city with colonies on either side of the strait. Grown wealthy from the produce of her tin mines, she also had a fleet of ships to transport her ore, and Herakles, wanting to borrow them, resorted to a method first employed by Perseus: armed threat. "The sun [object of the Tartessians' worship][7] having incommoded him on his voyage, he drew his bow and aimed an arrow at the god." (Apollodorus.)

The clergy inclined, as the text euphemistically implies: "Admiring his courage, the god gave him a golden goblet, in which he crossed the ocean. Upon reaching Erytheia, he spent the night on Mount Abas."

Diodorus: "Arriving in Iberia with his fleet, he met the sons of Chrysaor . . . The dog, having scented him, came running . . ."

The Battle at the Pillars of Hercules

Orthrus, unfortunately for him, was on guard. "Herakles killed Orthrus with his club, as well as the shepherd Eurytion, who had come to help him. Manoetes, who was tending the cattle of Hades nearby [sacred to Hades, that is], gave the alarm to Geryon, who met Herakles near the river Anthemon just as the hero was making off with the herd, challenged him to battle and was killed by his arrows."

Diodorus-the-realist sums up the battle that sealed Erytheia's fate

[7] Being "barbarians," they prayed to the star itself, rather than to Apollo in his chariot.

in the following words (Book V): "The [three] sons of Chrysaor commanded three armies. Herakles killed them in single combat, subdued Iberia, and took the famous herd of cattle away with him."

Then he planted the twin columns at Calpe and Abyle, to commemorate the Greeks' latest triumph over their Atlantid enemy; for centuries (and to this day), they remained the symbol of the strait.

The Enigma of the Fleet

At this point we confront the most tantalizing mystery of the hero's entire career: spurning the sea, he sets off home on foot, by the absurdly long route along the coasts of Spain, Celtica, and Liguria.

The Greeks were not unaware of the staggering trek ahead of them. They knew, at least roughly, how to calculate the length of the overland journey corresponding to the weeks of sea travel from the Peloponnesus to the edge of the ocean; and the Argonauts' trip up the Danube and down the Rhine gave them another means of estimating the breadth of the continent. If he had lost his own fleet and were unable to borrow someone else's, Herakles, who had demonstrated his abilities as a tactician on so many occasions in the past, ought to have built a new fleet, rather than affronting such an ordeal. Why did he give the "goblet" back to the Tartessians? And, for that matter, what had happened to his first, Cretan fleet? It may have been the very circumstances of its disappearance that caused the veteran Argonaut to prefer a long march to the uncertainties of the sea; but whatever his motive, it must have been a powerful one. The texts, truncated and lost (especially the twenty-five books of Diodorus), can no longer give us the answer.

The hypothesis most nearly borne out by the facts, however, is a tectonic upheaval, rendering the Mediterranean temporarily unsafe for sea travel.

The Tectonic Theory

In the twentieth century, seismic activity has been relatively attenuated: as the earth cools, its Plutonian heart is beginning to mellow. The solid crust enfolding its core of magma is thickening, and it is becoming increasingly difficult for lava to force a passage through to the surface.

The earliest convulsion recorded by human memory was the sinking of Plato's Atlantis, when the core, two thousand years younger, burst forth in an eruption that far surpassed all its subsequent efforts.

However, geologists are now agreed that there was a second series of major earthquakes in the Mediterranean and Atlantic in the sixteenth and thirteenth centuries B.C., whose over-all effects were almost as great as those of the first.

In addition, most of the Hellenic "myths" grew out of the seismic activity of a given period, e.g., Deucalion's "deluge" (earthquake and tidal wave), the explosion of Thera, the Symplegades, which collided as the Argonauts wriggled past, the floating pumice they saw off the Liparis, and the volcanic phenomena shortly to be witnessed by Herakles (rain of stones in the Crau, destruction of the port of Monaco, eruption of Vesuvius) in the generation preceding the "man-eating whirlpools" of Scylla with which Ulysses had to contend.

This list points to a period of intense volcanic activity along the crack in the earth's crust that runs across the Mediterranean and out to the Azores, which we may suppose to have been permanently abandoned at this point by the Phorcid descendants of Stheno, Euryale, and Medusa, anxious to avoid a repetition of the first Atlantic disaster.

The sea must have been in a dreadful state; with their rudimentary steering apparatus (an oar), the undecked Greek ships, propelled by oars or fixed single sails, could not dream of venturing out into such chaos.

Herakles in Celtica

Therefore, writes Apollodorus, "Herakles went to the country of Abdera [a town near Cádiz, according to Strabo, L. III]. Continuing up the Iberian coast, he came to Celtica."

This is confirmed by Diodorus, who adds: "He led his army

through the country, abolishing all the barbarian customs he found, including that of killing foreigners."

The daughter of one of the local kings had a son by him, Galatus, who gave his name to the Galatians (Diodorus, L. V).

The next trace of the passage of the Heraclids is found in the Rhône Delta, where, according to Apollodorus (who calls the region Liguria), "Alebion and Dercynos, sons of Poseidon, tried to steal the cattle away from Herakles."

Pomponius Mela (L. II, c 5), who calls the two chieftains Albion and Bergius, says they had armed the entire local population. The hero fought at great length and killed many men with his arrows, but at last his supply ran out and he was about to succumb when Zeus, whom he was earnestly invoking, caused a shower of stones to rain down upon his adversaries (still visible, in the Crau).

The Founding of Alesia

Herakles then explored the Rhône, as a possible branch of the "river with two estuaries" which the Argonauts had been looking for, and hence a shorter route to the east.

At the level of Lugdunum (Lyons), the Rhône Valley does veer to the right, but it soon enters the daunting landscape of the Alps and ceases to be navigable. The hero then tried the Saône, in search of a more propitious route; upon reaching the edge of the Langres plateau, he founded a settlement on a hummock that could be easily defended and would also provide a base for further explorations.

The place had been inhabited since neolithic times. Conveyors of quarried stone had made a fortified caravansary of it, an important halting place on their voyage from the flint quarries of the southwest to their large clientele in the plains of northeastern Gaul.

The mound is now some distance away from the main road, but tourists often make a detour on their way through the Côte-d'Or Department: by virtue of its rolling, wooded landscape and its history, the site is very romantic to the French, who feel that they are standing on the well springs of their own history, at Alise-Sainte-Reine.

"As Herakles' army was composed of voluntary soldiers hailing from every region, he founded a city which he called Alesia because of the distances his men had traveled [*ale,* in Greek, means a ceaseless wandering]. A great number of the local inhabitants were drawn to the place, and since they were more numerous than the others [the Greeks], the whole population gradually adopted the barbarians' way of life." (Diodorus.)

He goes on: "To this day the town is honored by the Celts, who regard it as the birthplace and heart of all Celtica. It remained free and impregnable from the time of Herakles until the present, but now Caius Caesar has attacked and subdued it . . ."

Herakles, founder of the future city of Vercingetorix.

In Cisalpine Gaul: Monaco

The Saône, however, flowed northward and proved equally unsuitable for his purpose, so Herakles abandoned the entire venture and, falling back upon the traditional route, crossed into Cisalpine Gaul.

He camped for a while on the rock of Monaco, a natural fortress used by pirates from time immemorial (conveniently borne out by the present-day castle of the Grimaldis), and the settlement spawned by the Heraclids retained its name of Hercules Monaeci Portus until the Roman Empire.

As though to engrave the hero's passage more deeply upon the minds of Provençal generations to come, the earth quaked while he was there, and, according to the legend, there was a landslide, after which the port of Monaco had assumed the shape of Herakles' foot, "the coast having crumbled beneath his step."[8]

Livorno, and on to Rome

One is not tempted to linger at the site of an earthquake. Pursuing their eastward journey, the hero and his men founded another coastal town: Livorno (Hercules Liburni Portus, in Roman times) and left another clue. "Then, from Liguria, Herakles went to the banks of the Tiber and camped on the very place where Rome stands today."

[8] The modern port installations have so altered the outline of the coast as to make verification impossible.

On the Palatine Hill, another natural stronghold then occupied by the Etruscans, "stood Rome, which was not founded as a city until several generations later, by Romulus, son of Mars [a soldier]." (Diodorus.)

The author's allegations are again borne out by our knowledge of the period when the Urbs crowned its first hill (thirteenth–tenth centuries). "A few natives lived on the Palatine Hill then, in a tiny settlement. Cacos and Pinarios, their foremost representatives, gave Herakles a solemn welcome and honored him with gifts."

Authors are not unanimous on this point, and Diodorus may be suspected of trying to show the thirteenth-century Latins in a flattering light that was not in keeping with the truth. Dionysos of Halikarnassos (L. I, c. 39), Virgil (*Aeneid,* L. VIII, v. 190 and ff.), and Ovid (*Fasti,* L. I, v 545 and ff.) say the hero killed Cacos, a "son" of Vulcan who had stolen some of his cattle, in Latium. And *kakos* means "bad" in Greek.

This victim was less offensive, however, than the tribes of colossi with whom Herakles' companions next had to contend on their southward journey.

The Phlegraean Plain

"After leaving the banks of the Tiber, Herakles came to the country of Cumae [near Naples], said to be the home of some very strong and evil men called giants . . . According to the mythologists, these were sons of the Earth," which is what farmers still like to call themselves.

"Hearing that Herakles had come, they all assembled and marched toward him in battle formation."

This encounter took place on the Phlegraean Plain (*phlegomai*—I burn), "so called because of a mountain that belched great quantities of flames . . . This place is now called Vesuvius, and many traces of the conflagration are still visible." (Diodorus.)

The Eruption of Vesuvius

This reference to an eruption is most enlightening. In ancient times the volcano was called Mount Somma (altitude 2300 meters) and had a single cone. An enormous explosion decapitated it, and another crater formed much lower.[9] That was the last eruption until the one that buried Pompeii and Herculaneum in A.D. 79 (between the two dates, a long slumber). Thus Diodorus, writing during the period of inactivity in the first century B.C., would appear to be referring to this "ancient" eruption when he speaks of the "mountain belching flames." But in that case, the explosion of Vesuvius coincides with the passage of Herakles; for, according to the "mythologists," "the hero crushed the Giants beneath the burning rock." Thus, by their appearance in the Heraclean "legend," these flames (the last emitted by the volcano before the time of Christ) help geologists to date the eruption that changed the aspect of the Neapolitan mountain—it must have taken place in the thirteenth century B.C., if Herakles was present.

The Battle with the Giants

A battle during an earthquake: "The struggle was fierce. At last, with the help of the gods, the hero emerged victorious." (Diodorus.)

Subsequent armies have invoked the gods no less earnestly: the crusaders' *Dieu le veult,* the appeal to the prophet of Allah by the knights of the Hegira, the Teutonic *Gott mit uns,* and the Te Deums sung on either side, are similar exhortations to the divinity to exterminate the infidel, whoever he may be.[10] The Giants did not worship Olympus, and were accordingly pagans in the eyes of the Greeks, so Herakles invoked Zeus and immediately became known as the "ally" of the "true" gods.

They heard his prayer: "The hero killed most of the Giants." The Giants—strange rock shapes rising up along the old Domitian Way near Cumae, in a landscape both desolate and serenely beautiful—"petrified" by Herakles. The local people, knowing only too well how eruptions will "fossilize" any victim they catch un-

[9] There have been sixteen major eruptions since the one that destroyed Pompeii, and in 1906 the phenomenon of the thirteenth century B.C. was repeated on a smaller scale, with the altitude of the volcano dropping from 1336 to 1277 meters.

[10] Even when a war is not specifically religious, the enemy is still anyone who challenges our faith in the destiny of our nation, in whose name wars are declared.

aware, have metamorphosed the anthropomorphic rocks into the "tall men" slain long ago by the Greeks.

Herculaneum

"Having pacified the region," Herakles and his company camped on the edge of the Phlegraean fields, to bury their dead, nurse their wounded, and repair their battle-damaged weapons.

Strabo says that in those days the region was ruled by Italic Pelasgians, a group of tribes of which the Giants were presumably members.[11]

As with their earlier settlements at Alesia and Monaco, the Greek encampment also attracted the neighboring people and led to the establishment of a permanent center. This was Herculaneum. In the first century B.C., Cicero referred to it as one of the most important towns in Campania. Here the eruption of A.D. 79 took the form of a downpour of scalding mud: the material ejected by Vesuvius, diluted by torrential rains (the traditional aftermath of a major eruption), poured into the town and flooded the streets. Then the magma hardened to rocklike consistency. Excavations have revealed the remains of a Roman town with a population of five thousand in which shipowners and tavernkeepers did business alongside marble craftsmen and skilled mosaic artists. The gulf provided sustenance for these simple folk: lures, ropes, and nets have been found, very similar to those used by the fishermen of Ercolano today.

From house to ruined house, the intimate details of everyday existence spring to life: a cupboard that was the tabernacle of the household lares and penates, a little chest where the lady of the house kept her jewelry, the breadbox, still filled with shrunken loaves . . . Sometimes, in their scratchings among the ruins, the teams of workmen turn up the sign of the first-century Christians—the fish, Ichthys (in Greek, the initials of Jesus Christ the Lord Our Savior).

In a villa set high on a promontory, a bronze Hermes has been

[11] The same author says it had previously been occupied by Oscians and Tyrrhenians.

unearthed, probably an effigy of the owner (who was, thus, a merchant).

Herculaneum had its hot baths, palaestra and theater, but they were humble indeed, in comparison with those of Pompeii; this was a port, where men crowded together to work, not a holiday resort for the rich and powerful.

Lake Avernus

The Heraclids remained here some time, for "the hero carried out various projects at Lake Avernus, which used to empty into the sea. They say he dammed up the outlet and built a road along the shore, which is still called the Heracleian road today." (Diodorus.)

This son of Zeus, already a great builder of dikes and dams, was continuing to strew his path with works capable in themselves of rendering him immortal.

Lake Avernus lies in a large oval crater at the foot of a precipitous bluff. Its muddy water reflects the overhanging summits like a mirror that has been faintly tarnished by some sulfurous exhalation. In ancient times the volcanic vapors drove birds away from the area, and the texts recount how Ulysses sacrificed to the forces of the Underworld in a nearby cave of forbidding aspect. Perhaps this was the seat of the oracle. There is no dearth of caves in the vicinity, but the earth's convulsions, in the course of it repeated volcanic upheavals, have buried every trace of the work of Herakles, and, failing some unpredictable and fortuitous stroke of the pick, buried they will remain.

All that has endured is the memory of the hero, who, after seeing that his companions had enjoyed their well-earned rest, resumed his interminable march to the south.

From Scylla to Charybdis

"He entered the land of the Poseidonites [a maritime colony] . . . At the narrowest point of the strait, between Reggio and Locris, he drove his herd of cattle across into Sicily."

Apollodorus: "He leaped into the sea and swam across." Diodorus: "Seizing a bull by the horns, he crossed the strait—a distance, according to Timaeus, of thirteen stadia [2400 meters]." Neither narrative makes any mention of the man-eating whirlpools, so they must have been temporarily at rest.

Pausanias reports that "Herakles crossed in the goblet given to him by the sun." Does this mean the hero was still receiving occasional aid from the Tartessian fleet (which other authors maintain was returned to the Iberians immediately after the victory over Geryon)? Swimming a herd of cattle across the strait would seem a hazardous undertaking, to say the least, even in a calm sea. One way or another, however, the channel was negotiated.

Eryx the Phorcid

"Herakles then came to the land of Eryx, son of Poseidon, in Sicily." (Apollodorus.) This was the territory of the Phorcid nymph, guardian of the strait and "daughter" of Poseidon herself, by virtue of her fleet (the one Perseus had previously borrowed).

More fighting ensued. "Scylla stole some of Herakles' oxen" (*Homerii scholii, Odyssey,* XII; Lycophron, v. 45, and scholiast).

Apollodorus writes: "Eryx, son of Poseidon and king of the Elymans, hid a bull which had escaped from Herakles in his own herd. After placing his cattle in the care of Hephaestos [god of Underworld fires, an indication that the Heraclids were approaching the slopes of Mount Etna], Herakles set out in search of the stray. He found him in Eryx's herd and demanded his return, but Eryx said he would give the animal back only if Herakles could beat him in a fight."

Diodorus also relates that the hero "was challenged by Eryx; Herakles offered his cattle as the prize, in exchange for the kingdom of Eryx." Another duel employing the principle of the "judgment of God."

"At first, Eryx was very angry, claiming that his kingdom was worth far more than Herakles' cows. But when Herakles pointed out that if he lost the sacred cattle [stolen from Geryon], he would also lose his immortality [because of the terms of the Delphis edict], Eryx accepted his conditions for the fight."

Apollodorus: "After throwing him to the ground three times, Herakles killed him."

Another version: "Having been vanquished, Eryx lost his kingdom. Herakles gave it to the inhabitants and told them to exploit it on their own account until a descendant of his should come to claim it. This happened when Doriaeus the Lacedaemonian came to Sicily several generations later, took possession of the land, and founded the city of Heraclea."[12] (Diodorus.)

Death and Rebirth of the Nymph Scylla

The scholia on Homer (*Odyssey,* XII) and Lycophron have the following to say on the subject of the hero's victory over Eryx: "Herakles pursued Scylla and killed her . . . But she was brought back to life by Phorcys, her father."

The Phorcids, but not the Corsican king himself (for Phorcys founded his dynasty long before the time of Herakles), could not abandon a position as strategically important as the Sicilian strait. The moment the Greeks' backs were turned, they rebuilt their stronghold at Scylla.

End of the Corsican Phorcids

This was their last display of strength. Recent research by the French Centre National de la Recherche Scientifique indictates that a great earthquake took place in Corsica "around the fourteenth or thirteenth century." Part of the eastern coast, between Bastia and Bonifacio, slid into the waves, while the west coast rose farther out of the water. At the same time, the agricultural Bronze Age culture of Sardinia—the nuraghe, those curious megalithic towers that have long puzzled the experts—also disappeared. This double disaster coincides approximately with the eruption that "decapitated" Vesuvius, giving added weight to the hypothesis of a period of intense and widespread tectonic activity in the western half of the Mediterranean.

Having established this, the geologists are still unable to provide more than a very approximate date for the annihilation of the Corsican Phorcids. The texts, however, do at least place a lower

[12] Doriaeus, son of Anaxandrides, who, according to Pausanias (L. III) tried to found a settlement in Sicily.

limit upon the catastrophe. If "Phorcys" was able to "resurrect" Scylla, then he had not yet been stricken by the earthquake. The Earthshaker did not, therefore, smite the Island of Beauty until after Herakles had gone to Sicily (around 1320, according to the Paros marble).

News from Greece: the Abduction of Persephone

"In the meanwhile, the hero continued his tour . . . and came to the city today known as Syracuse. There he learned of the abduction of Persephone." (Diodorus.)

The young priestess of Demeter had let herself be seduced by the Argonaut Pirithous, Theseus' boon companion. This profanation of the Eleusinian sanctuary had grave repercussions; it was sacrilege, aggravated by abduction. The two chief culprits were judged by the Sages and sentenced to life imprisonment in the caverns of Hades.

Popular as he was, even Theseus could elude the priests. He had helped Pirithous to kidnap the virgin sacred to Demeter, and so, condemned as his accomplice, he too set out for Cape Taenarum, site of the grotto of Cerberus and home of the "living dead."

Hoping to appease the wrath of Olympus incurred by his three friends, "Herakles offered . . . feasts and solemn sacrifices . . . and taught the inhabitants to repeat them every year in honor of Demeter." (Diodorus.)

Of "Nymphs" and "Sirens"

Syracuse was already acquainted with the Greeks; the island of Ortygia, parent colony of the city, had been the home of the nymph Arethusa, who had originated in the region of the Alpheus (Augeias' kingdom).

"Pursued by the god of that river," she had "thrown herself into the sea," crossed it, and settled in Sicily, where she was "transformed into a spring." Her persecutor, the god Alpheus, "who persisted in his love for her," caught up with her this time and proceeded to transform himself into a spring too, the better to press his suit.

This legend can be deciphered readily enough. In antiquity, every district claimed its own "patron saint," a pagan custom, like so many others, that has been perpetuated by Christianity.

These deities often lived in rivers, springs, or grottoes (as at Lourdes). The "sirens," for instance, were coastal gorges, where the water fell directly from the rocks into the sea, and so they are pictured as "half fish"—especially as sailors often visit them (who are also fishlike, in their dependence upon the same element).

And unless they have an enterprising and resourceful captain like Ulysses, a crew may easily be "led astray" (i.e., off course) by their "seductive singing" (the murmur of springs), for nothing captures the imagination of the parched seaman like the thought of a welling spring—unless, perhaps, it is the thought of a woman (the siren's other half). The Greeks, a seafaring people par excellence, always say that a young girl "is like cool water" and that a flirt "is playing the siren," still associating the two, as did their Heraclid and Odyssean ancestors.

Then there are the "nymphs," the fresh-water springs encountered fairly commonly near beaches (e.g., Scylla) and estuaries. Such was the legendary nymph of Syracuse. She had "originated in the Peloponnesus"; that is, one fine day in the fourteenth or thirteenth century (if the latter, at the very beginning), the tribe that worshiped the nymph Arethusa emigrated, fleeing a voracious tyrant who was exploiting the valley of the Alpheus downstream of Olympia. Propelled by sail or oar, the emigrants crossed the sea to the eastern shore of Sicily and settled on the island of Ortygia, near a spring which they baptized Arethusa, after their patron saint. The ships flying the colors of "the god Alpheus," launched in hot pursuit of the "faithless nymph," came ashore near the second spring, and so the god changed himself "into a spring." The inhabitants of modern Syracuse still take water from this stream, which they call "Occhio della Zillica."

Such was the hellenic ancestry of the Sicilian city, which explains why the natives had heard of Demeter; moreover, in order for news of Eleusis to reach the port, it must have maintained contracts with Greece, which was only natural, after all.

The "Nymph" Cyane

The Arethusa flows through the Città Vecchia, along the western quay just south of the headquarters of the port authorities. As early as the thirteenth century B.C. it was bordered by houses in which the Peloponnesian colonists preserved the traditions they had brought from their homeland (monochromatic ceramics and Mycenaean vases, preserved in the museum), but it was not a propitious place for the solemn rites required for the appeasement of Demeter, so Herakles selected another "nymph," the nearby Cyane.

"Near Cyane the hero sacrificed one of his finest bulls." (Diodorus.) The site is some four miles inland from Syracuse (along the Canicattini road); its aspect is utterly forsaken and quite disconcerting, for it evokes a landscape of the Upper Nile in the blast of the Sicilian sun. The silence that weighs upon the fish-filled water, bordered by a dense hedge of papyrus, is broken only by the steady drone of cicadas. Their strident call covers the silken murmur of the spring—or is it the lament of the nymph Cyane, who, "because she tried to prevent Poseidon from kidnaping Persephone, was changed into a spring by the angry god"?

Poseidon or Pirithous? An Argonaut was a sailor by definition and, as such, Poseidon was his god. Later generations have blamed the abduction upon the deity, since his "son" Pirithous could never have made off with the girl against the will of his own patron saint.

The Fate of Syracuse

It was only natural that the annual ceremonies that Herakles had dedicated to the goddess of the harvest should be supplemented by a market where the produce of the fertile uplands was sold. Arethusa's city prospered until it became the rival of Athens and, ultimately, of Carthage; it was able to resist both these sea powers at their zenith, and even to defeat them. In the fourth century B.C., under the tyrant Denys, it possessed a vast kingdom covering almost the whole of Sicily. Syracuse was a merchant city, but it was also an intellectual and artistic center; it built a theater with a capacity of fifteen thousand spectators, whose imposing ruins, leaning against the coastal cliffs, look out to the sea and the island of Ortygia.

Internal dissension alone could have undermined so great a power, and the hordes of expanding Rome took advantage of this process to destroy it; even then the city was besieged for two years before it fell (214–212 B.C.).

The Tomb of Archimedes

Archimedes (born in 287 B.C.) contributed to the defense of his native town by inventing the principle of the solar oven—mirrors which "concentrated the rays of Apollo" on Marcellus' ships and set them blazing like torches. When the soldiers finally entered the town, they found the sage pondering the solution to a problem in his bath. By some accounts, he was so engrossed in his thoughts that he did not respond to their commands; others say he requested permission to finish his calculation before having his throat cut. In any event, he was assassinated by an ignorant legionnaire in defiance of Marcellus' express orders—military leaders are always anxious to spare a brain that is capable of devising new instruments of warfare for them (whether burning mirrors or nuclear warheads), and the Roman general was concerned to save the life of the old genius. His tomb, near the theater, evokes at once the summits to which man's mind can attain, and the barbaric stupidity in which he wallows when it is a sword he is brandishing at the end of his fist, instead of a pen.

Herakles Conquers Sicily

"[Herakles] led his herd inland, and the Sicanians came to meet him with a considerable force of men, but he beat them off in a famous battle. He killed a great many of the foe, including Leucaspis ["man with the white shield"], Pediacrates, Brephonas, Gaugatas, Cygeos, and Critidas, all renowned chieftains to whom heroes' honors are still accorded today . . . Herakles next came to the territory of Agrigentum . . . where the inhabitants received him with many tokens of respect . . . In gratitude to those who had honored him so deeply, Herakles dug a lake in front of their city, with a circumference of four stadia (750 meters), and gave his name to it . . . He dedicated a shrine to the hero Geryon, who is still revered by the natives." (Diodorus.)

By honoring a vanquished enemy, you magnify your own courage.

"He dedicated another sanctuary to Iolas, his nephew and comrade at arms [his lieutenant, Iolas, who had never left his side since the slaying of the hydra], and inaugurated annual sacrifices in his honor which are still celebrated there."

Diodorus is continually referring to the survival of Heraclid institutions as customs which were "current" in his day, and thus, in some measure, vouching for them.

Akragas

The temples of the Sicilian's homeland are as tangible a record of his favorite hero as are his writings. Supported by the bare mountains of the southern coast, the ancient Akragas (or *akra-ge,* the "high-perched land") rises up in the center of a plain, twisted by cliffs and gullies into a landscape as tormented as its history. It surveys the horizon: the sea, from which so many civilizations have emerged and clambered up to live, one on top of the other, inside its walls.

The San Biagio church, for example, stands among the ancient monuments of Agrigento on the site of a temple of Demeter built in the fifth century B.C., its pagan foundations showing through the base of the Norman edifice.

The Mysteries of Agrigentum

The goddess of the harvest was extremely popular. A steep flight of stairs carved into the cliff face leads to a second shrine—also dedicated to Demeter—established in the seventh century B.C.; no one has yet penetrated its secret. First, there is a complex series of basins hollowed out of the tufa, then two deep grottoes, followed by corridors boring more than twenty-five meters back into the hill. What was their purpose? These shadowy precincts were presumably reserved for the initiates of some mysterious ritual similar to that of Eleusis. The priests had thought of everything, even the evacuation of waste water: a third tunnel contains terra cotta conduits similar to those used for the same purpose by modern Sicilians.

Farther along stands the wonderful sanctuary of Concord—architecturally so simple, and yet so commanding that one might mistake it for the Thesion of Athens. But this building dates from the fifth century B.C. and its inscription is in Latin:

Concordiae Agrigentorum sacrum Respublica.[13]

A few hundred yards away on the ridge, the temple of Hera-Juno is outlined against the cloudless sky, dominating another shrine believed to be dedicated to the Dioscuri (Castor and Pollux), who were companions of Theseus, Jason, and Herakles. Perhaps, however, this is still another altar to Demeter, for it is near the place chosen by the hero for his sacrifice to the great goddess.

The Temple of Zeus

The unchallenged ruler of all this was Zeus; in the fifth century B.C., at the height of their glory, his congregation of Akragas built one of the most grandiose sanctuaries of all antiquity in his honor.

The temple was far larger than any in Greece: 113 meters long, more than 56 wide. Visitors from all over the Hellenic world came to admire it. The entablature rested on a colonnade augmented by thirty-five gigantic statues. One of them, now recumbent, still welcomes the tourist; is it Atlas, Herakles himself, or one of the Giants he fought on the Phlegraean fields, when the gods of Olympus did battle by his side and gave the victory to him?

An earthquake has toppled everything else, but the column shafts remain; their fluting is wide and deep enough for a man to sink into them as into the hollow of his bed.

Herakles, Demigod of Sicily

Across from this mightiest temple of Magna Graecia, eight columns have been re-erected, as though to remind modern generations who was the first being, after his father Zeus, to set the seal of immortality on Agrigentum. At the same time, however, he was receiving it himself, for "his veneration by the Akragans

[13] In the museum; St. Gregory converted the temple into a Christian church in the fifth century A.D.

was the first he ever accepted, as a sign from the deity that the Delphic oracle would be fulfilled." (Diodorus.) The Pythoness had said, it will be remembered, that at the end of his labors, he would take his place on Olympus.

Perhaps his fabulous achievements had turned his head at last: the Caesars, too, "consented" to their deification during their lifetime, and temples for the worship of their persons were accordingly built (and subsequently rededicated to the Christian God).

The temple of Herakles at Agrigentum was built in 520 or 521 B.C. and is commensurate with the gratitude of the people. Six rows of fifteen columns each encircled the cella, where the faithful came to worship the bronze statue so highly vaunted by Cicero.

Demigod though he was, the murderer of Megara's children was still a slave. He had to return to Argolis and serve the remainder of his sentence; only then could he be a prince again, free to carve out his own kingdom somewhere in the wide world that was resounding with his exploits.

Up the Italian Boot

"Herakles and his cows went back into Italy." The author calls the continent by this name because "Italus was the Tyrrhenian word for bull"—the bull that had caused the destruction of Scylla and the death of Eryx?

Apollodorus: "[Herakles] having recaptured his bull, led it with the rest toward the Ionian Sea." Pausanias says (L. VII) he also took along the dead king's daughter, Psophis, by whom he later had two children in Greece.

"He continued up the coast, vanquished Lacinios, who tried to steal his cows . . . and accidentally killed Croton, whom he then buried with every honor. He erected a tomb for him and founded Crotona."

Huddled into a bay exposed to the Adriatic gales and dominated by the summits of the Calabrian ridge, the city still gazes out toward its Greek fatherland. Its inhabitants, exhausted by the blazing sun, sip cool drinks and appear to dream—of the desert drought of modern Mezzogiorno? Or of the exploits of their compatriot, the athlete Milon (sixth century B.C.)? Or of Pythagoras, who loved the place and spent years there, formulating the precepts that were to revolutionize his age?

Or are they imploring Herakles to come back and shake them from their age-old lethargy? But the hero has gone forever, along with the spirit that generated the great Hellenic achievements.

After performing the proper rites at the tomb of Croton, "and making the journey around the Adriatic coast on foot, he entered Epirus by way of the gulf." (Diodorus.)

The "Gadfly" of Epirus

As he was passing through the famous "gap" of Dodona in that region of northern Greece, "a gadfly sent by Hera stung his herd, which stampeded into the mountains." (Apollodorus.)

Was this an ambush laid by Eurystheus and the Argive Heraeum, warned that Herakles was on his way back with Geryon's sacred cattle, in an attempt to do him out of his latest labor?

The jealous Hera had spies in her husband's rival sanctuary at Dodona. Nor was this the first parasite Herakles had had to contend with. He had killed another—the hydra's lieutenant—back at the beginning of his career. And what better image for a cattle thief than a gadfly?

The outlaw of Epirus seems to have fared better than the crab of Lerna, however, and escaped the hero's avenging fist; Herakles was weary, and merely set about retrieving his livestock—an undertaking that led him far afield.

"He went in pursuit of his cattle; some he found near the Hellespont, but the others stayed behind [in the mountains] and became wild again. Having at last rounded up all he could find," he next had to cross the Thracian Strymon, which flows into the Aegean.

Crossing the Strymon

"[The god of] this river—which was then navigable—impeded his progress, so he filled up its bed with stones and made it impracticable." (Diodorus.) In fact, it was the seismic convulsions of the thirteenth century, coinciding with Herakles' presence in the region, that altered the course of the Strymon, and his name has remained linked with it, as with the landslide in Monaco and the Phlegraean eruption.

He did, however, build a dam across the Strymon, as he had done at Orchomenos and Lake Avernus. There were two imperative reasons for this: he had to provide a crossing for his cattle, and he also had to humiliate the "god" of the river (a "brother," one might say, of the "god" Alpheus, the "god" Achelous, or any other patron of a Hellenic river).

Under pain of losing prestige with his companions, Herakles, promoted to the rank of demigod during his stay in Sicily, could not allow a minor divinity to defy him, implying that some mere nymph might be more powerful than he. She must be punished. The custom survived for centuries: nearly a thousand years later, a Persian satrap ordered the insolent water of the Hellespont to be scourged with chains, for rebelling against the boats carrying his army through the strait on its way to invade Greece. And when, in 493 B.C., three hundred triremes of the Medic fleet sank in a storm at the foot of Mount Athos, Xerxes ordered a canal to be cut through the isthmus that linked the peninsula to the mainland. Whole populations of slaves perished at the task, whose sole object was to humiliate the holy mountain's tutelary gods (chiefly Apollo, the predecessor of Jesus and Mary in this part of the world).

At last, coming to the end of his great journey, "Herakles returned to the Peloponnesus . . . bringing the cattle to Eruystheus, who sacrificed them to Hera." (Diodorus.)

The Cities of Herakles

Thus ends the campaign of Herakles and his companions around the shore of the Mediterranean. It was on a scale larger than those of Perseus and Bellerophon, or any of the hero's earlier expeditions; the only venture comparable to it was the voyage of the Argonauts, with their transcontinental detour along the rivers and out into the ocean.

If the ancient authors were still able to give an account of it a thousand years later, it is primarily because of the survival of local traditions; native leaders fell to the swords of the Greek champions, but their memories lived on (except where supplanted by the cult of the conquering general) as objects of veneration.

Another reason for the survival of the tale is that, after each of his "pacifications," Herakles built upon his ruins, creating institutions that left an indelible mark upon the defeated: the mark of the early Helladic culture, easily recognizable a thousand years later.

Also, there were the cities founded on the Heraclid campsites: Alesia, Monaco, Livorno, Heraclea, Crotona. And the place names, such as the Pillars of Hercules and the Hercules Promontory (Cape Spartivento).

The Sword of Bronze

Lastly, there were the techniques which the Greeks taught the natives as they went—among them, that of the bronzesmith, who was the real engineer of the Heraclid victories, for it was he who placed the long-tongued sword in the hero's hand, rendering him invincible with only a handful of men.

Any organized company always travels with its armorers, who are needed to forge, sharpen, and repair its weapons. When an expedition remains in one place for any length of time (as in the Rhône delta and Liguria), local craftsmen begin to imitate the new methods, especially if they prove superior to their own.

Now, in the thirteenth century B.C., none of the colonies visited by the Heraclids possessed a weapon that was the equal of the Achaean sword, which is recognizable by the quality of its alloy (making possible its greater length), ornamentation of its blade (often a design of damascened lions), and solidity of its hilt (decorated with a Greek key or spiral).

Such swords have been exhumed by modern archaeologists near Barcelona (among the vestiges of a ship sunk in the shallows), in the Bouches-du-Rhône Department (Camp du Bois du Rouret) and along the river as far north as the Puy-de-Dôme; at Antibes and Nice on the coast, and in Liguria (Castelleta, Ivrea, and Turin).[14] This suggests the route followed by Herakles, especially

[14] See Déchelette's handbook of prehistoric archaeology.

as the towns named after him are located nearby. Excavations and Heraclid cities are found side by side, in the heart of the regions in which the hero's cult survived for over two thousand years.[15]

Prelude to Magna Graecia

If the sites of the buried swords are marked on a map and connected with those of the Heraclid cities, they will be seen to reconstruct the route of Apollodorus and Diodorus—the route of Herakles' return from Erytheia, on the trip that earned him and his companions their place among the gods of the sword of bronze.[16]

But a campaign on such a scale—like the raid on the Hesperidean ewes which was soon to follow—cannot be explained solely as a whim of Eurystheus.

In Libya and Egypt, along the Rhône, in Provence, Italy, and Sicily, Herakles selected every campsite so judiciously that most of them grew into towns which are still in existence today.

After the pacification of the Peloponnesus[17] and the bid for Aegean supremacy,[18] the third stage was the prospecting of the western Mediterranean, as a prelude to the colonization which effectively took place in the same regions in the classical period (Phocaea, the Italian coast, Sicily).

Herakles was both the precursor of Magna Graecia and its first pioneer.

[15] These swords cannot be claimed to have belonged to the Heraclids themselves, of course, but they offer one more indication of the passage of the Greeks in the thirteenth century, propagating the Mycenaean techniques.

[16] Madeleine de Loverdo, who has spent twenty-five years studying Mediterranean religions based on worship of the stars, was the first to propose using the bronze-sword caches to retrace the route of the Heraclid expedition.

[17] First labors (Nemea, Lerna, Erymanthus, Stymphalos).

[18] Aegean labors (Crete, Thrace, Thermodon, Troad).

Chapter XIII
FROM THE GOLDEN APPLES OF THE HESPERIDES TO THE GATES OF HELL

"He went to the garden where the Hesperides sing
And plucked their apples from the golden boughs
. . . Then he emerged unscathed from the Underworld
O justice, O fate, divine return."

EURIPIDES

". . . And Cerberus, cowering in his bloodstained lair,
Was dragged outside by that mighty hand."

VIRGIL

Who Were the Hesperides?

"The mythographers' account of Atlas and the origins of the Hesperides must not be omitted: in the land called Hesperitis [after *hesperos,* the "setting sun"], there lived two famous brothers, Hesperos himself, and Atlas." (Diodorus.) Well, no geographer will deny that the Atlas Mountains lie to the west of Greece.

"Hesperos had a daughter named Hesperis, whom he gave in marriage to his brother Atlas." A "Hesperis" colony—that is, one lying in the direction of the setting sun, and at the foot of the Atlas range—might well "marry" the mountains, in the mind of the Hellenes.

"Atlas had seven daughters by Hesperis, some called Atlantids after their father, and the others Hesperides after their mother." There were three Atlantids: Stheno, Euryale, Medusa (the Gorgons), and four Hesperides: Erytheia, whose sacred cattle Herakles had just made off with; Arethusa (Ortygia), whom the hero had met in the land of Scylla; Hestia, the "Virgin of Fire"[1] and, later, "goddess of the hearth" (suggesting a "haven" or harbor at the foot of a volcano); and lastly, Aglaia, about whom very little is known. These last two were probably two African "Graeae," known by some local name.

All of them belonged to the western Phorcid empire, for both Apollodorus and Hesiod (*Theogony,* 333) say they were guarded by "a hundred-headed, immortal dragon, son of Echidne and Typhon."

Pherecydes adds that the serpent "was the last of the children of Phorcys and Ceto." To imagine its appearance, we need only recall the earlier products of the same parentage: the multiheaded hydra of Lerna and the three-bodied Chimaera, both of whom brandished the image of the fire-belching ancestral volcano on their weapons.

The "golden apples"

The dragon had a hundred heads, say Apollodorus and Hesiod, but Pherecydes says it had only fifty. In any event, the defenders of the surviving Phorcids were numerous enough to overpower Herakles if he attacked them.

But, "Eurystheus refused to count either the cleansing of the Augean stabes or the slaying of the hydra, and ordered Herakles, for his eleventh labor, to bring him the golden apples from the garden of the Hesperides at the foot of Mount Atlas." (Apollodorus.)

What were these miraculous fruits? Diodorus' answer is categorical: "[Hesperos and Atlas] owned flocks of great beauty; their fleece was golden yellow, and as the Greek poets used the same word for both sheep and apples [*mela*], these flocks were called 'golden apples.'"

The Conquest of the Gardens

Herakles knew how to reach their pastures, for he had been there on his way to fight Erytheia, another Hesperide. Her African sisters aroused feelings of greed and lust in many a breast, more-

[1] The Romans called her Vesta, and the rites of her cult were performed by the vestals, who remained virgins—for such is superstition.

over, and even Pharaoh was tempted by the princesses' reputation: "As they were noted for their beauty and wisdom, Busiris, King of Egypt, was said to desire them." (Diodorus.)

No doubt he would have liked to employ them as a means of exacting tribute from the fortunate owners of the famous gardens.

Unfortunately for his plans, Herakles had killed him in the course of his previous campaign, so he had been unable to carry out his scheme, but this did not deter the raiding party he had sent out from seizing the first opportunity to plunder the Hesperid coast. They rued the day, however, for when at last they "found the daughters of Atlas playing in their garden, and swiftly bore them away to their ships," Herakles was already on the scene.

"Surprising them at their meal on the shore, he killed all the kidnapers and restored the daughters to their father, Atlas." Home safely again, the hostages agreed to reward their deliverer: "In return for this favor, Atlas gave Herakles what he had come for, and also instructed him in the science of astronomy."

The "Weight of the World"

Where had the Hesperides acquired this knowledge? Atlantis? Egypt? But if Plato is right in his assertions, via the priest of Saïs in *Timaeus* and *Critias,* the Egyptians themselves had learned astronomy from the Atlantid. Diodorus: "Atlas had fashioned a heavenly sphere most cunningly, and that is why he was said to bear the world on his shoulders." This image is not to be confused with the mountain that held up the sky, which is a purely visual legend.

"As Herakles was the first to bring the science of the sphere to Greece, he received much fame thereby, and that is why people say, allegorically, that Atlas gave him the weight of the world to bear." (Diodorus.)

Athena Returns the Apples

Thus the hero carried off the sheep with the golden fleece with the full consent of the Hesperides—although not the entire flock; as with the cattle of Geryon, he took only those animals that were sacred to the gods.

Others say Atlas did not give them to him, but that he "plucked them in the garden of the Hesperides after killing the serpent that kept watch over them." (Apollodorus.)

However it was, "he took them to Eurystheus, who gave them back again. Herakles then presented them to Athena, who returned them to the garden, for it was not right that they should be elsewhere."

Such generosity to the Phorcids on the part of Athena may be explained in terms of an exchange: Pallas would send the apples back to the Hesperid dragon in return for a promise that it would no longer employ its "countless heads" to hinder the Greek fleets in their efforts to conquer the Western world.

And Now to Hell

Apollodorus: "For his twelfth labor, Eurystheus ordered Herakles to bring Cerberus up from hell."

This is the usual translation of the text, and most readers instinctively interpret the word "hell" in terms of Christian imagery, i.e., as the place to which the souls of sinners are consigned after death.

Proceeding from this assumption, they construct a false syllogism: hell is the dwelling place of the dead, the dead do not come back to life, therefore the hell of the ancients is a myth. The correct line of reasoning is just the opposite: people come back from Hades; therefore, this is not a hell in the Christian sense of the word; therefore, this is not a mythical place, but a real prison.

"In Homer and Hesiod, Hades bears no resemblance to the Christian hell; there, in the form of visible shades, men continue to lead their former existences, going about their favorite occupations, keeping their former friends and enemies."[2]

In short, this is not hell as seen by Dante, but the caverns of Hades, where convicts existed "like living dead," a phrase used constantly in reference to penitentiaries and concentration camps of all sorts.

[2] *Grand dictionnaire universel larousse.*

Cerberus

Cerberus was the jail keeper: "This monster had three dog's heads, the tail of a dragon, and the heads of different types of serpents along his back." (Apollodorus.)

The dog is the ideal guard, so it is not surprising that the dignitaries (possibly priests) whose profession it was (hereditary, no doubt) to keep watch over the convicts should have adopted that animal as their emblem. Custom has ratified their choice: a good watchdog is now said to be a "Cerberus" (e.g., Orthrus).

"Heads" should be read "chiefs": three chiefs, or a trinity of guards. As for the serpents and the dragon's tail in their coat of arms, is it necessary to say where they came from? A "brother" of the Nemean lion, the Lernaean hydra, the Chimaera, and the Hesperid dragon, "Cerberus was born of Typhon and Echidne."

The multiplicity of the mouths of hell can be attributed to the fact that there were caverns in several parts of Greece which were suitable for use as prisons. "In Thessaly [at Eleusis] and elsewhere in Greece I was shown caves through which Herakles is said to have emerged, dragging the infernal monster [Cerberus] to the earth's surface. But the opinion most widely held is that the caves were those of Cape Taenarum in Laconia . . . There, in memory of this exploit, a temple was dedicated to Herakles after the underground passage had been blocked up."

It is, moreover, perfectly natural that Cerberus, as a son of Typhon and Echidne, should have adopted a cave as his stronghold, in the days when the monsters of the Echinadian fleet were proliferating all over the Peloponnesus.

Two Illustrious Inmates: Theseus and Persephone

When Herakles set out to capture the watchdog of Hades, the Laconian caves were harboring three inmates of note: "Persephone, Theseus, and Pirithous; all three were being punished for their crime."

On what charge had they been found guilty, and by whom?

"There were three judges."[3] The court was held in a place called the Field of Truth, where neither lies nor slander could approach. There princes stood stripped of their power and rich men of their wealth, no better than the poor and lowly; the guilty could look for neither support nor protection, and calumny could not blacken or even touch honest folk.

"Usually, the first two judges heard the cause and passed sentence; if they could not agree, he who sat in the highest place, between the two others [the seat first occupied by Minos I], intervened as arbitrator."

Now, how was it that Theseus found himself banished to the caves of Laconia, rather than the grottoes of Hades at Eleusis, where the crime was committed? The answer is that he was born at Troezen in the Peloponnesus, "where there were altars dedicated to the gods of the Underworld" (Pausanias), and this city undoubtedly came under the jurisdiction of the Cape Taenarum prison authorities. Or else, the judges in their wisdom had considered it prudent to remove the hero from the vicinity of Athens, where his popularity might have been an obstacle to his punishment.

The Key to Hell

The crime was a religious one; for added safety, therefore, Herakles, "before setting out, returned to Eumolpus at the sanctuary of Eleusis, to complete his initiation." (Apollodorus.)

Diodorus (L. IV) claims that the hero actually received his instruction from Musaeus, the son of Orpheus, who had succeeded him as director of the mysteries. Whether Eumolpus or Musaeus, it is only the office that matters, and not its occupant, for the sanctuary's archpriest was empowered to grant remissions for profaners of sacred objects.

Also, the caves of Hades were extremely well guarded. True, the hero had already taken part in the Eleusinian rites at the time of his purification, and so he knew about the infernal "ambushes" as they were demonstrated in the inner sanctum at Eleusis, but

[3] The first three judges were Minos I (the Wise); his brother, the law-maker Rhadamanthys; and Eachos, a "son" of Zeus, born on the island of Aegina.

the passwords often changed, and only the high priest knew the current phrase. He would not refuse to divulge it to the demigod, however—the cherished ally of Pallas whom the Athenians were beginning to call the Shield-bearer (bearer of the goddess's Aegis, against her enemies). Duly informed, then, "Herakles went to Laconian Taenarum, to the entrance of hell." (Apollodorus.)

The Road to Cape Taenarum

At first nothing could be easier to follow: the road is a kaleidoscopic succession of wooded hills, smiling valleys, tangled gorges, and white villages, a delight to the eye. From Eleusis it passes through Corinth, Argos, Tripolis, and Sparta, to Port Gythion at the extreme southern tip of the Peloponnesus, its harbor at the back of the cape. The caverns of Hades are forty-odd miles to the west, facing the opposite direction.

Here the difficulties begin: the main road goes no farther, and woe betide any driver gullible enough to believe the people of Gythion when they say the next portion of the road is "passible": at best, it is nothing but potholes and stony cowpaths, and at worst all trace of a road disappears in the wilderness of rock.

Only a jeep would have any chance of negotiating the mountain passes on the promontory. At first, there is a stretch of hilly country, with occasional cypresses and fig trees bordering an imposing assortment of ruts. It is impossible not to think of La Fontaine's "steep, dusty, difficult path," but soon the road ceases to deserve even that title, when it reaches the deep red gorges leading to the summit; the only forces that can negotiate them are the dry mountain torrents (with never a bridge) and the roots of oleander and thorn.

Beyond the summit lies the anonymous mineral world of the mountain—yellow in the sun, scarlet at dusk, always as naked as in the days when no plant grew on the face of the earth. When, at last, the sea reappears to the west—an improbably indigo-hued bath—it seems like a dream or mirage: there is a tiny town, clinging to the bare wall of this mineral universe, forever about to slip and slide into the gold-speckled bay.

What keeps the inhabitants of Areopolis alive? A mystery. If you ask them, they will mumble something about an invisible flock (but what could it find to graze?) or a field, in which wheat is alleged to grow, protected by a stone wall, ten or twelve miles away. They go out to it on mule back with their scythes over their shoulders, camp on the site, and return after the crop has been harvested. As for fishing: almost everywhere, the cliff falls into the sea like a guillotine.

Now the road becomes a mere goat path, littered with pebbles as sharp as the teeth of some tire-consuming dragon. Other villages lie beyond, however, Pirgos Dirou, and Drialos—inhabited by gaunt peasants with skins like parchment and a haughty mien. The black-garbed women carry their pails to water; as they are lowered, they clang noisily against the inside of the well, startling the cats that prowl the white-washed passageways in search of some hypothetical sustenance.

These people with the hawklike profiles, the women with their vases on their heads, the stone-edged wells: we have seen them before, in the Echinades. Cerberus' subjects are as much the "sons of Echidne" as the fishermen of Meganese.

Suddenly, with a thunderous roar, the bus from Gythion sweeps past, rattling and clanking, teetering on its skinny tires, groaning beneath the baskets lashed to its roof. It is coming back from the caverns, beyond the last hamlet, at the end of the world. The cloud of dust begins to settle and our vehicle resumes its slow progress toward the base of the cliff, carefully avoiding the trenches gouged among the loose stones, so deep that they will spring the axles even of the local carts, unless the cart horse assumes personal responsibility for avoiding them.

The Caverns of Hades

At first glance the site reputed to be the "mouth of hell" can be misleading: it has been almost totally buried by landslides, which have demolished the old temple of Herakles. But not far away there is an astonishing group of caverns which have, in a sense, supplanted it, and when the traveler finally reaches his goal at the back of the violet-hued inlet, he is more than repaid for the tribulations he endured in getting there.

The openings gape at the bottom of the cliff near a beach of murderous shale. Whether intentionally or not, the gates closing them off have been made to resemble those of a modern prison, and are so filled by aggressive iron grills that they can best be described by comparing them with the entrance to the Dépôt de la Santé in Paris (the chief prison).

A peasant wearing a guide's cap confronts the visitor; there is an admission fee, a few drachmas, to pay for electricity—the latest "development" effort of the local "town councils."

Behind the barred entrance, a concrete staircase disappears underground. The air becomes progressively more damp and chilly, and upon reaching the bottom step, no one who has read the ancient texts or visited a prison can refrain from exclaiming aloud.

Nature seems to have copied the plan of a modern penitentiary. The cave is roughly circular, with corridors opening off the perimeter. This star-shaped disposition is that of Sing Sing or Fresnes, except that here a forest of stalactites bristles from the vault, suspended more than fifteen meters above a corresponding thicket of stalagmites rising from the floor.

There is a hollow in the ground, where the occupants used to temper the clay for their pots. And farther along, underground, is the kiln in which they baked them, with a natural chimney that draws perfectly. Scrapings from its smoke-encrusted sides have been analyzed: the crust is thick and very ancient (fourteenth and thirteenth centuries B.C., the period of Persephone and Pirithous). In those days the prisoners were also potters; forced labor is not a modern invention.

Cerberus' Sentry Box

And here is "Cerberus' sentry box," although perhaps the name is only a lure for tourists. But there is a natural recess in the rock, with a kind of window in it. Sitting on a bench which the Creator has obligingly provided, a guard would effectively be able to keep an eye on everything that was happening within the cave, and also on the exit from the adjacent corridor, which stretches far back into the entrails of the earth.

This passageway slopes gently downward, slippery and ill-lit;

sometimes the dim glow of the lamps is lost in the soaring vault, and sometimes one has to stoop to pass under the ceiling. Along the walls on either side there are openings to the niches which used to be the prisoners' cells. Receptacles have been found in a hollow, which may have been a sort of pantry; there are fragments of pottery plates.

Farther along, in another hollow dug into the floor of the cave, speleologists from Athens have unearthed an ossuary; they have left one tibia behind.

A sudden gust of fresh air expands the lungs, and one emerges into a cavern hung with translucent "curtains." The vault arches thirty meters or more above the gallery floor, but has anyone even measured the depth of the subterranean precipice along which the passageway winds? The lanterns are strung along the stalagmites forming the handrail.[4]

Fifty yards ahead another opening leads into the largest cavern of all, with a motionless pool at the far end, below the level of the passageway (a steep pile of fallen rock, ten meters long, slithers down to the edge). The stalactites suspended overhead are mirrored perfectly in the still water, and the drops forming in the dome fall unendingly, one by one, jarring the smooth reflection.

In the past, this fresh-water pool probably communicated with the "subterranean Laconian Styx," less than a hundred meters away through the rock.

Here we can go no farther, however. In the passage on the right, at the end of a broad, deep fissure whose entrails remain plunged in total darkness, speleologists have discovered another ossuary. They have not yet explored it fully, but one day they will, and then perhaps they will find, among the heaped-up skeletons, the remains of Persephone, Pirithous, and other prisoners of note who died in the caverns of Hades on Cape Taenarum.

[4] Today the guide conducting the rare tourists who stray into this remote part of the world never fails to pause by an anthropomorphic formation in the passageway and exclaim, "Look! Wouldn't you say it's an exact replica of the profile of General de Gaulle?" (The resemblance is, in fact, striking.)

The Laconian Styx

Upon emerging from this visit to the dead, the daylight seems blinding. After a brief pause, we continue across the fifty or sixty yards separating the convicts' quarters from the orifice leading to the "Styx."

Another gate, iron grill, and staircase, all similar to the first. At the bottom, a gleaming expanse of water. A raft can be dimly perceived through the gloom, and flat-bottomed aluminum boats and oarsmen.

Visitors should watch their step, for the stream is as icy as the French Padirac, but there the similarity ends: the world-famous river of the Périgordine cavern bears about as much resemblance to the obscure Styx of Cape Taenarum as Cinderella in her homespun does to the princess arrayed in silks and bedecked with jewels.

The eight hundred meters of navigable subterranean waterway are one long succession of stalactites glittering like precious stones and transparent drapery like Roman togas. Guided by the boatman's pole, the bark glides through water so clear that one could believe one were floating over a bed of emeralds. The banks are formed by a vast population of statues carved out of ruby, topaz, amethyst, and diamond.

It is wiser not to touch them, they are too fragile; and yet it took nature twenty thousand years to model the tiniest stalactite.

For a whole hour the boat coasts along underground as though imprisoned inside a diamond.

Back in the everyday world, even the sun seems dull. You tip the boatman, who blurts out uncertainly, "You are a learned man, what did you understand? They say it's important."

Theseus' Release

When he reached the same doors that whisper Hades' secrets in our ears today, "Herakles found Theseus and Pirithous. Persephone welcomed him like a brother." (Apollodorus.) Was she hoping for escape? Did a knowledge of the password and "topography of hell" bestow such powers upon the hero?

"Reward and punishment were meted out according to virtue

and crime. There were acts that could not be pardoned, and sentence was for life; and there were less serious offenses, for which the guilty could be released after expiation."

Persephone, the virgin priestess, had allowed herself to be seduced, and so she received the maximum sentence. Regarding Pirithous and Theseus, opinions differ. Diodorus: "Herakles was allowed to free Theseus and Pirithous [not Persephone] and take them away with him." Apollodorus: "The hero did free Theseus [less heavily sentenced of the two] . . . But the earth quaked [in indignation?] when he attempted to release Pirithous [the principal in the crime] and he left him behind."

Perhaps the unfortunate ex-Argonaut was the victim of an ill-timed tremor which the guard-priests, furious at the loss of such a valuable prisoner, interpreted in their own fashion.

However, freeing Theseus and, perhaps, Pirithous, was only part of the task Eurystheus had imposed upon the hero.

Herakles and Cerberus

"Herakles asked Hades [the priests, that is] for Cerberus, and the god said he could have him if he could capture him without using any weapons. Wearing only his breastplate and lion skin, Herakles approached the animal near the gates of the infernal river,[5] seized him by the throat, and, although bitten by the dragon in his tail [or wounded by some attendant bodyguard], he would not let go, and the dog, to avoid being strangled, had to follow him."

This was not the first "monstrous" offspring of Typhon and Echidne to be so tamed by the hero. "He took him and returned to the earth's surface [reappeared in society] at Troezen," which was Theseus' homeland: before regaining Athens, the king undoubtedly wanted to offer a sacrifice on the infernal altars shown to Pausanias.

As for Herakles: "After showing Cerberus to Eurystheus, he took him back to hell." (Apollodorus.) Of late, the Greeks had grown more indulgent toward the Echinadians; they had crippled their power and were no longer afraid of them. Also, Cerberus

[5] Styx or Acheron?

benefited from the superstitious dread in which all gods were held —the fear that had impelled Athena to return the sacred sheep to the Hesperides. In this instance, it saved the priest of Hades from the fate suffered by his secular brothers (the lion and hydra, whom Herakles, having nothing to fear from Olympus on their account, had murdered).

End of the Delphic Mandate

Thus ended the twelfth and last of the labors; the Delphic Diktat expired with Herakles' emergence from the Underworld. After eighteen or twenty years of campaigning and never-to-be-forgotten battles, Herakles had atoned for the murder of Megara's children, committed in a fit of rage.

If one goes by the texts of the Paros marble, the hero must have been about fifty-seven years old (only forty, according to modern chronologists). Some people have been unable to believe he could have done so much (expeditions to far-distant lands, founding of cities) in so short a time. Yet it took Alexander ten years less to lead his phalanxes into India and found an equal number of cities. True, he did it a thousand years after Herakles, but the means of transport available to the Macedonians were no different: foot, horse, and similarly rigged vessels.

Chapter XIV
FROM THE CAPTURE OF TROY TO THE DEATH OF HERAKLES

"Herakles, although victorious at the tournament of Oechalia,
Was banished without receiving the prize: Iole's hand.
He killed Iphitus, atoned in servitude,
Then, freed at last, went to Troy
To slay Laomedon and set Priam on the throne."

after APOLLODORUS

The Contest in Oechalia

"His labors being terminated, Herakles returned to Thebes and gave his wife Megara in marriage to Iolas [his faithful companion]." (Apollodorus.)

Diodorus: "He hoped he would have better fortune with his progeny by some other woman." The custom of repudiation is still in use in some Eastern kingdoms.[1]

"Desiring to marry, he heard that Eurytus, King of Oechalia,[2] was offering the hand of his daughter Iole as a prize to any marksman who could outshoot him and his sons with bow and arrow." (Apollodorus.)

Since he would never wear the crown of Argolis, he thought he might obtain another one by marrying this princess who was being offered to a champion archer.

[1] *Vide* the Shah of Iran.

[2] Several cities were known by this name. Strabo (L. X) lists five, in Euboea, Trachinia, Thessaly, Arcadia, and Aetolia, and the authors disagree as to which was the one ruled by Eurytus.

"Herakles went to Oechalia and won, but Iole was not given to him. Iphitus, Eurytus' eldest son, thought the bargain should be kept." Having been an Argonaut, he knew Herakles.

"But Eurytus and his other sons refused, fearing, so they said, that if Herakles had more children he might kill them, too." This was either a very legitimate scruple on the part of a family of prospective in-laws, or another pretext. "Thus rejected, Herakles retaliated by stealing Eurytus' mares." (Diodorus.)

Homer also calls them "mares," as do Pherecydes (*Homerii scholii,* Od. XXI) and Sophocles (*Trach.* V), but Apollodorus says they were "oxen" and accuses Autolycos of the theft.

However, Iphitus set out to recapture his father's herd, and Herakles would seem to have been the culprit after all, for he hurled Eurytus' son over the parapet at Tiryns.

The Incident at Delphi

"Afflicted by an acute illness in punishment for his murder of Iphitus, Herakles went to ask the Delphic oracle how he might be cured. The Pythoness would not answer him, so he stormed the temple and, having carried off the sacred tripod, set up his own personal oracle." (Apollodorus.) Pausanias confirms this.

Herakles was never a man for half measures; and this way, at least, he need no longer fear the malicious intentions of the patron saint of Delphi. However, the god's priesthood was not at all pleased with the casual manner in which the rival institution had been established, and Herakles very nearly came to grief over it: "They began to fight with him . . . but Zeus hurled a thunderbolt and parted them." (Apollodorus.) Next, the clergy of Zeus "threatened the ruffian with their lightning," in order to calm the scandal, and the ruffled Pythoness gloried in her revenge: "Apollo sent Herakles an oracle, telling him that his illness would not be cured until he had been sold into slavery and given Eurytus the money from the sale, in compensation for his son's death; afterward he would have to serve as a slave for three full years." Blood money, and more forced labors in perspective, but it cannot be denied that Herakles was asking for trouble.

Herakles Goes to Omphale

According to Pherecydes (*Homerii schol.* Od. XXI), it was Omphale, Queen of Lydia in Asia Minor, who, for payment of the considerable sum of three talents, bought Herakles' services for the period stipulated by the oracle.

She wanted her money's worth: "While in her service, Herakles captured the Cercopes living near Ephesus, and put them in chains." (Apollodorus.) Homer describes these beings as "lying, deceitful, conniving creatures who performed unmentionable deeds, roaming the world in search of some new victim to cheat, never settling anywhere."

The hero also killed Syleus, who compelled passing travelers to till his land and cultivate his vines; and, as usual, various other local brigands.

Omphale was very impressed: "Marveling at Herakles' virtues, she freed him and married him. She even had a son by him.[8] After this, Herakles returned to the Peloponnesus and then marched on Troy, to take his revenge upon Laomedon." (Diodorus.) He had, it may be recalled, an old score to settle with this king.

The Rediscovery of Troy

The city that the hero was now preparing to sack had not yet become the mighty-walled fortress besieged by the Greeks in the following generation, when only the ruses of Athena (inspiring Ulysses) could bring it to its knees.

Actually, there have been six Troys—built, destroyed, and rebuilt, one on top of the other on the same site, so that, in the end, their superimposed foundations formed a hill.

After the disappearance of Troy VI, nature covered the entire mound with humus, and when, in the eighteenth and nineteenth

[8] Apollodorus says that "the expedition of the Argonauts and the hunt of the Calydonian boar took place while he was serving Omphale, and it was also during this period that Theseus came from Troy to rid the isthmus of pirates." But his affirmations do not tally with the Paros chronology as well as those of the other authors.

centuries, scholarly curiosity began searching for the site, there were several possible locations on the coast of Asia Minor.

There was one clue: Troy had originated near some springs (or "nymphs," as they might have been called), which Homer describes in detail and says that the temperature of the water of two of them was not the same as the rest.

Were they to be found among the thirty-six springs of the Turkish village of Bounarbashi, south of the plain of Troy? The neighboring hill of Bali Dagh bears some resemblance to an acropolis. But "every indication suggests that the distance from Ilium to the Hellespont was very short, hardly more than three miles, whereas Bounarbashi is eight miles away."

On the strength of this, Schliemann opted for the hamlet of Hissarlik. After spending the winter on the site in precarious conditions, he ordered his first team of eighty men to begin excavating the mound in the spring of 1872, equipped with "the best miners' bars and English picks and shovels."

Three foremen and an engineer were in attendance "to draw maps and plans," for it must not be forgotten that although the German visionary, the son of a drunkard, spoke sixteen languages and had amassed a huge fortune in the indigo trade, his sole qualification in the field of archaeology was unbounded enthusiasm.

And yet, he was proved right and the science of his day, which relegated the world of Homer to the mists of legend, was wrong. But what staggering perseverance he had, too: in this instance, faith literally had to move mountains, for he spent three years removing hundreds of thousands of cubic yards of debris.

In the winter, he wrote, the north wind (Boreas) blew through the cracks in the hut he had chosen as his residence "with such force that we could not light a lamp at night, and even though a fire was burning in the hearth, the thermometer registered nine degrees."

In the spring, malaria was rife in this mosquito-infested region, and at night, Schliemann adds, "there was the croaking of millions of frogs, and the hideous hooting of the myriads of owls that nested in our trenches; there is something sinister and repellent in their calls."

Even so, this was the best time of the year: "The leaves were beginning to unfold on the branches, and the Trojan plain was covered with flowers." Also, "the storks had returned," and he had another cause for rejoicing: some promising vestiges were coming to light—the remains of a series of superimposed cities, some "prehistoric, others more recent."

Which one had seen the famous war? He thought he would know it by the Scaean Gate, which Homer describes when speaking of the Trojan counselors: "They were excellent orators . . . sitting on top of the tower like cicadas perched on a tree in the woods, shrilling joyfully."

Schliemann actually found a segment of massive masonry on the south side of the hill and, somewhat rashly, baptized it the "great tower."

Somewhere, too, there should be some trace of the palace, in which Priam gathered together his most precious possessions to ransom the body of his son Hector, killed by Achilles outside the walls. "He weighed out ten golden talents, and he took two gleaming tripods, four caldrons, and a very beautiful goblet which the people of [nearby] Thrace had given to him when he went there as ambassador."

Nevertheless, Schliemann's discoveries were not conclusive, and the academic pens were spurting acid on all sides: this was not science, cried the archaeologists, this was tabloid sensationalism. The old man himself admits that after three years, having removed more than 250,000 cubic yards of earth, he was about to give up: "Now we are tired, and since we have achieved our purpose [identification of the site] and fulfilled the great ideal of our life, we are going to cease work at Troy, on June 15."

Beneath the Wall of Laomedon: Priam's Treasure

Miracles do happen: on June 14, the day before Schliemann's self-imposed departure, after making arrangements for the payment of his workers' final wages, he was standing by the building he thought was Priam's megaron, when he noticed a bronze object embedded in a layer of calcined red debris. Looking closer, he distinguished something bright.

He told the men to go, saying it was his birthday and they would be paid anyway. Then he crawled beneath the tottering wall that threatened to collapse at any moment and bury him alive. His faithful companion Sophia—his young Greek wife, who followed him with unequaled devotion—came with him. Schliemann borrowed her shawl to wrap up the treasure.

For, at the age of sixty-three, this merchant, who had been dreaming of the wealth of Troy since his earliest childhood, was now plunging his hands into a mass of jewels: there were two magnificent gold diadems—the larger made of a fine chain, from which were suspended seventy short chains and seventeen longer ones, each composed of little heart-shaped discs of gold (16,350 links in all) of exquisite workmanship. There were also six bracelets, a flask, a goblet weighing 601 grams, sixty earrings, 8700 rings, buttons, prisms, perforated bars, and other items—all of solid gold. They had been stored in a large silver container.

"I found all the objects together, or placed one inside the other, on the wall of the shrine attributed by Homer to Poseidon or Apollo"[4]—the very ramparts for which Laomedon had refused to pay the worshipers of these divinities who built them, thereby provoking their wrath and the visitation of the avenging "sea monster." Herakles had then freed the king of the monster, but without receiving his due, either.

The First Trojan War

"Such was the hero, valiant and intrepid, when he landed on these shores with only six ships [or twelve, or eighteen, depending upon the author] and a small group of warriors, demanding Laomedon's horses." (*Iliad,* V.)

One of the men "who had come with him of his own free will was Telamon. Upon reaching Troy, Herakles left Oicles [his companion] to guard the ships and, with the others, marched up to the city . . . But Laomedon and his forces attacked the boats and killed Oicles, who was defending them." (Apollodorus.)

Pausanias says (L. VIII) that his tomb was still shown to visitors

[4] In the last two paragraphs I have relied largely on Cottrell for my facts and quotations (in *Le Taureau de Minos*—Grasset).

in his day. "But Herakles repelled the king . . . and besieged the city for some time[5] . . . Then Telamon breached part of the wall and entered the town." (Apollodorus.)

At this point an incident occurred that was characteristic of the hero's new pride, the by-product of his labors. Jealous of his reputation, and wanting "to make certain that no one could boast of greater bravery than he, Herakles drew his sword and ran at Telamon."

But Telamon had his wits about him: "He quickly began to make a pile of some stones nearby. Herakles demanded what he intended to do with them: 'Raise an altar,' he replied, 'to the victorious Herakles!'" For this, he received a reward instead of a chastisement. "The hero praised his devotion . . . and, after capturing the city and killing Laomedon and his sons with his arrows, all except Podarces"—Podarces was the one who had wanted to give him the horses, as originally promised—"he gave Hesione to Telamon as a reward for his valor, and allowed her to choose whichever of the prisoners whose life she desired to spare." There were not many left, however, for "Herakles sacked the town and widowed its streets" (*Iliad,* V). Hesione chose her brother, Podarces. Herakles then told her "that he must first be sold as a slave, but that she could buy him back by giving up something of her own in exchange." Hesione gave her veil (probably a discreet euphemism), "and it was in memory of this that Podarces took the name of 'Priam' [from a Greek verb, *priamai,* "I repurchase"] in place of his former name."

Priam was a young man then. He met the Greeks again, in his old age, but on the second occasion Agamemnon was their leader.

The First "Odyssey"

"As Herakles was returning from the siege of Troy, Hera [his lifelong enemy] raised a violent storm against him." For this, the goddess was soundly rated by Zeus, in the terms recorded by Homer at the beginning of the fifteenth book of the *Iliad:* "This

[5] In his *Oration to Philip* Isocrates says that Herakles captured Troy in fewer days than it took the Greeks years (i.e., ten); Seneca confirms this (v. 865 of his tragedy on Agamemnon).

hero whom you, seducing the wind spirit Boreas to aid you in your evil designs, drove across the infinite sea and led astray on the opulent island of Cos."

In simpler words, Herakles' fleet was caught by one of the fierce northerly gales that still cause yearly shipwrecks in the Aegean (the most famous in classical times was the storm, mentioned previously, that sank three hundred triremes of the Persian fleet in 493 B.C. at the foot of Mount Athos).

Apollodorus: "When Herakles drew near Cos, the inhabitants took him for a pirate and drove him off with stones."

The Venetian scholiast says that Euripylos, king of the island, did try to prevent him from landing, but that Herakles succeeded in spite of him, and slept with his daughter Chalciope, by whom he had a son. Pindar seems to follow the same tradition, in a hymn quoted by Quintilian (L. VIII, c. 6) in which he says, "Herakles fell upon the Meropians, inhabitants of Cos, with the ferocity of a thunderbolt."

Plutarch relates the incident in great detail, in his *Greek Questions* (c. 58): "Returning from Troy with his six ships [Homer's figure], Herakles was caught in a storm and his entire escort destroyed with the exception of his own ship, which was driven aground on the Lacterian cape, and all he managed to salvage from the wreckage were his men and weapons.

"Coming across a flock of sheep, he said he would like to buy one, but Antagoras, the shepherd, was very boastful of his strength and proposed a wrestling match, promising to give Herakles the sheep if he won.

"Herakles accepted the challenge, but when the fight began, the Meropians rushed to assist Antagoras and the Greeks to aid Herakles. Since the Greeks were so few in number, however, they soon had to fall back, and Herakles took refuge in the home of a Thracian woman, where he disguised himself by putting on women's clothes."

Apollodorus writes that he was wounded in this fight by Chalcodon, son of Euripylos and Clytia (daughter of Merops, the patriarch of the entire island), and Theocritus confirms this in the seventh idyll.

Another Homecoming, Another War

But his luck still held; he survived again and found his way back to the Peloponnesus. Diodorus gives a clear picture of the reception he received there: "In Tiryns, Eurystheus accused Herakles of conspiring against the throne . . ."

Well, stranger things have been known to happen. As a result, "he was banished—he, Alcmene, Iphicles, and Iolas . . . Being compelled to leave Tiryns, Herakles and his companions went to live in Arcadia . . . There, hearing that a religious procession was on its way from Elis to the isthmus to celebrate the festival of Poseidon [when the isthmian games were held], and that Augeias' nephew Eurytus was leading the convoy," he was reminded of his grievances against that king, who had also refused to pay him for cleaning his stables.

"Herakles fell upon the procession, killing Eurytus near Cleonae, on the very spot where a temple of Herakles now stands."

Pausanias (L. V) has unearthed an interesting bit of information on the hero's ambush tactics: "He is said to have taken advantage of the moment when the Moliones were on their way to the isthmian games, protected by the general truce agreement in force during their celebration." Diodorus says, "he then marched on Elis."[6] In Apollodorus' version the order of events is reversed: "[First] he assembled an army in Arcadia, willingly joined by all the bravest of the Greeks. Augeias, forewarned of Herakles' attack, placed Eurytus and Cleatos in command of his army; they had only one body between them, and surpassed all others living at that time in bodily strength."

Eurytus, Another "Monster"

Pherecydes, quoted by the scholiast on Homer (*Iliad,* II), says that "Eurytus and Cleatos were double," with two heads, four arms, four legs, and a single body. Hesiod simply merged them into a "single body." These images recall Geryon (of the three

[6] According to the Paros marble, in 1308 B.C.—or 1215, according to modern chronology.

heads): Eurytus and Cleatos were generals, working "hand in hand," as the saying goes.

According to Apollodorus, Herakles began by suffering a reverse. "Having fallen ill during the trip, he made a truce with the Moliones, but they soon heard of his illness and attacked his army, killing most of the men and forcing Herakles to retreat. A short while late, however, the third isthmian games were scheduled to be held, to which the Eleans were sending a delegation of Moliones, so Herakles laid an ambush for them at Cleonae and killed them." In this case, he was merely returning treachery for treachery. "Then he led his army into Elis, took the town [of Elis] and killed Augeias and his sons."

This was a dreadful carnage. The scholiast on Homer (*Iliad*, II) says, according to Callimachos, that the Eleans perished virtually to a man, so Herakles ordered his soldiers to sleep with their widows, in order to repopulate the country. This is also implied by Pausanias (L. V, c. 3).

Herakles now remembered the banished son of Augeias who had upheld him at the time of the decision about his payment for cleaning the stables: "Herakles installed Phyleus on the throne." (Apollodorus, Diodorus.)

Pausanias alone (L. V, c. 3) claims that Herakles pardoned Augeias at the request of Phyleus, but this does not seem likely, for the hero appears at that time to have been in the throes of a positive mania of destructiveness: "After conquering Elis, he marched against Pylos." (Apollodorus.)

The Pylos of Neleus

The west coast of the Peloponnesus possesses some of the finest natural harbors in the world, made famous in modern times by the naval battle in which the combined navies of France, England, and Russia defeated the Turkish armada in 1827. Entering the harbor unannounced, they launched a broadside at the galleys of the Crescent and sank almost all of them, depriving the sultan of his best means of keeping the Greeks in check.

The view from the crenelated teeth of the old castle of Pylos, where the dazed Turkish artillery stood paralyzed, looks out to the vast lavender bay, protected from the open sea by steep-walled islands and strewn with islets ringed by golden circles of shallow water.

The lower stories of the houses of the little modern town of Pylos form a series of arcades, clustered around a square shaded by venerable plane trees, but the acropolis is more than ten miles inland, in the fertile, rolling country to the north—the acropolis, "with its bleached stones, always freshly whitewashed, where Neleus, son of Poseidon, used to sit and prove himself the equal of the gods in wisdom" (*Odyssey,* III).

The hill of Englianos seems initially to have been occupied by a middle Bronze Age village, before becoming, early in the thirteenth century, the site of the royal residence known today as the palace of Nestor (Neleus' son), while the town spread out into the surrounding hills.

Among the olive trees and the vineyards on the summit lie the foundations of the megaron, very similar to its contemporaries, the "palaces" of Mycenae and Tiryns. Surrounded by outbuildings and workshops, the edifice (50 by 32 meters) comprised a throne room with a circular central hearth, sleeping quarters, and storerooms. Wood was employed throughout: pillars, door frames, and ceilings. The outer walls, built of blocks of "poros," were strong enough to support a second floor, while a kind of plaster-coated conglomerate was used for the interior partitions. But the decoration was lavish: Piet de Jong has reconstructed it almost entirely from the scattered fragments. The throne room was paved with colored tiles, every one with a different design. Graceful frescoes danced along the walls—a dove in flight beside a lyre player, griffins, a lion, squid, fish—and continued out into the walls of the corridors.

Painted amphoras and coins have also been found, and, naturally enough, tholos tombs similar to those at Mycenae, as well as smaller tombs containing huge earthenware jars that served as coffins. Also, there were over a thousand tablets in Linear B script, some of which, found lying on the ground, described the location of the palace.[7]

[7] See preface by Professor Marinatos.

The building was burned by the Dorians around 1200 B.C., but when Herakles conquered it, the palace was at the height of its splendor.

The Rage of Herakles

"Having captured the town, Herakles killed Periclymenus, the bravest of Neleus' sons, who had assumed all kinds of different forms during the battle" (Apollodorus)—"there were fifty of him," or "he was everywhere at once," we might say. To no avail, however: "Herakles also killed Neleus and all his other sons, except Nestor who, being very young at the time, was reared by the Gerenians."

We meet him again later—aging, but rich in money and authority—among the Achaean warriors massed beneath the walls of Troy.

From Pylos the bloodthirsty Herakles now marched against Lacedaemon, "to avenge himself upon the sons of Hippocoön [King of Sparta], who had sent reinforcements to Neleus . . . Iphicles, the hero's twin brother, perished in this fight. After killing Hippocoön and his children, Herakles captured the city and restored Tyndareus to the throne [an exiled brother of Hippocoön] . . . Passing through Tegea [near Tripolis], the hero violated Auge, daughter of Aleus, without recognizing her; she bore him a son, Telephos."

Once again, images of the Middle Ages rise up before our eyes, with the Heraclid raiding parties melting into the costumes of the outlaw mercenaries of the Grandes Compagnies.

Chapter XV
THE DEATH OF HERAKLES

"Hearing from Lichas that Herakles loved Iole,
Deianeira sent him the tunic as a present.
Herakles ordered them to carry him to the summit of Oeta . . ."

DIODORUS

"Take a burning torch and light the pyre;
Come . . . O my stout soul, fasten a seal of iron upon
my mouth . . ."

SOPHOCLES

The Horn of Plenty

After his Pylian and Lacedaemonian escapades, Herakles, possibly disgusted by his own excesses, seems to have tried to settle down for a while. He may have been going through one of those periods of remorse that punctuate his life, alternating with his fits of rage.

"Having gone to Calydon, he asked to marry Deianeira, daughter of Oeneus [or "daughter" of Dionysos], and wrestled with the [god of the] river Achelous to win her hand . . ." (Apollodorus.)

The inhabitants of the river's rich valley may well have been apprehensive of this suitor, whose recent behavior clearly gave pause for thought. The Achelous "changed itself into a bull" for the match, and Herakles broke off one of its horns—probably in hand-to-hand combat. Ovid (L. IX) says this was the horn of plenty, or cornucopia, and Diodorus says the horn "was supposed to contain all the fruits of the autumn." He adds: "In this allegory, the horn represents the valley of the Achelous, and the fruits signify the fertility of its banks."

In short, Herakles won the country in a duel. "He married

Deianeira and returned the broken horn to the river." This largesse cost him little enough, since he had now become the legitimate heir to the kingdom.

"He then led an expedition, with the Calydonians, against the Thespiots . . . took Ephyra [Corinth] and, at a feast in the home of Oeneus, struck Eunomos a blow with his fist and killed him, just as he [Eunomos, "benevolent" or "well ordered"] was pouring water over his hands."

These outbursts of temper had plagued him all his life and were the cause of his eternal wanderings, but he was terrified of his own temper, and every demonstration of it was followed by a period of quasi-masochistic brooding. For although he was pardoned by the victim's father (understandably reluctant to argue with him), "Herakles insisted upon going into exile as the law prescribed, and he decided to settle at Trachis. He set out with Deianeira and came to the river Evenus."

The Philter of Nessos

And there he encountered an enemy of long standing, whose hatred he had incurred that time he drank too much wine while being entertained by the centaurs on his way to hunt the Erymanthian boar. For a fee, this centaur was now ferrying travelers across the river; ". . . he said the gods had granted him this concession on account of his righteousness." He entertained a rather curious notion of that quality, however: "Herakles preferred to swim across, and gave Deianeira to the centaur to carry, after paying the agreed fee, but halfway across, the centaur tried to rape her." Satisfaction of a long-cherished resentment? After all, Herakles had tried to kill him once. "Deianeira began to cry out, and Herakles, emerging from the water, pierced Nessos through the heart with an arrow." (Apollodorus.)

According to Diodorus (L. VI, c. 36), the aggression had been very nearly consummated: "Nessos was wounded while in the act, and so grievously that he died almost immediately, but just before breathing his last, he gave Deianeira the recipe for a philter that would, he said, prevent Herakles from ever desiring another woman."

The hero's amorous appetite was fabled throughout Greece, so the centaur could be sure his wife would one day have cause for jealousy and would resort to his lethal mixture.

"He told her to take his sperm and mix it with some oil and the blood flowing from his wound, and then to anoint Herakles' tunic with it, and then he died as soon as he had given her the recipe. Deianeira followed his instructions, placed the ointment in a vase, and kept it by her without telling Herakles."

. . . One moment of inattention by the river's edge where a centaur lay dying; that was all . . .

Herakles in Thessaly

After this incident, "Herakles crossed the river and went to the court of Ceyx, King of Trachis [near Thermopylae] and settled there, with his Arcadian troops."

But his violence-goaded brain would not let him rest for long. Apollodorus: "He set out again, to support Aeginios, king of the Dorians, who had been attacked by the Lapiths. Then he killed Laogoras, king of the Dryopians . . . Passing through Itonus, he was challenged to a fight by Cycnus [the swan], son of Ares [i.e., a warrior] and killed him. He went to Ormenium [near Volo], where King Amyntor tried to halt him, but Herakles slew him, too . . . He mustered an army against Oechalia and captured the town . . . After sacking it, he bore Iole away with him [she had been refused to him once before]."

Nicias says that Iole, knowing that it was on her account Herakles had invaded Oechalia, threw herself over the city wall, but the wind billowed out her skirts and she landed unhurt.

Herakles was satisfied: he had wanted Eurytus' daughter, and he had got her. Full of pride and amorous enthusiasm, "he went up the Cenaean promontory on the island of Euboea and raised an altar to Cenaean Zeus. Wishing to make a sacrifice, he sent a herald to Trachis to fetch his ceremonial robe." (Apollodorus.)

Diodorus writes: "He sent his servant Lichas back to Trachis to ask his wife Deianeira for the tunic he customarily wore at sacrifices." And the ultimate tragedy, brutal and inevitable, was played out (around 1300 B.C., according to the old chronologies —or 1209, according to more recent research).

The Poisoned Tunic

"Deianeira, hearing from Lichas that her husband was in love with Iole, rubbed the tunic with the ointment of Nessos the centaur. Lichas, not knowing what she had done, took the garment away for the sacrifice." (Diodorus.)

Apollodorus: "Herakles put on the garment and began to perform the sacrifice, but as soon as the tunic grew warm the poison began to penetrate his body."

What was this poison—the same one that Medea experimented with on Glauce? None of the hypotheses put forward thus far has offered a satisfactory explanation. Was it really a mixture of sperm and soured blood? True enough, ptomaine is deadly, but it would have had to enter his blood stream. If the texts said the victim had pricked himself with an open safety pin while fastening the tunic, for instance,[1] there would be no problem. But what could this potion be that could soak into a fabric and yet remain invisible (colorless) and produce the symptoms described? The pharmacopoeia of the ancients has kept the secret.

Diodorus: ". . . soon the poison began to work . . ." Apollodorus: "Herakles seized Lichas by the feet and flung him into the Euboean sea. He tried to rip off the tunic, but it stuck to his skin and his flesh tore away with it. In this pitiful state, he asked to be laid out on a ship and carried back to Trachis." Diodorus says he disbanded his army, and Apollodorus adds that "when she heard what had happened, Deianeira hanged herself." Herakles also "ordered Hyllus, his eldest son by Deianeira, to marry Iole as soon as he came of age."

The Martyrdom

"The disease was progressing rapidly, and he sent [a herald] to Delphi to consult Apollo. The oracle replied that Herakles and his military regalia must be conveyed to the top of Mount Oeta, and a great pyre must be built near him; Zeus would take care of the rest." (Diodorus.) Herakles was suffering the tortures of the

[1] Safety pins were in use as early as the fifteenth century B.C.

damned. Although the lament attributed to him by Sophocles is of no historical value, it does show the ancients' conception of his torment:

"Alas, unlucky wretch that I am, the pain is biting into me again, O gods! Without the help of Zeus, what magician, what artist of healing can ever still this pain that is killing me? It clings to me, O torture! Here it comes again . . . Ah, is there no one to give one mighty stroke and part my head from my accursed body? It's coming back, it's flowing back again, this agonizing, awful, searing pain that has done for me! O Pallas, Pallas, it's tearing me apart . . . Hades, son of Zeus, sweet Hades, put me to sleep, send me to sleep with sudden death, and put an end to my sufferings."

The Pyre on Mount Oeta

Mount Oeta overlooks both Trachis and Thermopylae, a little to the south of modern Lamia. It is part of a chain of mountains, several of whose peaks reach an altitude of two thousand meters. Its slopes are not as thickly wooded as they were in the heroic age: too many fires have gutted the forest, too many goats have nipped the buds from the saplings.

The summit overlooks Thessaly, part of Euboea and Boeotia. Othrys is visible to the north, above the gulf of Iolcos, Jason's homeland. The crest of Parnassus lies to the south, and to the east the horizon of Thebes, cradle of Herakles.

"Hyllus, you know the rock of Zeus atop Mount Oeta. You must carry my body there in your own arms. Cut down some deep-rooted oaks and many wild olives, male trees, too; lay my body on top of them and then take a torch of burning pine and set fire to them."

Apollodorus: "No one wanted to do it; but Poeas, a shepherd passing that way in search of his flock, said he would hold the torch, and in gratitude Herakles bequeathed him his arrows."

The fire was ignited; and here, in the final lines of Sophocles, are the last words spoken by Herakles: "Come; before my pain awakens again, O, my stout soul, fasten a seal of iron upon my mouth, seal my lips like two stones and stop my screams, for you must perform with joy this act that terrifies me."

Herakles Among the Gods

"They say he was enveloped in a cloud and borne aloft to the sky amid great peals of thunder." (Apollodorus.)

"When Iolas and his men returned to gather up his bones, there was nothing left, and that is why they believe Herakles had gone to live among the immortals, as the oracle had prophesied." (Diodorus.)

The greatest hero antiquity, the chevalier of the sword of bronze, was dead; it was only fitting that his funeral pyre should burn more fiercely than the setting sun.

Clearing the way for the Helladic colonists, he carried his weapons both east and west to the confines of the known world; he erected the Pillars of Hercules, looking out to the mysterious ocean of the Atlantides; and he founded more than twenty cities—in Thrace, in Bithynia, in Crete, Egypt, Gaul, Italy—that were to perpetuate his name until the age of Rome and afterward.

Everywhere they went, the Heraclids carried the skill of their bronzesmiths with them, and those who settled in foreign lands, Mycenaean sword in hand, broke ground for the civilization of Europe.

Chapter XVI
THE TWILIGHT OF THE HEROES

"Jason in misery, Theseus embittered:
Such was the tragic end of the greatest heroes."
Hellenistic carved stone slab

Death of Jason

Exiled in Corinth, Jason was about to suffer a fate hardly less dramatic than that of Herakles.

He had been living in peace for a decade when "Creon, King of Corinth, promised him the hand of his daughter Glauce, whereupon Jason repudiated Medea in order to marry her." (Apollodorus.)

Like Herakles, the Thessalian prince was looking for a throne, to make up for the loss of Iolcos, where he would never reign.

He little knew his Colchian sorceress, if he imagined she would take this affront lying down: "Medea sent [her rival] a poisoned cloak that burned both her and her father, who had come rushing to her side." This garment with the vesicant properties is reminiscent of the tunic of Nessos the centaur.

"Then Medea killed her children by Jason and fled to Athens, where she married Aegeus, by whom she had a son named Medeius." From the days of the Argonauts, Theseus knew what his mother-in-law was capable of, and he watched his step—which was, no doubt, what saved him: "Medea then tried to kill Theseus, so that Medeius might inherit the throne of Attica, but they were both driven out of the country."[1]

[1] When Medeius grew up, "after defeating numerous barbarian tribes, he gave the name of Media to the countries he had conquered. He then set out on an expedition to India, during which he lost his life." (Apollodorus.)

Apollodorus then asserts that "Medea returned to Colchis incognito," and adds that upon her arrival she found Aeëtes dethroned by his brother, Perses, slew the usurper, and restored her father to the throne. But this is untrue, for the "eagle of the Caucasus" had been killed by Herakles.

According to Diodorus, "Jason, having lost his wife and children, took his own life." Another tradition relates that, while sleeping under the *Argo,* which was then on dry land (having been dedicated to Poseidon somewhere in the isthmus), a wooden beam accidentally fell on top of him and killed him—a pitiful end for a hero who had campaigned his way to the far shore of the Black Sea and been one of the first Hellenes to explore the interior of the European Continent.

The Incident at the Panathenaia

Although he was no longer bedeviled by Medea, Theseus' troubles were not over. Upon his return from Hades, at the height of his popularity, he undertook his most enduring achievement, the federation of the Attic demes (town councils), as a preliminary to Athenian supremacy in the Golden Age.

His place among the immortals was assured for his institution of the new regime, as much as for his military exploits; in the fifth century B.C., the Athenians erected a magnificent temple to his memory in the Agora.[2]

A great four-yearly procession commemorated the event for generations, with the citizens and *metekhi* (aliens, with no pejorative connotations), preceded by magistrates, sacrificers, musicians, and maidens bearing offerings, marching in a long line to the Parthenon to present Pallas Athena with a new tunic and crown her with gold. The crowd would flock to the top of the Areopagus, seat of the new Senate, and the Pynx, covered with the hovels of the poor, as to some great fair. The Agora, at the foot of the

[2] The temple of Theseus and its heroön, built by Cimon in the fifth century B.C. as a shrine for the hero's remains, stood on the southeast side of the Agora; the building known today as the Theseion was actually dedicated to Hephaestos, and acquired its other name by virtue of its bas-reliefs, most of which depict events in the life of Theseus.

festive Acropolis, was alive with people, and the great pillared stoas buzzed like hives.

In our century, when thousands of brightly dressed tourists pour down from the Parthenon on summer Sundays to visit the vast ruins where the heart of Athenian commerce used to throb, one can imagine the spectacle of that other throng, in its unique setting.

But the games that were part of the festivities on that first occasion led to an incident that had disastrous consequences for the city. Among the princes and ambassadors who had come from all over Greece to take part in them was one "Androgeos, son of Minos, who defeated all other contestants and became a favorite of the Athenians." (Diodorus.)

Champion athletes were adored by the people then as now, when the exploits of top performers can even open the doors of cabinet ministries.

"Aegeus was jealous of his popularity and, fearing that the son of King Minos [whose predilection for meddling in his neighbors' affairs has already been noted] might take advantage of it to dispossess him of his throne, laid a trap for him. He chose a moment when Androgeos was journeying to Thebes, and had him basely killed by a few Oenoenians." This was a fatal political error; the sovereign from Knossos was not likely to pass up such an opportunity.

"Upon hearing of the death of Androgeos, Minos hurried to Athens to demand justice for the murder. Obtaining no satisfaction, he declared war upon the Athenians, calling on Zeus, with many imprecations, to visit every conceivable calamity upon their heads."

His sincerity was increased by the fact that, as a result of her persistent commissioning and promoting of the heroic campaigns, "Athena" was becoming a dangerous rival to Cretan hegemony on the high seas.

He blockaded the port, causing a famine in Attica (where the soil is extremely poor), further aggravated by drought. "The situation grew so critical that the Athenians were forced to consult the [agrarian] Oracle of Apollo, who told them to give Minos whatever he might ask as retribution for the murder of Androgeos. Minos demanded seven young men and seven maidens, to be delivered to him every nine years as food for the Minotaur, so long as the monster should live."

Theseus and the Minotaur

It looked as though this tribute might have to be paid forever, for there would always be a high priest to don the mask of the bull.

During the first nine-year period Theseus bided his time and made his plans, then, "Minos returned to Attica with a large fleet, to take delivery of the fourteen youths and maidens." (Apollodorus.)

In league with Aegeus, Theseus joined them as one of the sacrificial group, and even though he was now a grown man,[3] the Cretan sovereign was delighted: the heir to the Attic throne would make an ideal hostage. The Minotaur obviously was not aware that his prisoner had sworn to kill him, but the ship's pilot was in the plot: "Just as they were setting sail, Aegeus told the pilot to hoist a white sail at his return if Theseus had killed the Minotaur, but to keep the black sail [as a sign of mourning] if he had perished." (Diodorus.) And the craft rode away toward Crete.

The "Labyrinth" at Knossos

Theseus was faced with a double problem: how to kill the Minotaur and how to escape from the labyrinth in which the monster kept his prey imprisoned. And this, as may be seen from a trip to the site, was no easy task.

He landed in what is today the charming little Cretan port of Iraklion, to which that other knight—*sans peur,* if not altogether *sans reproche*—had already bequeathed his name. From it, the road passes through several white hamlets and joins the Minoan highway near a little café—a place to pause for a cooling drink in the shade of an arbor, before setting out to explore the megaron of Knossos.

Just beyond the café there is a fork in the road; the left branch leads to the palace theater—a rectangular stage surrounded by mounting stone tiers (five hundred places were reserved for the guests of Minos). In the time of Theseus, boxing matches

[3] Many authors place the battle with the Minotaur in Theseus' youth, but the Paros marble would seem to indicate that it took place later.

and athletic contests were also held there, in addition to theatrical performances and a form of ballet, whose attitudes and movements have been preserved on frescoes and painted jars.

The other branch of the road passes over some foundations (those of the first palace) and stops at a portico, dominated by red-colonnaded propylaea. Their low, hulking proportions are reminiscent of Egypt, but on a less gargantuan scale. From the top of the staircase, the picturesque cypress-studded valley stretches out below. The monumental stairs open directly onto the second floor of the palace; like most of the structures here, it has been painstakingly rebuilt by Schliemann's successor, Sir Arthur Evans.[4] There were two more floors; from his terraces at the top, Minos could survey his whole empire: the sea.

In the center of this incredibly complicated edifice is a courtyard where a tower used to stand. On the left side of the courtyard is the throne room, with its griffin fresco and the stone seat with its undulating back on which the monarch used to take his place.

It is useless to attempt to describe the rest of the palace coherently—it is a maze of corridors, pantries, cryptlike chambers (going back to the period of the first megaron), moats, caches for the treasure, staircases, interconnected vestibules, cells, storerooms (the alignment of the jars is still visible), corridors ending in cul-de-sacs, pillared halls, bastions, balconies, servants' quarters, temples, prisons, and sewers—all inextricably intermingled.[5]

It was Evans' belief that the "labyrinth" simply referred to the priest-king's entire palace, in which he imprisoned the sons of the Athenian patricians.

Daedalus and Icarus

Most of this curious architectural conglomeration was the work of a high-born Athenian exile. Great-grandson of King Erechtheus of Athens, "son" of Hermes, and an artist and kinsman of the Orpheus of Eleusis, Daedalus was also the inventor of the level

[4] Schliemann identified the site, but, discouraged by the high price which its owner was asking for it, died without having investigated it, leaving to Evans the honor of excavating the palace of Daedalus.

[5] See plan of the megaron of Knossos.

and the drill, and the precursor of modern cybernetics: "He made statues which could walk and move by themselves."

His presence in Crete was the consequence of a crime: he had killed his nephew out of jealousy and was sentenced to death by the Areopagus, whereupon he fled to Minos, who set him to work enlarging his palace. He and his son Icarus were the first victims of the dungeon, for Minos, wishing to make certain that its secret could be kept, "locked them inside it. But they escaped," knowing, as they must, every twist and turn of the corridors for which they themselves had drawn the plans.

Daedalus improvised some wings—after all, he was the engineer who first "replaced oars by sails" on small craft, then, to divide their pursuers, he and Icarus sailed off in different directions. But they must have built their boats in such haste that they were not solid. (The Greeks still say that any loose bond is "stuck together with wax.") Icarus was unlucky: a gust of wind wrenched his sail from the flimsy mast, and he drowned in the sea which was thereafter known as the Icarian. Only his unhappy father escaped, to land either at Cumae in Italy (according to Virgil), in Sicily, near the home of King Cocalos (the "gaunt"), or perhaps at Memphis in Egypt, where it is said that the inhabitants worshiped him after his death, on account of his great creations.

It was not child's play, certainly, to escape from the labyrinth, but as he was being led into it, Theseus could console himself with the thought that someone had done it before him.

Ariadne's Thread

Quite unexpectedly his task was facilitated: "Ariadne, the daughter of Minos, fell in love with Theseus, who was exceptionally handsome; she spoke to him and offered him her help." (Diodorus.) Without further ado, the hero put his plan into action. "He slew the Minotaur and escaped from the labyrinth, Ariadne having shown him the way . . ." The legend speaks of a thread which the princess gave him to help him find the exit.

As the crowning stroke in his humiliation of the "malevolent Minos" (*Odyssey,* XI), "Theseus secretly kidnaped Ariadne before returning to his own country. He sailed out of the port by night and came to the island of Dia, now called Naxos.

"It was there, legend has it, that Dionysos was blinded by Ariadne's beauty and stole her away from Theseus. He married her and was always deeply devoted to her."

Unless he had lived for more than a century, this Dionysos could not be the same adventurer with whom Perseus had come to blows. It must have been one of his descendants, heir to the vines which the "god" planted on Naxos.

Perhaps the fickle Ariadne, who dearly loved "fine-looking men," was a willing victim, and perhaps the wine grower took her by force, but in either case Theseus, with only one ship, was in no position to retaliate, so he set sail again without his fair companion, and in the depths of despair.

The Baptism of the Aegean

The hero was so distraught that "he forgot Aegeus' orders and sailed into Attica without striking his black sail. Aegeus, seeing the ship from afar and believing his son dead, bravely took his own life . . ." (Diodorus) by throwing himself into the waves, thus giving a name to the Greek sea which it has kept ever since.

"Theseus succeeded his father."

The Tragedy of Phaedra

His reign was not, however, an auspicious one. In order to re-establish relations with Crete, he married Phaedra, another of Minos' daughters, but she fell in love with Hippolytus, Theseus' son by Hippolyte (the Amazon).

The young man would not satisfy her passion, so the vindictive Phaedra accused him of trying to force her (as Stheneboea before her, prompted by the same motive, had accused Bellerophon in front of his father).

In his fury, Theseus sent Hippolytus to suffer the vengeance of Poseidon.

The legend says that Theseus soon saw what he had done, and the horrified, remorseful Phaedra finally hanged herself in desperation. The hero never recovered. The man who, in his younger days, had slain so many robbers on the road from Troezen to Corinth, killed the bull of Marathon, hunted the Calydonian boar, and shared in the tribulations of the Argonauts, and in his adulthood released Pallas from the Cretan extortion, killed the Minotaur, and, most important of all, federated the Attic cities, launching Athens on the road to economic, naval, and political supremacy in Greece—"Theseus, son of Aegeus, a godlike man" (*Iliad,* I), went off to die an exile on the island of Scyros, bitter, inconsolable at the loss of his son, and also a victim, although indirectly, of Phaedra's calumny.

Chapter XVII
THE SWORD OF IRON

The days of the gods with the sword of bronze were over.

"Leaving Trachis, the Heraclids took refuge in Attica, where they were pursued by the fury of Eurystheus, who threatened to declare war on Ceyx [the successor of Theseus] if he did not surrender them immediately." (Apollodorus.)

Aristotle says (L. VII, c. 6) that Herakles had seventy-two children by the various women whose beds he had shared: seventy-one sons and one daughter. Apollodorus lists their names, and adds that "they went to Athens and stood as suppliants before the altar of Pity, imploring the Athenians for help."

If Euripides and Pherecydes (*Anton. Liber.* 32) can be trusted, they were given asylum by Demophon, son of Theseus, but Diodorus (L. IV, c. 57) and Pausanias say it was Theseus himself who took them in and defended them against their enemies.

Apollodorus: "The Athenians refused to surrender them, and went to war with Eurystheus, who, when leaving for the campaign, entrusted the government of Mycenae and the kingdom to Atreus, his mother's brother, because of their kinship." (Thucydides, *Peloponnesian War,* L. I.)

The Athenians defeated the Argive forces "and killed five of the king's sons. Eurystheus fled in his chariot, and Hyllus pursued him beyond the Scironides rocks and killed him." But Pausanias and Pindar say it was Iolas who cut off his head, near the Mocarian spring. Whichever it was, "the head was taken to Alcmene, Herakles' mother, who stabbed its eyes with her shuttle."

Apollodorus writes: "Eurystheus being dead, the Heracleans entered the Peloponnesus."

But it is Thucydides who sees the deeper implications of this final tragedy: "Since Eurystheus did not return, Atreus, having won the people by flattery, seized the throne with the consent of the Mycenaeans, who feared the Heraclids and believed Atreus would be a good king; and the Pelopids were more powerful than the Perseids.

"That, in my opinion, was Agamemnon's legacy; also, his navy was the most powerful of all, and so he was able to organize the great campaign."

That is why, when the time came to set sail for Troy,[1] he was named commander-in-chief of the Greeks.

But the Dorians had already crossed the mountain barriers of the Pindus and Rhodopes, driving back the Achaeans with their swords of bronze, and soon supplanted them throughout Greece.

The Perseids had buried their dead; these new tribes cremated them.

But most important of all, they brandished a new weapon: the sword of iron.

[1] 1218 B.C., according to the Paros marble; 1192 B.C., according to modern scholars.

COMPARATIVE CHRONOLOGIES OF THE LIVES OF HERAKLES, THESEUS, AND JASON

Year[1]	*Year*[2]	*Herakles*	*Theseus*	*Jason*
1362	1261	Birth		
		Childhood and		
1340		Youth	Birth	
		in Thebes	Childhood	Birth
		Lion of Cithaera	=Herakles' visit	
			to Troezen	Childhood
		Orchomenos	Youth at	in care of
		Marries Megara	Troezen	Chiron
1330		Slays children		
		Delphi		
		First labors		
1326		*Purification at*		
		Eleusis		
		Tauros in Crete	In the isthmus	
		Diomedes	Tauros at Marathon	At Iolcos
		Hippolyte	Calydon	=
	1225	Argo	=Argo	=Calydon
		Caucasus		Argo
1320				
		Geryon		
			Amazon Wars	
			Abduction of	
			Persephone	Corinth
		Hesperides	In Hades	
		Hades		
		Oechalia	Release from	
		with Omphale	Hades	

[1] Paros marble (264 B.C.).
[2] Will Durant's *Story of Civilization* (French edition, 1962).

Year[1]	*Year*[2]	*Herakles*	*Theseus*	*Jason*
1310				
		Troy		
1308		*Elis*		
			Medea in Athens	Glauce
				Death of Jason
		Calydon		
		Deianeira		
		Thespian War		./.
	1209	Death of Herakles		
1300				
			Panathenaia	
1295			Athens and Minos II	

[1] Paros marble (264 B.C.).
[2] Will Durant's *Story of Civilization* (French edition, 1962).

CHRONOLOGIES

(ancient and modern)

OF THE PERIOD FROM THE FOUNDING OF ATHENS TO HOMER

Generally accepted at present		*Paros*[1] *marble*		
1582		1582	Cecrops, King of Athens	
		1574	Deucalion on Mount Parnassus	
1433	or	1529	Deucalion—flood in Thessaly	
1313	or	1519	Cadmos at Thebes (Thotmes I in Egypt)	First fifty-oar vessel First chariot, imported from Phoenicia
		1510	Danaos in Argos	
		1506	Minos I	
		1409	Demeter and the Eleusinian Mysteries (Amenhotep III in Egypt)	Cereal culture in Attica
		1399	Orpheus, Eumolpus, and Musaeus	
1241	or	1326	Purification of Herakles in Athens	
		1308	Herakles in Elis	
		1295	Athens and Minos II	
1213	or	1251	Adrastos and the Seven against Thebes	
1192			Trojan War	
1183			Fall of Troy	
		1087	Ionian emigration Founding of Miletus	
900	or	937	Homer and Hesiod	

[1] Modern historians propose several intermediary chronologies; the one on the left is taken from Will Durant (*The Life of Greece,* French edition of 1962). All are approximative, but whichever is adopted, the order of events remains the same, and that is what matters.

PRINCIPAL SITES OF THE HEROIC AGE

N.B. Variant spellings, i.e., Latin, or different transliterations of ancient or modern Greek, may occur elsewhere in the book.

Achelous R.
Aegean
Aegina
Agrigentum
Akragas (see Agrigentum)
Alesia
Alpheus
Arcadia
Argive Heraeum
Argos
Athens
Atlas
Avernus, Lake
Azores

Bosporus Thracius
Byzantium

Calydon
Canaries
Carthage
Celtica
Charybdis, Reggio
Cnossos or Knossos
Colchis (modern Georgia)
Copais, Lake
Corcyra (modern Corfu)
Corinth
Corsica
Cos
Crau (the "Story Plain")
Crete
Crotona
Cumae

Damala (Troezen)
Danube
Delphi
Dodona

Echinades Is.
Elba
Electras
Eleusis
Elis (city and region)
Epidaurus
Epirus
Erymanthus
Erytheia (see Gades)
Euboea
Evenos

Gades (also Gadire, Erytheia; modern Cádiz)
Gadire (see Gades)
Gortyna

Hellespont (Dardanelles)
Heraclea
Herakleion (Iraklion)
Herculaneum
Hercules, Pillars of

Iberia
Inachos R.
Iolcos

Lemnos
Lerna
Leucadia (modern Levkas)
Libya
Livorno
Lycia

Marathon
Meganese (modern Taphos)
Messina, Scylla
Monaco
Mycenae
Mysia

Nauplia
Nemea

Oechalia
Oeta
Olympia
Orchomenos
Ormenion
Ortygia

Paros
Peloponnesus
Piraeus
Pisae
Pontus Euxinus (Black Sea)
Pylos

Reggio, Charybdis
Rhine
Rhône
Rome

Santorini (formerly Thera)
Scironides
Scylla, Messina
Seriphos
Strymon
Stymphalos
Symplegades (see Bosporus)
Syracuse

Taenarum, Cape (Hades)
Taphos (Meganese)
Taravo
Tartessus
Tassili
Thebes
Thera (Santorini)
Thermodon R.
Thessaly
Thrace
Tiryns
Tomi
Tretos
Tritonis, Lake
Troezen (Damala)
Troy

Vesuvius
Volos

BIBLIOGRAPHY

PRINCIPAL CLASSICAL AUTHORS CONSULTED
(*original, and texts of scholiasts*)

APOLLODORUS OF ATHENS: *Bibliotheca* (French; Clavier tr.), Paris, 1805. (Generally considered spurious.)

DIODORUS SICULUS: *Historical Library* (French; Hoefer tr.), Paris, 1865–66.

EURIPIDES: *Works* (French, L. Parmentier and H. Grégoire trs.), Paris, 1923.

HERODOTUS: *Works* (French; P. E. Legrand tr.), Paris, 1944.

HESIOD: *Works and Days* (French), Paris, 1863.
Shield of Herakles (French), Paris, 1834. (Considered spurious.)
Poems (French), Paris, 1873.

HOMER: *Iliad* and *Odyssey* (French; Pléïade edition), Paris, 1957.

OVID: *Heroides* (French), Lyon, 1573.

PAUSANIAS: *Description of Greece* (French; C. Poncelin tr.), Paris, 1797.

SOPHOCLES: *Plays* (French; Rochefort tr.), Avignon, 1810.

THEOCRITUS: *Idylls* (French; edition prepared by a Société d'Héllénistes); Paris, Hachette, 1847.

THUCYDIDES: *History of the Peloponnesian War* (French; J. Voilquin tr.), Paris, 1936.

and the other works quoted in the book.

NOTE: The oldest important sources of material on the Greek heroes are Homer and Pherecydes, authors flourishing at least four centuries after the events of which they purport to give a "fictionalized" account. To give readers some perspective, then, their allegations may fairly be accorded the same degree of accuracy as the *Chanson de Roland,* composed by the bard Turold between four and five hundred years after the battle of Ronceveaux to glorify the deeds of the knights of Charlemagne. The same critical processes have been employed in both cases to distinguish between history and the legends elaborated by oral tradition.

PRINCIPAL MODERN AUTHORS CONSULTED

English

J. ALSOP—*From the Silent Earth,* New York, 1962.
WILL DURANT—*The Story of Civilization* (in French), Paris, 1962.
ENGBERG—*The Hyksos Reconsidered,* Chicago, 1939.
E. EVANS—*De Scripta Minoa,* Oxford, 1909.
——*The Palace of Cnossos,* London, 1921.
HALL—*Old Civilisation of Greece,* London, 1901.
J. HARLAND—*The Peloponnessos in the Bronze Age,* Cambridge, 1923.
J. H. HARTLAND—*The Legend of Perseus,* London, 1896.
KANTOR—*The Aegean and the Orient in the 2nd Millennium B.C.,* Bloomington, 1947.
A. LANG—*The World of Homer,* London, 1910.
S. MARINATOS—*Crete and Mycenae,* London and New York, 1960.
H. J. SPINDEN—*The Reduction of Mayan Dates,* Cambridge, 1924.
I. VELIKOVSKY—*Worlds in Collision* (in French), Paris, 1955.

French

J. BÉRARD—L'Homère des anciens n'est-il plus? (*Figaro littéraire,* 4.9.1954).
——*Recherches sur la chronologie mycénienne,* Paris, 1950.
V. BÉRARD—*Les Phéniciens et l'Odyssée,* Paris, 1927.
——*Calypso et la mer de l'Atlantide,* Paris, 1929.
——*Ithaque et la Grèce des Achéens,* Paris, 1938.
——*Pénélope et les barons des îles,* Paris, 1928.
H. BOUCHER—*La dispute du trépied et les vases peints à sujets héracléïens*), Paris, 1913.
F. CHAMOUX—*La civilisation grecque,* Paris, 1963.
P. COMELIN—*Mythologie grecque et romaine,* Paris, 1956.
L. COTTRELL—*Le Taureau de Minos,* Paris, 1956.
——*La porte des lions,* Paris, 1965.
E. DAVIN—*La crau antique,* Toulon, 1940.
DÉCHELETTE—*Archéologie préhistorique.*
F. DIEL—*Le symbolisme dans la mythologie grecque,* Paris, 1952.
H. D. DISSELHOFF—Les grandes civilisations de l'Amérique ancienne, Paris, 1963.
E. DOBLHOFER—*Le déchiffrement des écritures,* Paris, 1959.
E. DROULERS—*Dictionnaire des attributs, allégories, etc.*

GATEFOSSÉ ET ROUX—*Bibliographie de l'Atlantide,* 1927.
GLOTZ—*La civilisation égéenne,* Paris, 1923.
R. GROSJEAN—*Les statues menhirs de Corse* Centre national de recherches scientifiques, 1957, 1958, 1959, 1960.
R. HENNING—*Les grandes énigmes de l'univers,* Paris, 1957.
P. HIRMENECH—*Hercule préhistorique,* Le Mans, 1909.
H. KITTO—*Les Grecs, autoportrait d'une civilisation,* Paris, 1959.
LAGRANGE—*La Crète ancienne,* Paris, 1908.
M. LAUNEY—*Le sanctuaire et le culte d'Hercule à Thasos,* Paris, 1923.
P. LE COUR—*L'Atlantide,* Paris, 1950.
R. L. LEFÈVRE—*Héraklès,* Paris, 1930.
G. MASPÉRO—*Histoire ancienne des peuples de l'Orient,* Paris, 1895–97.
R. MATTON—*La Crète antique,* Athens, 1960.
MONTESSUS DE BALLDORE—*Ethnographie sismique et mythologie,* Paris, 1923.
G. POISSON—*L'Atlantide devant la science,* Paris, 1945.
——Tantale, roi des Hittites, *Revue archéologique,* 1925, p. 75.
E. POTTIER—*Pourquoi Thésée fut l'ami d'Hercule,* Paris, 1901.
L. PURPER—*La résurrection de la mythologie,* Paris, 1894.
E. RECLUS—*L'Homme et la Terre,* Paris, 1905.
N. K. SANDERS—*Les derniers secrets de la planète,* Paris, 1957.
D. SAURAT—*L'Atlantide et le monde des géants,* Paris, 1954.
H. TAZIEFF—*Quand la terre tremble,* Paris, 1962.
——*Cratères en feu,* Paris, 1957.
J. VERCOUTTER—*Essais sur les relations entry Egyptiens et Préhellènes,* Paris, 1954.

German

H. BESIG—*Gorgo und gorgoneion,* Berlin, 1937.
H. SCHLIEMANN—*Illion,* Leipzig, 1888.
——*Mykene,* Leipzig, 1877.
——*Troja,* Leipzig, 1883.
O. WASER—*Skylla und Charybdis,* Zurich, 1894.
and the other works quoted in the book.

NOTE: Having observed how often the "*Guides Bleus*" are used by tourists in Greece and Italy, I have attempted to simplify identification of the sites by adopting, whenever possible, the order of the visit and condensed historical form employed in those popular publications.

INDEX

Abas, 34
Abas, Mount, 190
Abdera, 146, 192–93
Abderos, 146
Abyle, 191
Acastus, 167
Achaean age, similarity of Christian Middle Ages to, 119, 236
Achaeans, 22, 26, 29–70, 119, 162, 177, 184ff., 252
Achaean sword, 210–11
Achaeos, 22
Achelous River, 29, 237–38
Achilles, 23, 167, 229
Acrisios, 34–36, 37, 50
Acrocorinthus, Corinth, 57–58
Acropolis, Athens, 29, 153–54; Panathenaia, 244–45
Admete, 147
Aeëtes, 162–63, 164, 166, 173–74, 175–77, 178, 183, 244
Aegean civilization, development of, 15ff., 19ff.
Aegean Sea, 163n, 164; naming of, 249
Aegeus (father of Theseus; ninth king of Athens), 29, 93–94, 151, 156, 181, 243, 245, 246, 249, 250
Aegina (island), 166, 180
Aeginios, 166, 239
Aegios, 129
Aegyptos, 30
Aenos, 150
Aeolians, 22
Aeolos, 22
Aeschylus, 1, 38
Aesclepiades (Bellerophon), 61–69. *See also* Bellerophon
Aeson (father of Jason), 94, 180–81
Aethlios, 23
Aethra, 93–94
Aetolia (Aetolians), 23, 68, 158–59, 166
Aetolos, 23, 166
Africa, 15–16, 17, 28. *See also* specific countries, individuals, locations
Agamemnon, 2, 8, 103, 168n, 231, 252
Agathon of Zante, 9, 166
Agenor, 23
Agora, Athens, 143; temple of Theseus, 244–45
Agriculture, 123, 124, 125
Agrigentum, 204–7; temple of Herakles, 206–7; temple of Zeus, 206
Ajax, 167
Akragas, 205–7
Albion, 193
Alcaeos (later Herakles), 79, 80–82. *See also* Herakles (Hercules)
Alcaeus, 70, 73, 74, 116, 148
Alcinous, 179
Alcmene, 73, 74, 75–76, 78, 79, 80, 84, 86–88, 233, 251
Alebion, 193
Alesia, 193–94, 210
Alexander (the Great), 12, 23, 224
Alphabet, brought to Greece by Phoenicians, 62
Alpheus, 72, 139, 141, 143, 201–2, 209
Althaea, 54–55
Altis, 139, 142, 143, 144
Amazons, 54, 63, 167, 168; of the Thermodon, Herakles and, 147–49; Theseus and, 181
Amon, 47; oracle of, 47
Amphiaraos, 156
Amphibia (Nicippe), 74, 85, 109
Amphitryon, 73, 74–79, 80–82, 84–86, 87, 89, 90, 91, 92, 98, 125
Amphoras, 13, 25, 235; painters, 122
Amycos, 170–71
Amymone (river), 117
Amyntor, 239
Anaxo, 73, 74
Ancaeus, 166, 172
Androgeos (son of Minos), 245
Androgeus, 148, 150
Andromeda, 47–48, 50, 56, 74, 150
Animal totems, 11
Antaeus, 188, 189
Antagoras, 232
Anteia, 34, 61
Antilochus, 3
Antinoë, 180–81
Aphrodite, 48, 168
Apis, 21
Apollo, 31, 102–3, 128, 141, 149, 190n, 209, 240; temples of, 31, 100–4
Apollodorus, 12, 243, 244; on Amphitryon, 70, 73–74; on Bellerophon,

63, 64, 130; on Herakles, 18, 90, 94, 97, 98, 104, 109, 110, 111, 114–20, 126–30, 134, 135n, 137, 138, 146–69, 183, 185, 186, 190, 192, 193, 198, 199, 207, 208, 211, 213, 215–17, 222, 223, 225, 231–42 *passim;* on Jason and the Argonauts, 160, 162–64, 166, 167, 169, 170, 171, 175, 176, 179, 180–81, 243, 244; on Perseus, 34, 35, 37–42, 45, 46, 47, 49, 50, 54, 56; on Theseus, 151, 246
Apollo Musagetes, 103
Apolonius Rhodius, 74, 109, 120, 130, 166, 169, 175, 178, 179
Apsis, Mount, 31, 33
Apsyrtus, 175–76
Arcadia, 119, 120, 121, 127, 128, 233
Archaeology (archaeologists), 1–5, 12, 141–42, 165–66, 228–30 (*see also* specific individuals, locations); mythological process and, 6–14
Archimedes, 204; tomb of, 204
Areopagus, Athens, 244–45, 248
Areopolis, 218–19
Ares (god of war), 41, 147, 186
Ares, island of, 130
Arethusa, 201–2, 203, 212–13
Argive Heraeum, 82–84, 86–87
Argo (ship), 164–81, 244
Argolis (Argives), 30, 34ff., 51–56, 70, 73, 74, 80ff., 104ff. 115ff., 184, 225. *See also* specific events, individuals
Argonauts, Jason and the, 160–81, 209; map of voyages of, 161; muster roll of, 166–68
Argos (city), 31–34ff., 50–56, 58, 73, 74, 75–79, 80ff., 92, 105ff., 150, 164; plain of ("cask of the Danaans"), 33
Argos (founder of Argos, the city), 92, 164
Argos (port on island of Elba), 178
Argos (son of Phrixos), 164
Ariadne, 248–49
Aristotle, 90, 169, 251
Arkhala Khori, 26–27
Armor (armorers), 112–13, 210. *See also* Helmets; Shields; Swords
Arrian, 176
Artemis, 69, 127, 128, 158
Ascalaphos, 167
Asia, (Asians), 15, 19, 70, 73, 75, 120, 162. *See also* Asia Minor; specific individuals, people, places
Asia Minor, 17, 19, 59, 70, 123, 147, 169, 170, 183, 227, 228. *See also* specific individuals, people, places
Asklepiades, 140
Asparus, 176
Asterion, 167
Asterodeia, 175
Asterope, 180–81
Astrology, 125
Astronomy, 214
Atalanta, 167, 175
Athalia (Elba), 178
Athena, 123, 144, 145, 156, 218, 227, 244–45; and Athens, 141, 145, 154–55, 156; and Bellerophon, 64, 67–68, 123; and Jason and the Argonauts, 164, 172; and golden apples of the Hesperides, 214–15; and Herakles, 111, 130, 141, 189, 208–15, 218; Panathenaia, 244–45; and Perseus, 39, 41, 42, 45, 49, 55, 56; statues in Parthenon of, 154–55
Athenaeus, 92
Athena Oxyderkes, temple of, 31
Athens (Athenians), 39, 76–77, 144, 145, 156, 152–56; Acropolis, 153–54; Atlantides and, 18; Herakles and, 141, 189 (*see also* Herakles); Panathenaia, 244–45; Parthenon, 154–55; Polis, 155–56; Theseus and supremacy of, 244ff.; twelfth-century B.C., 155–56; twentieth-century A.D., 152–55
Athletes (athletics), 140–41, 144, 245, 247. *See also* Games; Olympic Games; Wrestling matches
Atlantic Ocean, earthquakes in, 192
Atlantides, 18, 27, 28, 185ff., 212, 214, 242
Atlantis, 192; disappearance of, 17–18, 28, 43
Atlas, 16, 43, 127, 212. *See also* Atlas, Mount; Atlas Mountains
Atlas, Mount, 16, 43, 127, 185, 212, 213, 214
Atlas Mountains, 16, 127, 128, 212, 213
Atreus, 75, 168n, 251, 252
Attica, 29, 55, 76–77, 122, 123, 138, 155, 156, 157, 181; Theseus and federation of cities of, 243, 245ff.
Auge, 236
Augeias, King, 167, 233–34; Herakles and Augeian stables of, 131–34
Autolycos, 89, 113, 166, 226
Automedusa, 115
Avernus, Lake, 198, 209
Azores, 17n, 18, 43–45, 192; map of, 32, 60

Bacchantes, 54, 120, 121
Bali Dagh, 228
Bebryces (Bebrycans), 148, 170–71
Bellerophon, 18, 56, 61–69, 185, 186–87; and Amazons, 63; labors of, 62,

63ff.; and Pegasus, 64ff.; slays Chimaera, 62–63, 64
Belleros, King of Corinth, 61, 62
Bergius, 193
Birds of prey, Herakles and, 129–30, 183–84
Bistones, 146
Black Sea, 147, 162, 166, 172, 177, 244
Boars, 11, 119; Herakles and Erymanthian "boar," 119–22, 157; Theseus and Calydonian "boar," 157–59; Theseus and Crommyonian "boar," 152
Boeotia, 29–30, 78, 95, 163. *See also* specific cities
Boreas (north wind), 13, 132n, 166, 171, 188, 228, 232
Bosporus, 172, 176, 177
Bouletiron, Olympia, 143
Bournarbashi, 228
Brephonas, 204
Bronze, use of, 20, 26, 27, 184, 210, 242; swords, 27, 210–11, 242, 252
Bulls (bullfighting), 132–33, 179, 203, 207, 237; Europe and Cretan "bull," 23–25; Herakles and Cretan "bull," 137–38, 187; Jason and, 173–75; Theseus and "bull" of Marathon, 156–57
Busiris, King of Egypt, 189, 214
Butes, 167
Bybon, 140
Byzantium, 176
Byzas, 176

Cacos, 195
Cádiz, 28, 42
Cadmos, 23, 29–30, 54, 75, 92, 163
Caieta, 178
Calais, 166, 171
"Caldron, The" (La Caldeira), 44, 45
Callimachos, 234
Callirhoë, 185
Calpe, 191
Calydon (Calydonians), 158–59, 237–38
Campania, 197
Canary Islands, 18
Cape Cyclops, 38
Cape of the Sword, 38
Carians, 19, 25
Carthage, 185, 189, 203
Cassandra, 9
Cassiopeia, 47, 56
Cassiterides Islands (Tin Isles), 26, 178, 184
Castalian spring, Delphi, 101, 102, 103
Castor and Pollux (the Dioscuri), 158, 166, 178, 206
Cattle (livestock) (*see also* Bulls; Goats); Herakles and, 184–91, 198–99, 203, 207, 208, 209, 214
Caucasus (Caucasians), 162, 163, 170, 173, 175, 177, 183–84
Caverns (Hades), 215–24
Caves of Hercules, 188n
Cecrops, 29, 76, 156
Celtica. *See* Celts (Celtica)
Celts (Celtica), 177, 178, 191, 192, 194
Centaurs, 119–22, 135, 238–39
Cephalus, 76–77, 78, 79
Cepheus, 47–48, 166
Cephises (stream), 95, 97
Cerberus, 201, 215, 216, 219, 220–24
Cercopes, 227
Cercyon, 152
Cereals, cultivation of, 123, 125
Ceres, 123, 124. *See also* Demeter
Cerynean "hind," Herakles and the, 126–28
Ceto, 27
Cetos (ship), 48
Ceyx, King of Trachis, 239, 251
Chalciope, 232
Chalcodon, 232
Charioteer statue, Delphi museum, 100–1
Chariots (chariot races), 54, 71–73, 89, 122–23
Charybdis, 40, 179
Chemical analysis, use in archaeology, 13
Chemicals, trade in, 26
Chimaera, 59, 62–63, 64, 115, 123
Chiron (centaur), 94
Chott Depressions, 16, 39–40, 179
Chrestomathia, 3
Chrysaor, 59, 61, 63, 184–86, 190–91
Cicero, 197, 207
Cilicians, 19
Cilix, 23
Cimon, temple of Theseus built by, 244n
Circe, 173
Cithaeron, Mount, Herakles and killing of lion of, 91, 93, 99, 105, 109, 114
Città Vecchia, 203
Cius, 169
Cleatos, 233–34
Cleite, 169
Clement of Alexandria, 170
Cleomenes, 104n
Cleonae, 111, 233, 234
Clymenus, 96
Clytemnestra, 181
Clytia, 232
Cocalos, King, 248
Colchis (Colchians), 159, 160–64, 170, 173–76, 184, 243, 244
Comaetho, 78
Concord sanctuary, Akragas, 206

Copais, Lake, 95
Copper working, 16, 20, 26
Copreus, 115, 121
Corcyra (Corfu), 179
Corinth, 21, 52, 53, 54, 57ff., 68, 129, 178, 238, 243; Acrocorinthus, 57–58; Bellerophon of, 57–69; description and remains, 57–59; isthmus, 58–59; Peirene fountain house, 57; Peribolae, 57
Corinth, Gulf of, 29, 39, 129
Corone, 150
Corsica, 27, 60
Corvo (island), 44
Corytas, 101, 102
Cos, 232
Creon, King of Corinth, 243
Creon, King of Thebes, 75–76, 78, 96–98
Crete (Cretans), 20, 23–29, 77–78, 137–38, 145, 148, 245–49 (*see also* specific events, individuals, locations); Argonauts and, 179–81; collapse of Minoan civilization (earthquakes and fire), 5, 13–14, 26–27; Herakles and, 137–38, 187ff.; Herakles and "bull" of, 137–38; Knossos palace, 6, 9, 13–14, 20, 25, 246–47; as naval power, 77–78; Theseus and the Minotaur of, 245–49
Cretheus, King of Thessaly, 94
Critias (Plato), 15n
Critidas, 204
Crommyonian "boar," 152
Croöntiades, 98
Croton, 207–8
Crotona, 207–8, 210
Cumae, Italy, 195, 196, 248
Curetes, 158–59
Cyane, 203
Cyclades, 20, 25, 26, 49
Cyclops, 33, 48–49, 50, 51, 52, 58, 108, 119n
Cycnus, 239
Cygeos, 204
Cymbals, Herakles and use of, 130
Cyrene, 145, 167
Cyzicus, 168, 169

Daduchos, the, 125, 126
Daedalus, 7, 247–48
Damala, 93
Danaans, 33–34. *See also* Danaos
Danaë, 12, 34–39, 49, 50, 56
Danaos, 30, 31, 33–34, 36, 55, 70, 75, 80n, 92
Danube River and valley, 19, 176, 177–78
Dardanelles (Hellespont). *See* Hellespont (Dardanelles)
Deianeira, 55, 135, 237–40
Deicoön, 98
Deino, 28, 39–40
Delphi, 98–104; *Charioteer* statue, 100–1; museum, 100; oracle, 11, 101–4, 207, 224, 226, 240; ruins, 99–100; sacred forest, 99; Sacred Way, 100; secret of, 101ff.; temple of Apollo, 22, 100–4; Treasury of the Athenians, 100
Demarates, 104
Demes (town councils), Attic, 244
Demeter, 201, 202, 203, 205–6; Eleusis sanctuary of, 122–26
Demophon, 251
Denys, 203
Dercynos, 193
Deucalion, 21–23, 94, 162, 163, 192
Dexamenos, 135
Dia (Naxos), 249. *See also* Naxos
Diktys, 37, 49, 50
Diodorus Siculus, 12, 80; on Dionysos, 80, 96–97, 99, 101, 102; on Herakles, 18, 80, 96–97, 99, 101, 102, 114, 116, 117, 119, 120, 121, 122, 125, 135, 139, 140, 146, 147, 148, 183–217 *passim,* 223, 225, 226, 227, 233, 234, 238, 239, 240, 242, 251; on Jason, 163, 167, 169, 170, 175, 176, 177, 178, 181, 244; on Theseus, 151, 246, 249
Diomedes, King of Thrace, Herakles and "mares" of, 145–47
Dionysians, 54–55. *See also* Dionysos
Dionysos, 54–55, 102, 120–21, 135, 144, 145, 167, 189, 249
Dionysos of Halikarnassos, 195
Dioscuri, the, 158, 206. *See also* Castor and Pollux
Dnieper River and valley, 19
Dniester River and valley, 19
Dodona, 9, 164–66, 208
Doliones, the, 168–69
Doriaeus the Lacedaemonian, 200
Dorians, 22, 236, 239, 252
Doros, 22. *See also* Dorians
Dragons, 63, 122–23, 162–63, 185, 213, 215, 223; "teeth" of, 163, 173
Drialos, 219

Eachos, 217n
Eagles, 11, 162–63, 183–84
Earthquakes, 13–14, 17, 57, 58n, 65, 110, 172, 191–92, 196–97, 200–1. *See also* Volcanoes (volcanic eruptions); specific locations
Echidne (the Spider), 28–29, 59, 60, 63, 109, 115, 162, 173, 183, 213, 216, 219 (*see also* Echinades Islands); death of, 67–68

Echinades Islands (Echinadians), 28–30, 42, 61, 74, 77, 78–79, 108, 127, 135, 173, 216, 223; pirates from, 39, 59, 64–68, 128, 129, 171
Egypt (Egyptians), 16, 19, 20, 21, 26, 29–30, 47–48, 51, 77n; "darkness over Egypt," 13–14; Herakles and, 183, 189, 211, 214; Pharaohs, 11–12, 20, 47, 77n, 189, 214
Eileithyia, 82
El Djerid Chott (Gulf of Gabès), 40
Electra, 181
Electryon, 70, 73, 74–75, 76
Eleios, 131n
Elektras River, 24
Eleusis, 122–26; mysteries of, 124, 125–26; Persephone in, 182; Sacred Way, 124; sanctuary of Demeter, 182, 201, 202, 217
Eleutherios (stream), 83
Elis (Eleans), 23, 109, 111, 115, 121, 131–35, 138, 139, 233–34
Elysian Fields, 126
Englianos, 235
Enyo, 28, 39–40
Epeios, 23
Ephyra, 20–21, 58
Epidaurus, 53–54, 151; theater, 53–54
Epirus, 164–65, 208
Eratosthenes, 40
Ercolano, 197
Ereb, 24, 29
Erechtheion, 155, 156
Erechtheus, King of Athens, 76–77, 155, 156
Erginios, 172n
Erginus, 96–97
Erymanthian "boar," Herakles and, 11, 119–22
Erytheia (*see also* Gades); 28, 42, 47, 59; Herakles and cattle of, 184–91, 212–13
Eryx (the Phorcid), 199–200
Ethiopia, 17
Etna, Mount, 41, 123, 199
Etruscans, 195
Euboea, 169, 239
Euboean Gulf, 94
Eumolpus, 90, 125n, 126, 217
Euneos, 168
Eunomos, 238
Euphemos, 167
Eupolemos (architect), 83
Euripides, 34, 53, 95, 99, 137, 183, 212, 251
Euripylos, 232
Europe, 23–25, 29–30, 137
Euryale, 28, 42, 44, 46, 116, 212–13
Euryalos, 167
Eurydice, 34, 73, 74
Eurystheus, King of Argos, 62n, 73, 85–86, 167; death of, 251–52; and labors of Herakles, 104, 105ff., 114–15, 118, 121–22, 126, 128, 131, 133, 135, 138, 145–47, 150, 184, 208–9, 213, 215, 223, 233, 251–52
Eurythos, 90
Eurytion, 135, 185–86, 190–91
Eurytos, 166
Eurytus, King of Oechalia, 225–26, 233–34, 239
Euxinus. *See* Black Sea
Evans, Sir Arthur, 6, 9, 12, 247
Evenus, 238
Exedra of Herodes Atticus, 142
Extortion, 11, 95, 109, 111, 119, 121, 137, 250. *See also* Pirates (piracy); Tolls

Faial (island), 44, 45
Faustina, 144
Fertility worship, 84–85, 102–3, 147, 237
Field of Truth, 217
"Fifty" (number), Greek use of to indicate many, 92, 117, 236
Fleece, 11. *See also* Golden fleece
Flores (island), 44
Foxes, 11, 76–77, 91

Gades, 184, 190, (*see also* Erytheia); straits of, 178
Galatians, 100n, 193
Galatus, 193
Games, 234, 244–45. *See also* Athletes; Olympic Games
Ganymede, 150
Gaugatas, 204
Gaul, 193, 194
Geryon, 59, 63, 78n, 109, 185–86, 187, 199, 205, 208, 233–34
Ghea (Mother Earth), 27, 102–3, 139, 165
Giants, 55, 59, 195–98, 206
Glaucos, 61, 69
Goats, 63, 101
Golden apples of the Hesperides, 213–15
Golden fleece, 11, 160, 162–81, 213, 214–15
Gorgons, 27, 28, 39, 40, 42–46, 49, 59, 60, 116, 127, 184ff., 212–13
Gortyna, 24, 138
Gothic arch, Cyclops' use of, 119
Graeae, 27, 28, 39, 40, 42, 45, 127, 185, 213
Great Britain, 26n, 178
Great Ehoiai (Hesiod), 163
Greece, 22ff. (*see also* specific aspects, developments, events, individuals, places); archaeologists and (*see* Ar-

chaeology; specific individuals, places); development of Aegean civilization, 15ff., 19ff.; war between Atlantides and, 18
Greek Questions (Plutarch), 232
Gymnasium, Olympia, 142, 143
Gythion, 218, 219

Hades (hell), 124, 125–26, 182, 186, 190, 199, 215–24
Hadrian, Emperor, 144
Harpies, 171–72
Hecate, 173
Hecatompylos, 189
Hector, 229
Helios, 70, 79
Hellanicos, 186
Helle, 163
Hellen, 22–23, 26
Hellenes, 22–23ff., 59, 147, 165, 212
Hellespont (Dardanelles), 163, 168, 219
"Helmet of Hades," Perseus and use of, 41–42, 45, 47, 49
Helmets, use of, 113. *See also* "Helmet of Hades"
Hephaestos, 111, 141, 166, 173, 199, 244n
Hera, 23, 31–33, 82, 147, 165; goddess of fertility, 82–84; and Herakles, 82–87, 98, 148, 208, 209, 231; temples of, 31–33, 34, 82–84, 139, 144, 145 (*see also* Heraeum; specific locations); and Zeus, 23, 31, 82, 84, 86
Hera Akraia (Hera of the Cliff), 31n
Heraclea, 210
Heracleum, 189–90
Heraeum: Argive, 82–84, 86–87; Olympia, 139, 140
Herakleion, 188
Herakles (Hercules), 7, 11, 18, 30, 55, 62n, 74, 75, 79, 80–88, 89–94, 95–136, 168; and Aeëtes, 175; and Amazons, 147–49; and Augeian stables, 131–35; birth of, 79, 80–86; brings Cerberus from Hades, 215–24; and cattle of Erytheia, 184–91ff.; in Celtica, 191, 192–94; and Centaurs, 119, 120; and Cerynean "hind," 126–28; children of, 251; cities of, 209–11; contest in Oechalia, 225–26; and Cretan "bull," 137–38; death of, 237–42; and death of "eagle," 183; at Delphi, 99–104; and Dexamenos, 135; early achievements of, 95–98; education, 80–90; in Egypt, 189; at Eleusis, 122–26; encounter with "giants," 195–98, 206; and Erymanthian "boar," 119–22; and Eurystheus (*see* Eurystheus); and Eurytus, 233–34; and first "Odyssey," 231–32; and founding of Alesia, 193–94, 210; and "gadfly" at Epirus, 208; at Gates of Troy, 149–50; and "golden apples" of the Hesperides, 212–15; height of, 140; and "hydra," 108, 115–19; and Hylas, 167, 170, 183; and Jason and the Argonauts, 166, 167, 168n, 169–70; at Lake Avernus, 198; map of labors of, 136; map of voyages of, 81; and "mares" of Diomedes, 145–47; marooned by Argonauts, 169–70, 183; and Nemean "lion," 108, 109–15, 116; and Nymphs, 199–200, 201–2, 203; at Olympia, 138–45; and Omphale, 227; physical appearance of, 91; at Pillars of Hercules, 190–91; as politician, 187; and Pylos of Neleus, 234–36; rage (temper) of, 90, 98–99, 236, 237, 238, 239; and serpents, 86–88; and Sicilian conquest, 204–5; "son" of Zeus, 12, 79, 80, 139; and Strymon, 208–9; and Stymphalian Marsh "birds of prey," 128–30; and Theseus, 93–94; at Troy, 149–50, 227–31; virility of, 91–92, 238–39; youth, 89–94
Herculaneum, 196, 197–98
Hercules, Pillars of, 15, 18, 190–91, 210, 242
Hercules Promontory (Cape Spartivento), 210
Hermes, 38–39, 49, 131, 141; Praxiteles' statue of, 142, 144–45; "sons" of, 166; statues at Herculaneum of, 197–98
Herodes Atticus, Exedra of, 142
Herodorus, 90, 91, 92, 172
Herodotus, 15–16, 20, 157, 190
Hesiod, 12, 15, 31, 46, 62, 63, 92, 109, 115, 163, 171, 185, 213, 215
Hesione, 149–50, 231
Hesperides, 28, 39, 42, 212–15
Hesperis, 212
Hesperitis, 212
Hesperos, 212
Hestia, 213
Hesychios, 146
Hierokeryce, the, 125
Hierophant, the, 125, 126
Hind, Cerynean, Herakles and the, 126–28
Hippocoön, 236
Hippocrates, 84
Hippodameia, 38, 71–73
Hippolachos, 69
Hippolyte (daughter of Dexamenos), 135

Hippolyte, Queen (Amazon wife of Theseus), 93, 135, 149, 181, 249; Herakles and "girdle" of, 147–49, 150
Hippolytus, 149, 181, 249
Hipponomaea, 73, 74
Hippothoea, 68
Hirmenech, P. H., 6
Hissarlik, 8, 228
Homer, 1, 2, 3–4, 8, 11, 12, 18, 22, 23, 34, 41, 74, 84, 126, 138, 168, 171, 215, 227, 234; epitaph on Perseus, 55–56; on Bellerophon, 63, 69
Horn of plenty (cornucopia), 237
Hydra, Lernaean, Herakles and, 11, 108, 115–19
Hyginus, 66, 109, 135
Hyksos, 189
Hylas, 167, 170, 183
Hyllus, 240, 241, 251
Hymn to the Mysteries (Homer), 126
Hypsipyle, 168

Ialmenos, 167
Iberia, 26, 184ff., 190–91
Icaria, 55
Icarios, 55
Icarus, 7, 248
Ichthys, 197
Ida, Mount, 23, 24, 25
Idmon, 167, 172
Iliad, 2, 3, 34, 55–56, 61, 63, 82, 84, 122, 159, 171, 230, 231–32, 234
Inachids, 21, 30, 33
Inachos, 20–21, 33
India, 224
Indian Ocean, 17
Indo-Europeans, 19, 177
Iobates, King of Lycia, 34, 62, 63–64, 69
Iolas, 98, 115, 117, 118, 205, 225, 233, 242, 251
Iolcos, 94, 160, 180–81, 243
Iole, 225–26, 239–40
Ion, 22–23
Ionian Islands, 65
Ionians, 23
Ionian Sea, 207
Iphicles, 73, 79, 86–87, 89, 98, 115, 158, 233, 236
Iphitos (Iphitus), 167, 175, 226
Iraklion, 246
Iran, 17, 19
Iron swords, 252
Isander, 69
Isocrates, 231n
Istros, 164
Italus, 207
Italy, 177, 178, 197, 207–8, 211

Itea, 99, 100, 104
Ithaca, 28, 67, 68
Ithacos, 68, 74
Itkinos, 154
Ixion, 120

Jason, 23, 160–81, 186; and the Argonauts, 160–81; birth, 94; death of, 243–44; and the Golden Fleece, 173–81; map of voyages, 161; and Medea, 160, 173–76, 180–81; and Theseus, 159
Joannina, 164–65
Justin, 20

Kallicrates, 154
Kinship (relationship), figurative, 11–12
Klearchos, 146
Knossos, 6, 9, 13–14, 20, 25, 26, 27, 138, 245, 246–48; Theseus "labyrinth" and Minotaur at, 246–48
Kourtaga, castle of, 158
Kronion, Mount, 141, 142
Kronos, Mount, 139
Kypria Epic, 3

Labyrinth, Theseus at Knossos, 246–48
Lacedaemon(ians), 104n, 236
Lacinios, 207
Laconia, 216–18, 221–24
Laertes, 167
Lambadophores, 125
Laodamia, 69
Laogoras, 239
Laomedon, 149–50, 225, 227, 230–31, 236
Larissa, 31, 33, 50
Laurel wreaths, Olympic athletes, 141
Lava flows, 43n, 44, 45. *See also* Earthquakes; Volcanoes
Lebanon, 20
Legends. *See* Mythological process
Leitos, 167
Leivadi, 36
Lemnos, 168
Leon the Protospathairean, Church of, 95–96
Lepreus, 134
Lerna, Herakles and "hydra" of, 11, 108, 115ff.
Lethe, 24
Leucadia, 65–66, 67
Leucas, 28
Leucaspis, 204
Levadia, 95
Libya, 18, 23, 27, 28, 183, 188, 190, 211
Lichas, 239–40
Liguria(ns), 178, 191, 193, 194, 210
Linguistic symbolism, 10–12

Linos, 90–98
Lion Gate, Mycenae, 52
Lions, 11; Herakles and, 11, 91, 93, 94, 105, 108, 109–15, 116
Liparis, 41
Livorno, 194, 210
Lucan, 103
Lugdunum (Lyons), 193
Lycia (Lycians), 19, 34, 48, 59, 62, 63, 64, 69
Lycimnios, 74, 75
Lycophron, 150
Lycos, 172
Lydia (Lydians), 19, 227
Lynkeos, 34

Macchiavelli, Niccolo, 188
Madeira, 18, 42
Magna Graecia, Herakles as precursor and pioneer of, 185, 206, 211
Maikop, 163n
Manoetes, 186, 190
Marathon, Theseus and "bull" of, 138, 156–57
Marcellus, 204
"Mares," 145–47, 226
Marinatos, Professor S., 4–5, 14
"Mask of Hades," 41–42, 49–50
Medea, 160, 173–76, 180–81, 243–44
Medeius, 243
Media, 243n
Mediterranean Sea (and area), 15, 17, 19, 20, 25–30ff., 47, 53, 184ff., 209–11; culmination of Bronze Age in, 26; volcanic activity in, 191–92, 200–1
Medusa, 28, 29, 38, 42, 44–46, 49, 212–13 (*see also* Gorgons); "blood" (genealogy) of, 59–61, 63, 64, 116
Meganese Island, 66–67, 78
Megapenthes, 50, 51, 55
Megara, 95, 97, 98, 224, 225
Meleager, 158, 166, 175
Melkarth, temple of, 20
Memphis, Egypt, 248
Menelaus, 3
Menetios, 167
Merops (Meropians), 232
Mesopotamia, 19
Messenia, 2–4
Messina, 40, 41, 185
Mestor, King of Mycenae, 68, 70, 74
Midea, 33, 51, 73, 74, 75, 76
Migrations (emigrations), 9–10, 15–17, 18, 19, 164, 202. *See also* specific people, places
Milon, 207
Milos, 36
Minoa, 23, 25ff. *See also* Crete
Minoan civilization of Crete, collapse of, 5, 13–14. *See also* Crete
Minos, 9, 13–14, 27, 245–46, 247, 248; king of the *minoa*, use of term, 25n; Minos I, 25, 137, 217n; Minos II, 77–78, 137, 138; sired by "Zeus," 12
Minotaur, the, 9; birth of, 24–25; Theseus and, 246–47
Mnesimache, 135
Moliones, 233–34
Molorchos, 111
Monaco, 194, 210
Monastiraki, 83
Monsters, 29, 184, 186n, 216, 233–34, 246–48. *See also* Bulls; Dragons; Gorgons; Lions; Minotaur
Müller, Max, 7
Musaeus, 125n, 217
Mycenae (Mycenaeans), 2ff., 6, 8, 10, 51, 52–53, 73, 74, 75, 82, 83, 114, 118, 128, 150, 251, 252 (*see also* specific individuals); heroes and expansion of civilization of, 10ff.; Lion Gate, 52; script, 2; tholos tombs, 52, 53n; throne of Perseus, 53
Myrtilos, 72, 73
Mysia (Mysians), 19, 148, 169, 170
Mysteries, Eleusis, 124, 125–26
Mythological process, 6–14; ancient writings (texts) and, 7ff.; connection with the gods, 11–12; deciphering myths, 7–8; definition of "myth," 6; key to history, 9–10; techniques of historical investigation, 12–14; technology and, 13–14

Narhavales, 178
Natron (embalming chemical), 26
Nauplia, 33
Navigation, 19, 26, 29, 42, 49. *See also* Sailing
Naxions, twin sphinxes of Naxos, 100
Naxos (Naxians), 100, 120, 249
Nebrophonos, 168
Neckar (river), 178
Neleus, 235, 236
Nemea, Herakles and "lion" of, 108, 109–15, 116
Nereids, 47, 179
Neritos, 74
Nero, Emperor, 100, 143
Nessos, 121, 238–39, 240
Nestor, 2–4, 235, 236
Nicephorus Callistus, 171
Nicias, 239
Nicippe, 84, 85
Nike of Paeonios, 142
Nile River, 16, 17, 36, 203

Notos (south wind), 132n
Nuraghe, 200
Nymphs, 27–28, 39, 40–42, 175, 199–200, 201–2, 203, 209, 228

Occhio della Zillica, 202
Ocean, 42, 173, 178. *See also* Pontos
Ocypode (Ocypete), 171
Odyssey, 3, 24, 25, 40, 42, 94, 108, 235
Oechalia, 225–26, 239
Oeneos (Oeneus), King of Calydon, 54–55, 68, 157–59, 237, 238
Oenoë, 127
Oenomaos, King of Pisa, 71–73
Oeta, Mount, 121, 240–42
Oicles, 230
Oïleus, 167
Olenus, 135
Olives (olive cultivation), 55, 123, 155, 156, 158, 165
Olympia, 116, 138–45; Games, 8, 139–41; Heraeum, 139; Herakles at, 138–45; ruins, 141ff.; museum; 46, 72, 140, 144; Stadium, 139–41; 142, 143; Treasuries, 142–43: Zeus temple, 143, 145
Olympias, 103
Olympic Games, 139–41; first (776 B.C.), 8; Stadium, 139–41, 142, 143; Gymnasium, 142
Olympus, Mount, 38, 189, 192, 201, 207
Omphale, Queen of Lydia, 227
Onassis, Aristotle, 68
Oracles, 47, 50, 99, 101–4 (*see also* Priests; specific individuals, places); at Amon, 47; at Delphi, 99, 101–4, 105, 207, 224, 226, 240, 242; of Hera, 50; Jason and, 160, 163, 164–65; and kings (succession), 12, 34–35
Oration to Philip (Isocrates), 231n
Orchomenos (Orchomenians), 95–98, 105; acropolis, 95–96; tholos tomb, 96; Treasury of, 96
Orestes, 181
Ormenium, 239
Orpheus, 124–25, 217; and Argonauts, 168, 176
Orthrus, 59, 63, 78n, 109, 185, 186, 190–91
Ortygia, 201, 202, 204, 212–13
Othrys, Mount, 94, 241
Ovid, 39, 40, 76n, 115, 176, 180, 195, 237

Paeonios, 72, 142, 144
Palaemon, 166
Palaestra, Olympia, 142
Palatine Hill, 195
Pallas Athena. *See* Athena
Panaghia Vrashou (Madonna of the Rock), 31n
Panapeus (of Phocis), 78
Panathenaia, 244–45
Parian marble (*see also* Paros marble chronology); Hermes statue of, 144
Parnassus, Mount, 22, 99, 101, 162
Parnis, Mount, 153
Paros, island, 92, 148. *See also* Parian marble; Paros marble chronology
Paros marble chronology, 21, 22, 29, 123, 124, 125n, 156, 162, 168, 224, 227, 246n, 252
Parthenon, Athens, 153, 154–55, 244–45
Pasiphaë, 138
Paul, St., 10
Pausanias, 1–2, 24, 54, 72, 104n, 117, 123, 125, 131n, 141, 155, 157; on Herakles, 92, 96, 104n, 129, 131n, 141, 142, 144, 157, 199, 200n, 207, 217, 226, 230–31, 233, 234, 251; on Perseus, 51, 55
Pediacrates, 204
Pegasus, 18, 59, 63, 184; Bellerophon and, 64–69; "fleet of the winged horse," 7, 46, 61; mythological process in, 7
Pegasus, Gulf of, 94
Peirene fountain house, Corinth, 57
Pelasgians, 19, 20, 21, 22, 23, 33, 164, 165, 169, 197
Peleus, 167
Pelias, 94, 160–62, 173, 180–81
Pelion, Mount, 94, 120
Pelopeion, Olympia, 143
Pelopids, 74, 115, 121, 252. *See also* Pelops
Peloponnesus, the, 18, 20ff., 31, 58, 73ff., 105ff; Herakles and pacification of, 105ff., 183–211ff.; map of Labor of Herakles, 106–7
Pelops, 11, 19, 71–73, 74, 75, 115, 121, 128, 143, 172. *See also* Pelopids
Pemphredo, 28, 39–40
Peneleos, 167
Peneus (river), 22, 134, 135
Pentelichos, Mount, 152
Pericles, 29, 154
Periclymenes (Periclymenus), 167, 236
Peripatetics, the, 153
Peripatos esplanade, Acropolis, Athens, 153
Periphetes (nicknamed Corunetes), 151
Peristeri, 4
Peristhenes, 90
Perseids, 8, 73–79, 80ff., 105ff., 114ff., 252 (*see also* Perseus); family tree

of, 73–74; Law of Succession of, 80–86
Persephone (Proserpina), 126, 167, 182; abduction of, 201, 203; in Hades, Herakles and, 216–18, 220, 222–23
Perses, 70, 224
Perseus, 18, 30, 31–56, 120, 162, 186–87 (*see also* Perseids); and Andromeda, 47–48, 50, 74; birth of, 12, 35–36; and Cyclops, 48, 49, 50, 52; death of, 55–56; and Dionysus, 54–55; map of voyages of, 32; and Medusa, 38–46, 49–50; and Mycenae, 52–53; reign of, 53–56; revenge of, 50; "son of Zeus," 12, 35–36; sons of, 68, 70–79, 80
Persia(ns), 70, 232
Phaedra, 249–50
Phaestos, 24, 138
Phaëton, 132
Phalerum, Bay of, 153
Phanos, 167
Pharaohs, 11–12, 20, 47, 77n, 189, 214
Phasis, 170, 173
Phedriades, 99, 101, 102
Phedriades rocks, 99
Pherecydes, 12, 34; on Herakles, 86, 120, 169, 183, 213, 226, 227, 233, 251; on Perseus, 36, 38, 42, 49
Phidias, 143, 154
Phikia, 52
Philammon the Egyptian, 90
Philippeion, Olympia, 142
Philonoë, 69
Phineus, 47–48, 163–64, 171–72
Phlegraean Plain, 195–98
Phocaea, 211
Phoenicia (Phoenicians), 19, 20, 23ff., 29–30, 33, 48, 169, 189
Phoenix, 23–24, 48. *See also* Phoenicia (Phoenicians)
Pholoë, 120
Pholos, 120–21
Phorcids, 27–29, 42, 46, 49, 59ff., 64–68, 116, 123, 162, 163, 184, 185, 199–200ff., 213, 215 (*see also* Phorcys); genealogy of "monsters," 28; map of Empire and "monsters," 60
Phorcys, 27–29, 39, 40, 42, 123, 185, 200, 201. *See also* Phorcids
Phoroneos, 20–21
Phrixos, 163, 164, 171, 173
Phrygia, 63, 70
Phthiotis, 22
Phyleus, 111, 133, 134–35, 234
Pico ("the peak"), La Caldeira, 44
Pigs, 123
Pillars of Apollo, 57
Pillars of Hercules, 15, 18, 190–91, 210, 242
Pinarios, 195
Pindar, 18, 251; on Bellerophon, 57, 64, 68; on Herakles, 18, 91, 94, 99, 120, 127, 132
Piraeus, 29
Pirates (piracy), 33, 37, 74, 91, 119, 120, 227n; Cretans and, 23, 25, 26, 137; Echinadians and, 35, 59, 64–68, 74, 129; Jason and, 171; labors of Herakles and, 91, 108, 109, 111, 129, 137
Pirgos Dirou (village), 219
Pirithous, 167, 182, 201, 203, 216–18, 220, 222–23
Pisa, 139, 143
Pisander, 170
Pisander of Camirus, 117
Pison, 120
Pittheus, King of Troezen, 92–93
Plaka district, Athens, 153
Plato, 15, 56, 214; on Atlantis, 17, 18, 43n
Pliny, 133
Plutarch, 232
Pluto, 124, 126
Podarces, 231
Poeas, 167, 241
Poisons (poisonings), 173, 174, 180, 240–41, 243
Poleyn, 122
Polis, 155–56
Pollux and Castor (Dioscuri), 158, 170–71, 206
Polydectes, 37–38, 49, 162
Polyeides, 64
Polygonus, 150
Polyphemus, 167, 169
Polytos, 150
Pompeii, 196, 198
Pomponius Mela, 193
Pontos, 27, 28. *See also* Ocean
Pontus Euxinus. *See* Black Sea
Porgos, 183
Poseidon, 137, 138, 160, 203, 233, 235, 249; and Athena, 155; daughters of, 47; and Herakles, 141, 149; Phorcys as son of, 27; son of, 23, 27, 33, 134n, 150, 163, 167, 199, 203, 235
Poseidonites, 198
Praxiteles, statue of Hermes by, 142, 144
Preveza, Gulf of, 65
Priam, 19, 168n, 225, 229, 231
Priests (priestesses; priesthood), 15, 16, 18, 82, 86, 104, 127, 128, 147, 156, 165–66, 205–6, 217–18, 223, 224, 226. *See also* Oracles
Proclus, 3
Procris, 77, 78
Procrustes, 152

Proetos, 34–35, 50, 51, 61–62, 64
Promachos, 180, 181
Prometheus, 21, 162, 183–84
Propontis, 176
Proteus, 150
Protohistory, 7ff., defined, 27n
Prytaneion, Olympia, 142
Psiloriti (Mount Ida), 23, 24, 25
Psophis (mother of two children by Herakles), 207
Psophis (a region of Arcadia), 120
Pterelaos, 68, 74, 78
"Putting on the mask," 41–42
Pylos, 2, 3, 234–36
Pyrrha, 22
Pythagoras, 207–8
Pytho, 101
Pythoness (oracle), Delphi, 99, 101–4; Herakles and, 99, 103–4, 207, 224, 226

Quintilian, 232
Quirini, Cardinal, 141

Radioactivity, archaeological analysis by use of, 13
Rameses, 77n
Ransom payments, 121. *See also* Extortion; Pirates (piracy); Tolls
Reggio, 40, 41
Rhadamanthys, 25, 217n, law of, 90
Rhea-Cybele, 144
Rhine (river and valley), 177, 178
Rhône (river and valley), 177, 193–94
Roland, 7
Rome, 185, 194–98, 204
Romulus, 195
Roncesvalles, 7

Sabrina (island), 43
Sahara Desert, 16, 39
Sahu-Ra, Pharaoh, 20
Sailing (navigation; ships and shipping), 25–26, 42, 137, 245. *See also* Pirates (piracy); Navigation; Trade; Wings
Saïs, priest of, 15, 16, 18, 214
Salamis, Gulf of, 123
Salmydessus, 171
San Biagio church, Akragas, 205
Santa Maria (island), 43
Santorini, 77. *See also* Thera
São Jorge (island), 43–44
São Miguel (island), 43
Saône River, 193–94
Sardinia, 200
Sarpedon, 150
Scaean Gate, Troy, 229
Schliemann, Heinrich, 2, 4, 6, 8–9, 12, 52, 96, 228–30, 247
Schliemann, Sophia, 230
Science (technology), archaeology and mythography and, 13–14
Sciron, 152
Scironides, 152
Scylla, 45, 123, 179, 192, 199, 201, 202; nymph "daughter" of Phorcys, 28, 40–41, 49–50, 185, 202
Scyros (island), 250
Scythia (Scythians), 181
Semele, 54
Seneca, 231n
Seriphos, 36–37, 38, 39, 49
Seti I, 77n
Shields, 31, 114, 118; invention of, 34; Medusa-head, 46, 49; use of, 72n, 114
"Shower of gold," 35, 36
Sicily, 28–40, 123, 185, 198, 199–200, 201, 202, 203, 211; Herakles conquers, 204–5, 211; Herakles as demigod of, 206–7; temples, 205–7
Sinis (nicknamed Pityocamptes), 151
Sirens, 202
Sisyphus, 61
Skorpios (island), 67
Sneferu, Pharaoh, 20
Solon, 15, 18
Solymians, 63, 69
Somma, Mount, 195–96
Sophocles, 53, 175–76, 226, 237, 241
Spain, 187n, 191
Spanish Civil War, 187n
Sparta, 138
Spectography, 13
Sphinx of Giza, 16–17
Stace, 135
Stadium, Olympia, 137–41, 142, 143
Staphylos, 55, 167
Sterope, 72
Stheneboea, 34, 35, 50, 61–62, 69
Sthenelaos, King of Argos (son of Perseus), 70, 73, 74, 75, 80, 82, 86, 110, 147n
Sthenelaos (son of Androgeus), 148
Stheno, 28, 42, 44, 46, 116, 212
Strabo, 26, 42, 64, 124, 197, 225
Strophades, 171
Strymon, 208–9
Stymphalian Marsh, Herakles and "birds of prey" of, 128–30, 135
Styx, 221, 222, 223n
Succession, Perseid law of, 80–86
Suidas, 64, 69, 90n
Sumerian civilization, 19
Swords: of bronze, 27, 210–11, 242, 252; of iron, 252
Syleus, 227
Symbolism, linguistic, 10–12
Symplegades (rocks), 172, 192

Syracuse, 201, 203–4
Syria, 19, 20, 23, 48

Tacitus, 178
Taenarum, Cape, 201, 216, 218–24
Talion, law of, 90
Talos, 179
Tanais, 177. *See also* Danube
Tangier, 188
Tantalos, King of Phrygia, 11, 19, 70–71
Taphos ("Taphians"), 68, 74, 78
Taravo, valley of the, 27
Tartessus (Tartessians), 26, 190, 191, 199
Tassili frescoes, 16
Tauros, 137–38, 156–57, 179n. *See also* Bulls
Taurus Mountains, 19
Taygetus, 127, 128
Tebessa, 40
Technology (science), archaeology and mythography and, 13–14
Tectonic upheavals. *See* Earthquakes; Volcanoes (volcanic activity)
Tegea, 236
Telamon, 167, 170, 178, 230–31
Teleboas (Teleboans), 68, 74, 75–77, 78, 79
Telegonus, 150
Telephos, 236
Terceira (island), 43
Teutaros, 90
Thasos, 150
Theatre, Epidaurus, 53–54
Thebes, Egypt, 29, 77n, 189
Thebes, Greece, 29–30, 54, 75–78, 79, 84, 86, 89, 95ff., 105ff., 163, 225, 241, 245
Theimacus, 98
Themis, 22
Themiscyra, 148
Theocritus, 87–88, 89, 90, 91, 109, 111–14, 131, 170, 232
Theogony (Hesiod), 62, 109, 115, 171, 213
Thera (Cyclades), eruption of, 5, 13–14, 26. *See also* Santorini
Thermodon, Amazons of, 147–49, 161, 181
Theseion, 244n
Theseus, 29, 126, 138, 151–59, 181–82, 227n, 243, 251; and Amazons, 149, 181; and Ariadne, 248–49; and "boar" of Calydon, 157–59; and "bull" of Marathon, 156–57; death of, 250; and Herakles, 93–94, 156, 216–18, 222–23; and Hippolyte, 93, 149, 181, 249; incident at Panathenaia, 244–45; and Jason and the Argonauts, 159, 166; and Medea, 243, 244; and the Minotaur, 246–49; and Persephone, 126, 167, 201; and Phaedra, 249–50; released from Hades, 222–23; temple in Athens to, 244–45; youth of, 151–59
Thespians, 175
Thespiots, 238
Thessaly (Thessalians), 21–22, 94
Thestios, 91–92, 99
Thetis, 179
Thoas, 168n
Tholos tombs, 52, 96, 235
Thoosa, 28, 40–41, 49
Thrace (Thracians), 145, 150, 164, 168n, 171, 181
"Three times a day" (Greek idiom for "incessantly"), 179
Thucydides, 21, 22, 25, 73, 76, 120, 251, 252
Thyestes, 75
Timaeus (historian), 176, 199
Timaeus (Plato), 15n
Tin, 26, 184, 190
Tiphys, 166, 172
Tiresias, 79, 82, 84, 86, 88, 105
Tiryns, 33, 34, 50, 51–52, 61, 73, 74–75, 76, 233; Herakles at, 104, 105ff., 131; palace and fortifications (walls) of, 51–52, 108–9
Titus, 144
Tolls, levying of, 11, 58, 95, 109. *See also* Extortion; Pirates (piracy)
Tombs, 235. *See also* Tholos tombs
Tomi, 176, 177
Torone, 150
Trachis, 238, 239–40, 241
Trade (commerce), 25–60, 111. *See also* Sailing
Treasuries, 142
Tretos, Mount, 109–14
Tripolis, 116
Triptolemy, 123
Triton, 179
Tritonis, Lake, 39, 179
Troezen, 92–94, 217, 223
Troubadours, ancient writings as work of, 7
Troy, 6, 8; founding of, 19; Herakles at, 149–50, 227–31; location of original city, 227–28; rediscovery of, 6, 227–30; Trojan War, 3, 8, 9, 42, 167–68, 187, 229, 230–31; wooden horse, 42
Turkey, 228, 234
XXVth Idyll (Theocritus), 131
Tyndareus, 236
Typhon, 59, 60, 63, 109, 115, 162, 173n, 183, 186, 213, 216

Tyre (Tyrians), 20, 23, 24, 29
Tyrrhenia, 18, 27, 28, 178

Ulysses, 167, 192, 202, 227
Umbrians, 177
Underworld, the, 124, 125–26, 218–24. *See also* Hades (hell)

Valerian Flaccus, 150
Velikovsky, I., *Worlds in Collision by,* 27n
Vercingetorix, 194
Vesta (and Vestal virgins), 213n
Vesuvius, Mount, eruption of, 195–97, 200
Vidhi, 93
Virgil, 80, 195, 212
Volcanoes (volcanic activity), 13–14, 17–18, 26–27, 41, 44–45, 191–92, 195–97. *See also* Earthquakes; Lava; specific locations, volcanoes
Vonitsa, 65
Vulcan, 195
Vulcan Island, 179

Weapons (*see also* Armor; Swords); Herakles and, 210–11
Wheat cultivation, 123
Wilhelm, Kaiser, 142
Wine-drinking (and wine cultivation), 4, 98, 102, 120–21
Wingless Victory, Temple of, Athens, 154
Wings (symbolism), 7, 41, 46, 49, 61, 64, 171, 248; chariots, 122–23; horses, 7, 46, 61, 64; sails (ships), 7, 41, 46, 61, 64, 123, 171, 186, 248; sandals, 41, 49
Wolfsbane (aconite), 173
Women of Colchis, The (Sophocles), 175–76
Wooden horse, Trojan War, 42
Wrestling, 142, 188, 232

Xenophon, 103
Xerxes, 209
Xuthos, 22

Zenobius, proverbs of, 179
Zephyr, 171
Zetes, 166, 171
Zeus, 23, 25, 72, 78, 79, 101, 150, 156, 164–66, 176, 189; and Athena, 156; and Demeter, 125; Hera and, 23, 82, 84, 86, 231; Herakles (son of) and, 79, 80–82, 105, 139, 188, 196, 226, 231, 240, 241; Parthenon statue, 155; Perseus and, 35, 36; sons of, 12, 35, 36, 54, 79, 80–82, 103; temple, Akragas, 206; temple at Dodona, 164–66; temple at Olympia, 139, 143, 145